A New Pastoral Care

Women in Travail and Transition

edited by
Maxine Glaz &
Jeanne Stevenson Moessner

Fortress Press   **Minneapolis**

John A. Hollar

WOMEN IN TRAVAIL AND TRANSITION
A New Pastoral Care

Scripture quotations unless otherwise indicated are from the New Revised Standard Version of the Bible, copyright © 1989 by the Division of Christian Education of the National Council of Churches.

Cover design: Patricia Boman
Interior design: Karen Buck

Library of Congress Cataloging-in-Publication Data

Women in travail and transition : a new pastoral care / edited by
  Maxine Glaz & Jeanne Stevenson Moessner.
        p.   cm.
  Includes bibliographical references.
  ISBN 0-8006-2420-3 (alk. paper)
    1. Women—Pastoral counseling of. 2. Women—Religious life.
3. Women—Psychology.   I. Glaz, Maxine, 1940-   . II. Moessner,
Jeanne Stevenson, 1948-   .
BV4445.W65   1991
259'.082—dc20
                                                         90-26299
                                                         CIP

The paper used in this publication meets the minimum requirements of American National Standard for Information Sciences—Permanence of Paper for Printed Library Materials, ANSI Z329.48-1984. ∞™

Manufactured in the U.S.A.   AF 1-2420

01   00   99   6   7   8   9   10   11   12   13   14

Contents

Preface

Greater knowledge of women's experience, we believe, will enable all caregivers (both female and male) to provide better pastoral care by reconsidering gender-specific presuppositions. This volume is a *new* pastoral care because it focuses on the gender needs of women. It is the first book to address the broad range of women's pastoral care needs, although we acknowledge the contributions of other authors on specific gender issues.

We hope that readers will feel the passion with which the contributors wrote this book. A team of women collaborated in its production because currently no individual woman in our field could undertake the complete project. We believe that the combined effort of five women who work in clinical settings and four women in academic positions strengthens the book in several ways. Our cooperation avoids the tendency to separate theoretical from practical concerns; each of us has given attention to both in our respective areas of research. The contributors' team sought to speak from and to its diverse denominational background: American Baptist, Southern Baptist, Disciples of Christ, Episcopalian, Methodist, Presbyterian, Roman Catholic, and United Church of Christ. Discussions among the contributors have made the resulting book a richer synergism.

As contributors, however, we also recognize our cultural limits. We are aware that women behave differently in other cultures and that culture itself bears analysis. As editors, we hope that companion volumes will be written by nonwhite, ethnic, non-middle-class women within Western culture and by other women elsewhere throughout the world.

Nevertheless, we hope that this book will make a contribution to the lives of women by affirming women's experiences in such a way as to revive the church's capacity to give care to women. Many pastors, theologians, and laypeople are committed not only to understanding dehumanizing forces but also to combating them. We share this commitment with both contributors and readers. It is an apt response to the experience that motivates us all—hearing a cry as of a woman in travail (Jer. 4:31).

The Society for Pastoral Theology was the milieu for this book's conception. We first began to talk about its composition in a research seminar in 1988. Our effort reached a crucial stage when the editors, Maxine Glaz and Jeanne Stevenson Moessner, along with John A. Hollar, editorial director of Fortress Press until his death, and four of the contributors met for two days at the society's 1989 meeting.

This book is dedicated to John A. Hollar. When he got off the plane in Denver to meet with the editors and contributors, John had just finished reading Chapter 3, "Women Who Work and Love: Caught Between Cultures." He was extremely excited about the issues raised and the tensions depicted. Only after we knew him better did we realize that John had had some of these same struggles in trying to combine working and loving. He taught us, above all, that caring for generations, nurturing babies and books, and investing one's growth in relationships are not gender-specific. John's love for his family lingers with us as much as the facility of his editorial pen. Although John did not live to see this volume in print, his comments and concerns affect each chapter. His presence with us in Denver made its indelible imprint. Later, by phone, the last four words he spoke to us were "God be with you." And with you, John.

Jeanne Stevenson Moessner
Decatur, Georgia

Maxine Glaz
Denver, Colorado

. . . .

Contributors

. . . .

Mary Louise Cullen, R.M., M.S., O.C.N., currently works as a women's health care nurse practitioner and in vitro coordinator at the Institute of Reproductive Health and Infertility, Rochester, New York. A member of the Oncology Nursing Society and founding council member of the Society of Gynecologic Nurse Oncologists, she has conducted workshops at national conferences and written numerous articles.

Mary James Dean, M.A. English, M.A. Religious Studies, D.Min. Family Therapy, is a clinical consultant in family therapy at the Rochester Mental Health Center, where she is developing family therapy programs in the treatment of schizophrenia and chemical dependency. A clinical member of the American Association for Marriage and Family Therapy (AAMFT) and a credentialed alcoholism counselor in New York State, she has published several articles and conducted numerous workshops and training sessions. She trained at the University of Rochester Medical Center.

Priscilla L. Denham, M. Div., is Associate Director of Pastoral Care in charge of clinical education at Jeanes Hospital, Philadelphia, Pennsylvania. She was ordained by the Southern Baptists and receives her ecclesiastical endorsement from the American Baptist Churches, U.S.A. Among the articles she has written is "Toward an Understanding of Child Rape" (*Journal of Pastoral Care*, December 1982). She is a clinical member of both AAPC and AAMFT.

JoAnn M. Garma, Ed.D. Psychology and Counseling, is Director of Pastoral Care at Children's Hospital, New Orleans, an accredited training center with the ACPE. She is an ordained Episcopal deacon and an ACPE supervisor. She served as chaplain for more than seven years with the Orleans Parish Criminal Sheriff's Office and as a board member with the Metropolitan Battered Women's Board, New Orleans.

Maxine Glaz, Ed.D., is Director of Pastoral Care and Education at Presbyterian/Saint Luke's-Swedish Health Care System in Denver. She is an ordained minister of the United Church of Christ and a CPE supervisor in the ACPE. Her previous appointments include those of Associate Professor of Pastoral Care at Colgate Rochester Divinity School and Clinical Associate Professor of Community Health Services at the University of Rochester School of Medicine. She is a past member of the steering committee of the Society for Pastoral Theology and an author of several scholarly articles and papers.

Bonnie J. Miller-McLemore, Ph.D., is Assistant Professor of Religion, Personality, and Culture at Chicago Theological Seminary. She is also associate staff at the Center for Religion and Psychotherapy of Chicago. She has worked as a hospital chaplain and as an associate minister with the Disciples of Christ. She is author of *Death, Sin and the Moral Life: Contemporary Cultural Interpretations of Death* (Scholars, 1988) and related articles. Her current work on women and work is part of a larger research interest in images of adulthood and women's experience.

Jeanne Stevenson Moessner, Dr.Theol., is Adjunct Professor of Pastoral Theology at Columbia Theological Seminary, Decatur, Georgia, and a resident in pastoral care and counseling at Georgia Baptist Hospital. Her doctorate is with honors from the University of Basel, Switzerland. She has also been a research fellow at Candler School of Theology, Atlanta. She is currently in process for AAPC certification, as well as a candidate for ordination in the Presbyterian Church U.S.A. She is author of *Theological Dimensions of Maturation in a Missionary Milieu* (Peter Lang Verlag) and several scholarly articles.

Christie Cozad Neuger, Ph.D. Personality and Theology, an ordained United Methodist minister, is currently Assistant Professor of Pastoral Theology at Princeton Theological Seminary and coordinator of its CPE program. Previously she was a pastoral psychotherapist and director of the resource center Foundation for Religion and Mental Health. Her doctorate is from the School of Theology at Claremont.

Nancy J. Ramsay, Ph.D., D.Min., an ordained Presbyterian minister, is Associate Professor of Pastoral Theology at Louisville Presbyterian Seminary and is progressing toward AAPC certification. She served as an associate pastor in North Carolina and earned her Ph.D. in Religion and Personality at Vanderbilt University after attaining a D.Min. at Union Theological Seminary, Richmond.

Acknowledgments

. . . .

An edited volume such as this requires special support. Each of us has many persons to whom we would like to offer thanks. We also came to appreciate the significance of the Society for Pastoral Theology, which serves both as a forum for conversation and as the silent critic whose respect we sought to earn. First, the contributors and then the coeditors would like to acknowledge other benefactors.

We wish to thank the women interviewed while researching our chapter. Their shared experiences teach us all and make possible a new vision for pastoral care with women's physical issues. M.J.D. and M.L.C.

I want to thank Ms. Betty Jacobson who graciously, supportively, and skillfully typed revision after revision. I also wish to express love and thanks to Donald, my husband, and Isaac, my son, who accepted my limited family time and encouraged me when I grew fainthearted. P.L.D.

I want to thank Martha Brewer, Judith Harris, Edna Koffskey, Carol Lindsey, Mindy Milam, and the women in the Mamou Riding Club. I also want to thank Barbara Davidson with the Louisiana Coalition against Domestic Violence. J.M.G.

My deeply felt thanks go to those with whom I work and whom I love at Chicago Theological Seminary, the Center for Religion and Psychotherapy, and within my own family. In each setting, many persons—Susan Thisthlethwaite, Dorothy Bass, William Myer, Terry Lyon, Susan Pangerl, Marie McCarthy, Mark Miller-McLemore, my two sons, Christopher and Matthew (whose in utero contributions were quite significant), and the many other women and men who have shared their own struggles to work and to love—have all in different ways provided the kind of holding environment that allowed my ideas to germinate and come to fruition. B.M.M.

My thanks go to Win, Dan, and Cathy for providing a context of support and empowerment in my life and work. In addition, I would like to express my gratitude to the community of feminist scholars for providing a context of entitlement and new visions. C.C.N.

I am grateful to Maxine and Jeanne as well as to Elizabeth Liebert, Martha Kenney, and Carolyn Lindsey for their willingness to review versions of my chapter and offer improvements. Especially, I wish to thank those women survivors of sexual abuse in the Louisville chapter of Parents United who shared their experience with me in behalf of this project. I hope that I have kept faith with their trust. N.J.R.

My family's humor and good grace carried me through the more difficult moments of working on this text. I acknowledge a special gratitude to Stuart A. Plummer for his thoughtful discussion of the content of my chapters and his unwavering encouragement during the process of writing and editing. Nancy Plummer Murrow and Bruce Murrow provided both emotional and computer support that culminated in a memorable midnight rescue of millions of bytes of data that had disappeared with a mistaken touch of the delete button. Who knows how chapter 2 might have ended without them! M.G.

For the students who participated not only in my classes but also in the vision of this book, I am grateful. For the support of Columbia Theological Seminary, for the typing assistance of Mandy Lape-Freeberg, and for the opportunity to deliver chapter 10 in lecture form at Duke Divinity School, I am indebted. For the encouragement of my sisters, Alice Dudas, Nancy Foster, Nan Hawkes, Blanche Montesi, Melinda Rhett, Judy Stones, Flo Seger, and Susan Sharpe, I am blessed. A special thanks to David Moessner and Stevenson Moessner, and to George S. Flinn, Jr., who in his own way cares for women in travail. J.S.M.

John Hollar's death forced this manuscript into the able editorial hands of Timothy G. Staveteig and Reneé Fall. We are indebted to them for seeing the book through its several drafts and for accepting the complexities of simultaneously editing the work of seven contributors and two editors. The enthusiasm of Pamela Johnson and others at Fortress Press was deeply felt. The book is stronger because of their understanding of what this book, as a whole, is meant to be. J.S.M. and M.G.

Introduction:
I Heard a Cry

JEANNE STEVENSON MOESSNER AND
MAXINE GLAZ

· · · · · · · · · · · ·

"For I heard a cry as of a woman in travail,
anguish as of one bringing forth her first
child. . . ."

Jer. 4:31 (RSV)

We use this passage from Jeremiah as an intentional paradigm for linking women's productivity in parturition to the minister's capacity to be involved with her in her time of need. Pastoral care takes on a different sensitivity and perspective when the cries of women are heard. Most ministers have not been helped to understand women's experience. Basic psychology, as taught in seminaries, does not facilitate comprehension of the themes intrinsic to female development. Even the best care can fail when it is insensitive to a woman's experience.

One Failed Moment

The true story of June is an example of a failed moment in pastoral care. As with many of the accounts of women and their ministers in this book, better care could have been provided had the minister been available to the woman's experience.

June, a mother for the first time, had had a harrowing delivery: she nearly died in childbirth. Exhausted and frightened, she lay awake in her hospital bed unable to close her eyes. She was glad that the birthing process was finished, but the baby, she felt, had nearly killed her. When her pastor arrived, five hours had passed since the ordeal.

She could not bring herself to describe her feelings: the pastor, aware that she had been near death, did not enquire. Instead, after introductory

1

talk, the pastor repeated how grateful to God she should be for the wonderful new life that had been entrusted to her. June felt even worse after the visit because one major part of her experience had not been acknowledged: the baby as threat to her own life.

June did not establish a nonambivalent relationship with her infant. In therapy years later, she concluded that the emotions formed at the birth and sealed inside by the pastor's oblivious remarks were a significant factor in her lack of bonding with her child. Because she could not bring herself to share her feelings, she felt victimized, increasingly guilty, and cornered as the mother of this child. The outcome of this, she surmised, was a troubled adolescent.

June did, however, have two more children. Although she would not tell her husband the reason, she asked him to keep the minister away from her during her hospital stay at each birth. These two births were uncomplicated; June felt much better in her mothering of each. Because the youngest child seemed to do as well as her first child did poorly, June inferred that the minister's absence was far more helpful than his presence.

Can a thirty-minute pastoral visit have such reverberations for a mother when the unspoken cry of her plight is missed or ignored? June thought so. Listening to many other women and their stories of missed pastoral opportunities convinces us that lack of sensitivity to sexual and gender experience in pastoral care has helped to create many women like June; silent and confused about their feelings, they avoid particular people and situations as a means of coping.

Entrance into Pain

Each cry of travail calls for a response from us, but what will it be? Shall we presume to utter the same cry and claim familiarity with an experience that is probably not our own? Do we cringe in the face of agony and flee? Are we overwhelmed with guilt, and do we become either defensive or skeptical? We face the universal temptation to avoid what is real but painful to others. However, this avoidance of pain is not the only possible response. As we begin to understand those whose lives are not like our own and learn that their experience may not conform to our preconceptions, we brave a new confrontation with reality. Then not only is our capacity for others enhanced but we also mature in self-understanding.

Until the last two decades, considering women as an identifiable constituency with emotional and religious concerns growing out of the experience of being female was deemed unnecessary for churchpeople.

Christianity has seen itself as a catholic faith. For centuries women themselves believed that, because Christianity intended to be universal, it needed to be interpreted as universal. So what if the sermons women heard, the rituals in which they participated, their pastor's care of them, and Scripture itself seemed designed for men by being masculine in tone and style? Women adapted in spite of their doubts. More recently, many women first wondered if "mankind" and "brotherhood" really included them, then took seriously such inner dialogue with quiet reservation. Some women accepted institutional reassurance and complied with the dominant mind-sets, but increasingly other women felt torn and distanced from theological questions that were not congruent with their own questions and answers to those questions that were unresponsive to their needs.

Many pastors, seminarians, laypeople, and counselors may still be uninformed about the issues presented here. This ignorance is more than unfortunate; it is dangerous. Marie Fortune, for example, cautions abused women about continuing counseling with pastors who are not prepared to deal with topics such as sexual abuse: "Although they [the ministers] care deeply about you and want to help, their lack of knowledge and skill will prevent them from being the support that you need. . . . God will provide other pastors or priests who may be more knowledgeable and prepared to help."[1]

The purpose of this book is to foster a greater number of knowledgeable and prepared caregivers. After two decades, we are less sanguine about a pool of such persons forming on their own.

The Voice Heard

This book underscores the changes that have occurred in women's thinking about themselves, their experience, and their faith since the onset of the second wave of feminism in the 1960s.[2] Recent research in the psychology of women is voluminous; between 1967 and 1982, more than eighteen thousand articles were published in the psychological literature.[3] When interdisciplinary articles on women are counted in neighboring fields such as sociology, medicine, and anthropology, the articles and books relevant to a psychology of women published in the last two decades approach a hundred thousand units.[4] Our book utilizes material from this vast body of research and then moves beyond it by exploring its relationship to the development of pastoral theology and by highlighting its importance for ministers concerned with the pastoral needs of women. The contributors and editors have also drawn on their graduate theological education, training in Clinical Pastoral Education, the American Association of Pastoral Counselors, the American Association for Marriage and Family Therapy, and the advanced psychotherapy seminars of the Denver Psychoanalytic Institute and Society.

Yet, we readily acknowledge the limits of our experience and study. We do not claim to speak for all women and not even most women like us—white, middle-class, North American women primarily in church settings. The research is likewise limited in scope and generally based on a white, nonethnic, middle-class population. As early as 1964, psychoanalyst Clara Thompson acknowledged this deficit; she noted that psychoanalysts observe Western women in patriarchal culture in a state of transition. Thus isolating or drawing conclusions from some "biologic woman" is impossible. Women behave differently in different cultures. They may also live a different emotional life because of their culture. Freud's sample of middle- and upper-class women in Europe was wrongly taken to be "women in general."[5] The writers and editors of this book are aware that women behave differently in different cultures and that, therefore, culture itself needs to be analyzed.

This book deals forthrightly with issues both of gender and of sex. When we describe gender issues, we intend the psychological qualities of being "feminine" and "masculine" associated with cultural and societal categories, and we use these adjectival terms in this sense. In comparison, sexual issues are related to biologically based categories of male and female. The realization of gender differences often results in an uncomfortable sense of separateness; what was assumed as universal experience is recognized as privileged. This awkward recognition may provoke guilt, denial, or anger, depending on the person's new understanding of his or her position in relation to others. Yet we are at a point in the history of culture when we can and need to understand the importance of gender issues if we are ever to achieve a family of faith that is not divided. We have also come to recognize that *differentiation* (the process of distinguishing oneself and one's views from those of another individual or group) can both strengthen individuals and moderate divisiveness.[6] A critique of culture with its categorization of gender, then, is an undercurrent through this book, not only when it is explicitly raised but also when it is subtly implied.

Beyond opening up the possible tensions related to gender, sex, and culture, this book raises deeply troubling concerns—those that frequently have been hidden, ignored, or unknown. Our hope is that readers—women and men—will appreciate a book that gives voice to previously unvoiced thoughts of women. Elizabeth Cady Stanton wrote to Susan B. Anthony in early summer 1860, "One word of thanks from a suffering woman outweighs with me the howls of all Christendom."[7]

The authors and editors share her spirit. Ours may not be safe work, but if there are howls from Christendom, then those wails will be outweighed by the value of this book even for one person.

An Overview

Part One addresses the basic questions intrinsic to the psychology of women: To what extent are the psychological differences between women and men biological or cultural? What are the effects of biology on women's psychology? What are the effects of culture on women's psychology? What social-psychological patterns of reinforcement shape feminine behavior? To what extent are these patterns stable or fluid? What occurs to women in the sequence of normal development? In what ways does developmental experience shape feminine character and particular psychological issues? To what extent are the differences between women and men of greater or lesser magnitude than the differences among individuals within each gender?

Chapter 1 presents a reconstruction of a psychology of women which is placed within the context of later psychoanalytic material.[8] In this chapter the focus is on such questions as how the developmental experience modulates character. Chapter 2 historically reviews women's contributions in the field of the psychology of women. We evaluate models of pastoral theology with two criteria: their adequacy as psychological theories and their fidelity to fundamental convictions of Christian theology.[9]

We hope that Part One will enhance the awareness of those involved in pastoral theology in three ways. First, life is embodied in the unique experience of gender and gender identification, however much men and women may be more like each other among genders than different from each other within each gender. No human being exists as "disembodied spirit."[10] Gender differences, whether biologically, developmentally, or socially grounded, modify religious and psychological experience. Male-organized theological reflection and understandings miss concerns that are existentially important to women. Second, the impact of feminist scholarship on the church's discussion of anthropological concerns is derived from the literature on psychology of women. These concerns are central to our pastoral theology. This impact is shown from the literature on the psychology of women. Pastoral care suffers when a minister is too easily swayed by an outdated or male-oriented psychology. It also suffers when the minister does not comprehend the conflict between a seductive psychology and a comprehensive faith.

Specifically, the minister who does not understand the biological, experiential, and cultural contexts of the person who silently cries for ministry inevitably inhibits an adequate interpretation of the Christian gospel for struggling people. Third, descriptions of a nondominant female perspective provide a perspective from which to examine the male-dominant one of the church, both ancient and modern.

Part Two gives a hearing to women experiencing particular crises, including women who are suffering battering or sexual abuse, struggling with divorce or the loss of a partner, balancing pressure to work and to love, and enduring times of depression. In addition to addressing specific times of travail, we also look at the broader social significance of women's changing place in culture and hear the sounds of deliverance from oppression.

Chapters by Nancy J. Ramsay, JoAnn M. Garma, and Mary Dean and Mary Louise Cullen help the reader identify with the experience of being female in North American culture. Christie Cozad Neuger offers a feminist cultural critique to evaluate pastoral care approaches to women's depression. Priscilla L. Denham and Bonnie J. Miller-McLemore rethink contemporary life-styles of women: Miller-McLemore considers the underlying metaphors in two distinct feminist approaches to women's changing place in society and to our changing self-understanding; Denham challenges typical pastoral thinking about women whose life-styles have moved beyond the usual couple status. Each of these chapters raises questions about psychology and culture and reinforces the importance of theological reflection in pastoral care.

Part Three posits a new model of ministry that better expresses women's growing self-understanding both as ministers and as persons who cry—silently or aloud—for ministry. One chapter gathers up the practice of pastoral care with women as modeled and suggested by the earlier chapters. In the other chapter Jeanne Stevenson Moessner articulates a new approach in pastoral theology and ministry: pastoral care is not given by an authority figure who "shepherds" a flock; rather, ministers can better view themselves as neighbors who minister because they too have received ministry as people "by the side of the road."

This work begins a revision that can modify our approach to the pastoral care of men as well. We believe that this book approaches a significant revision of pastoral theology from the standpoint of women's experience. As it does so, it directs us toward a gender-free perspective that, until now, has been missing and that is possible only through the inclusion of women's voices.

NOTES

1. Marie Fortune, *Keeping the Faith* (New York: Harper & Row, 1987), 76.
2. See pp. 47–49.
3. Margaret W. Matlin, *The Psychology of Women* (New York: Holt, Rinehart and Winston, 1987), 7.
4. Ibid.
5. Clara M. Thompson, *Interpersonal Psychoanalysis: The Selected Papers of Clara M. Thompson*, ed. Maurice R. Green (New York: Basic Books, 1964), 232.
6. For a fine overview of how processes of differentiation strengthen individuals and reduce friction in relationships, see Edwin H. Friedman, *Generation to Generation: Family Process in Church and Synagogue* (New York: Guilford Press, 1985), esp. 27, 32, 34–35, 228–49. Although feminism may seem divisive to some, others believe that as women become differentiated unconscious friction between men and women subsides.
7. Elizabeth Cady Stanton, "Letter to Susan B. Anthony, June 14, 1860," in *Elizabeth Cady Stanton, as Revealed in Her Letters, Diary, and Reminiscences*, ed. Theodore Stanton and Harriet Stanton Blatch (New York: Harper and Brothers, 1922) 2:82.
8. Stephen A. Mitchell, *Relational Concepts in Psychoanalysis* (Cambridge: Harvard University Press, 1988), presents an evaluation and integration of psychoanalytic theory that serves as an intellectual foundation for this reformulation of the psychology of women. In particular, Mitchell construes psychoanalytic theory as moving beyond a monadic view of mind toward an interactive, relational view. This approach offers a psychological perspective that is decidedly more congruent with a Christian anthropology. For a practical illustration of this, see Mitchell's chapter "The Problem of the Will," 239–70.
9. Cf. Don S. Browning, *Religious Thought and the Modern Psychologies* (Philadelphia: Fortress Press, 1987), 5–6, 29–31.
10. Although some notions of spirituality build on a division of body and soul (or worse, as in some gnostic heresies, suggest the preeminence of spiritualized being dissociated from the earthly sphere), this position has been rigorously rebutted in Christianity. The present theological opinions are decidedly in favor of a more holistic view of spirit and personality as expressive dimensions of bodily being. We are our bodies, although perhaps of more significance than our corporeal forms, and do not have souls that dwell in some material shell. See, for example, James B. Nelson, *Embodiment: An Approach to Sexuality and Christian Theology* (Minneapolis: Augsburg, 1978), 11–36.

PART ONE

Women

CHAPTER 1

A New Pastoral Understanding of Women

MAXINE GLAZ

• • • • • • • • • • • •

We continue to be a racist, classist, sexist people in spite of the gospel announcement of parity in Christ: "There is no such thing as Jew or Greek, slave and freeman, male and female; for you are all one person in Christ Jesus" (Gal. 4:28 NEV). Modern psychological theory, which has as its purpose an understanding of the mind and of individual behavior, also has a heritage of sexism. Just as Christian conventions too often acceded to the conditions of culture as far as women have been concerned,[1] early psychological theory was skewed by the social and historical views of women which preceded its development. The results are disappointing: a church that fails to practice what it has announced, followed by a psychology that claimed women's moral inferiority.[2]

The perspective of women's experience—thinking about being human from a woman's vantage point—allows us to reexamine both the ancient Christian message of God's redemptive love and care for all people and modern psychology's basic assumptions. Carol Gilligan has argued that Lawrence Kohlberg's theory of human moral development is based on male norms and data.[3] A pastoral care that is strongly influenced by such psychological and developmental theories has imported this male bias. Nevertheless, modern empirical theories of psychology, sociology, and anthropology offer important insights for understanding people. Psychology in particular has a continuing influence on methods of pastoral care in the church. Yet psychology cannot serve as the core of pastoral theology, even though anthropology is an integral element in the interpretation of divine activity.[4]

Psychological theory has served as an important reference point for discussions in pastoral theology since Freud, but it is met with increasing skepticism as a foundational metaphor. Pastoral theologians such as Don Browning, Donald Capps, Charles Gerkin, and Thomas Oden remind us that the church's ministry is essentially a theological undertaking based on a rich tradition of interpreting God's being and activity among people.[5] The pastor needs to recognize the dissonance between the positions of modern psychology and Christian thought when insights offered as science give rise to ethical and cultural beliefs that are competitive with or critical of a Christian interpretation of life.[6]

The need to be analytic in one's psychological perspective and to begin to reconstruct pastoral theology as a theological discipline is evident. I depart from the position of the writings noted in an effort to identify the gender-biased psychological assumptions that pervade the pastoral care literature. Because pastoral theology has given credence to psychological theory and because a male psychological bias exists, we must also critique the male norms within pastoral thought and practice. We can learn from new interpretations of women's psychological experience just as we do from current discussions of gender issues in the fields of biblical studies, church history, and theology. Our assessment of the masculine distortion of pastoral care ultimately supports the argument of current pastoral theologians, that pastoral care has been uncritical in the appropriation of psychology. Taking psychology as a metaphor in tension with the Christian tradition, we turn to women's experience in order to recover a pastoral approach to women. From this point, we construct an understanding of four themes in women's experience that change how pastoral care is undertaken.

We are aware of the need to maintain a theological focus. We are also aware of a dissociative process: people of a dominant perspective emphasize a new theme or status symbol as people of an alternative perspective become adept in the former theme.[7] Yet, for two reasons we pursue this course. Heuristically, we cannot leave the discussion of a psychology of women to our past. Pastorally, we cannot abandon psychological inquiry at the point of imminent revision in gender perspectives because ignoring women's issues invites continuing frustration and anger in women like June who have already endured misunderstanding and harm in the name of ministry.

DEVELOPMENTAL THEMES IN WOMEN'S EXPERIENCE

The psychological view of feminine experience developed in this chapter is based on a reconstruction of psychoanalytic perspectives. Psychoanalytic theory is not limited to drive theory but includes object relations, ego-psychology, and self-psychology as theoretical developments.[8]

In particular I am attracted to the emerging syntheses in psychoanalysis as suggested by Stephen Mitchell's *Relational Concepts in Psychoanalysis* and Joseph Lichtenberg's *Psychoanalysis and Motivation*.[9] These reconstructions have been augmented by my own reading of clinical-observational studies, by further consideration of developmental understandings of human being and becoming,[10] and through the review of empirical work on social-psychological behavior.[11] My view is Freudian in that it participates in current conversations in psychoanalysis regarding women's psychology. Furthermore, although I regard the effort to understand persons as part of an essential interpretive task,[12] I am also interested in the interaction of biology and neurology with behavior and therefore in the question of causality, or at least predisposition.[13] A psychology of women based within a psychoanalytic framework relies on an understanding of the unconscious[14] and includes attention to the oedipal configuration of child in the triadic relationship to mother and father. I assign great importance, however, to the pre-oedipal relationship of mother and child in the development of gender identity.

This description of a psychology of women focuses on a developmental question: What happens to women within the process of normal human development which is distinctive and primarily related to the fact of their gender? Whatever these differences, which are substantial, my own conviction is that differences between women and men are less substantial than differences among men and among women. Although I present human psychological issues in a way that describes the distinct experience of women, this psychology is neither disconnected from male experience entirely nor necessarily descriptive for all women. Even though I think that something of what I describe is universal in women's experience, such a claim is inherently risky.

How women are different from men and whether we attribute differences to biology, culture, or development are separable issues. In any case, the examination of gender distinctness does not necessarily lead to hierarchical conclusions. If women prove to be more interested in social relationships than in success or more worried about being harmed than about beating a competitor, that does not justify relegating them to secondary positions or to the "mommy track."[15] The recognition that sexual or gender differences are used to prescribe social roles and behavior is precisely where the feminist movement has been most correct about sexism and culture. Because determination of sexual or gender differences has often been formulated from within a patriarchal position, thinking clearly about those differences remains difficult for us. Our anxiety about the exploration of differences should be acknowledged, but it need not deter us from an exploration of what and how issues may be truly "women's issues."

Object-Relations as the Foundation

No child is raised outside a social field that, at the beginning of life, may be as limited and as filled with possibility as the relationship of mother and child. Human babies develop in relationship, or, to paraphrase D. W. Winnicott, babies alone do not exist![16] The baby also exists as a sexual being to her or his parents from its birth, if not before. Inevitably this means the relationship of mother-daughter, mother-son, father-son, or father-daughter is unique to the pair with an operative and distinctly assigned sexual meaning.[17] Observers find many differences reflected in the interaction of parents to girl and boy children, including distinct patterns in holding, touching, verbalization, and eye contact.[18] Even if you do not assign your child to a specially hued nursery, you will interact with your child differently if you have a girl than if you have a boy. As a baby is understood as a sexual being from very early in life, she or he comes to understand herself or himself in this way from birth. One mother, who is a competent seminary professor with feminist passions, recently said that her three-year-old boy informed her that "boys eat *blue* ice cream and girls eat *pink* ice cream!" As humans we develop a primal, mostly unconscious, distinct self-understanding that, if not written in the genes, may be written in the phylum and is certainly culturally transmitted, if one considers culture to include the nearly universal social unit of mother and child.

Beyond this base of differential treatment of the sexes by the primary caretaker(s) are at least four ways in which an explicitly feminine experience emerges through normal developmental crises, as follows:

1. Intrusion anxiety rather than castration anxiety
2. Interpersonal relationship styles that develop around issues of identification, attachment, and separation, which in girls are dealt with from the context of similarity to their mothers, rather than distinctiveness from them
3. The rhythmicity of the feminine experiences of puberty, menstruation, pregnancy, delivery, and lactation
4. Maternal identification that includes the toleration of self-deprivation in the service of both the ego and the development of the young, but that is not to be equated with masochism

Intrusion Anxiety Rather than Castration Anxiety

The establishment or internalization of core gender identity is complete, according to Robert Stoller, by eighteen months.[19] The child knows herself or himself as a girl or boy and begins to build and incorporate that awareness and its significance into a system of self-understanding. One's genitals become important, if not fascinating, and so do the genitals of others. Freud wrote extensively of castration anxiety and extended this concept to females as well as males, wrongly deducing an understanding of penis envy as the female corollary of male castration anxiety. Karen Horney suggested instead that the young girl often has experiences of hurting herself in the tender genital area.[20] These episodes inform her sense of internal threat. We might think of this anxiety as parallel to but different from male castration anxiety. A female undergoes her own avenue of threat, the dangerous and hurtful possibilities of invasion or intrusion. She is not worried about being a castrated male. She is concerned, though, about bodily harm, and so her sexual interest has a threatening aspect as well.

The young girl, barely more than a toddler, deals with less visible, less obvious, and less concretely examinable genitalia but nevertheless apprehends her own personal and sexual vulnerability. The fear of invasion anxiety becomes informative for the adult woman's psychology, as is exemplified in June's experience (see pp. 1–2). June almost died while having a baby. A common fear during pregnancy is that the child will take over the mother or kill her, or be hurt itself in delivery. Not only did June have to face the reality of her own mortality, but also she had to resolve an intense conflict over the meaning of her sexuality. Being a woman and being sexual had put her in a life-threatening situation; the childhood (but not childish) threat of intrusion and bodily harm had in some sense been confirmed even though she had lived.

June's ambivalence about her baby was profound. Her pastor identified with the part of her ambivalence most removed from her initial exhaustion and thus reinforced the cultural expectation that June's maternal instinct should carry the day. June felt reprimanded for her doubts about this child and the threat the baby had posed to her. We might speculate that she was reprimanded because her minister could think only of the precariousness of the infant and of an identification with it.

Whereas the male defense against his own impulse and his own aggression through castration anxiety may be passivity or a compensatory aggression—a larger gun, if you will—the female's defense in the face of the threat of harm and of her own impulse seems to be more usually withdrawal and avoidance of threat. In the illustration, June withdrew while her minister became more insistent. In particular when men begin to get aggressive or violent, women often turn inward to worry, What is wrong with me? Although Jo Ann Garma focuses on the social context and realities of battering and abuse in chapter 6, the defensive reactions of males (compensatory) and females (withdrawal) toward aggression[21] and the outcomes of aggression in family violence are connected. The simplistic attribution of a woman's tolerance of abuse to her submissive or masochistic nature is a view both too naive and hostile toward women.

Invasion anxiety describes sexual differences in one's sense of one's self and in one's defenses, that is, the formation of intra- and interpersonal character, or character armor. We could argue that the girl initially has a vaguer sense of herself as sexual and perhaps has a heightened sense of uncertainty or apprehensiveness about what or who she is, partly because she "knows not yet what she is," even though she has some sense of the possible meanings of her body's form. For very large numbers of girls and women, invasion anxiety becomes invasion reality. Belenky, Clinchy, Goldberger, and Tarule, in the book *Women's Ways of Knowing,* found that 20 percent of their upper- and middle-class sample had been victims of sexual abuse or seduction by their fathers, brothers, mothers, teachers, ministers, therapists, or a rapist.[22] An even greater number, 50 percent, of lower-class women had similar experiences.[23] As Nancy Ramsay describes in Chapter 5, much human pain, brokenness, and inhibition is the result. Nevertheless, even without actual experiences of incest, abuse, or rape, I assert that the fantasy fear of invasion anxiety is an important component of feminine psychology.

Identification and Separation

Mahler, Stern, Lichtenberg. The second focus of women's psychology is extrapolated from normal developmental tasks in the process of separation-individuation. The delineation of separation-individuation themes in the development of character formation is described in the mother-child observational studies of Margaret Mahler.[24] This description of the developmental sequelae of separation-individuation should not be construed as evidence that Mahler advocates separateness as the aim of human development. Mahler presents attachment and separation as the two psychological valences essential in the child's working model of self-in-relationship. A behavioral repertoire, once established in relationship to the primary caretaker, tends to be repeated and consistent; patterns of ego development in association to the caretaker, therefore, can be used to account for individual personality.[25] Because of Mahler's dependence on Freud, she might be described as aligned with the culture of detachment.[26] Her description of human development, however, is an effort to organize observations of the process of attachment and disengagement rather than an endorsement of separateness as normative for healthy personality.

When Mahler's position is augmented by those of Daniel Stern and Joseph Lichtenberg (each informed by studies in infant research), the drama of separation-individuation can be extrapolated both from metaphors of detachment and from the consequent pessimism about persons. Lichtenberg, in particular, suggests that human intimacy and attachment is achieved in several spheres: through physical regulation, through disengagement, through shared thinking, and through affiliation with groups.[27]

Stern presents a picture of the infant who develops in relationship with numerous others and with a sense of self that is continually evolving through processes of learning, internalization, and identification.[28] Accordingly, a foundational self is established in the early months of the child's development but is open to continual transformations, dependent on the quality of new and changing object relations. From this vantage point, the primary caretaker's influence is less central to the formation of character, and the push-pull of attachment and separation is a less prominent reality. Stern's position identifies a certain plasticity in human personality. It may also be viewed as a correction of the psychoanalytic tradition's enormous and misunderstood attention to mothering and its vicissitudes.

The Mahlerian tradition, unfortunately, has not been disseminated well at the popular level and fosters undue anxiety in most mothers about their parenting. In many cases, a woman has felt blamed outright for her child's neurotic personality. Nevertheless, Stern's position, if romanticized as a description of the essential relatedness of humans and of perpetual openness in personality formation, may err in the direction of what Browning calls "a pervasive metaphor of harmony."[29] Even though metaphors of harmony may seem to point toward continual human change and growth as a possibility, they do not offer reasonable explanations for the realities of the intransigent problems of individuals and of culture. Writers like Nancy Chodorow and Dorothy Dinnerstein[30] base their analyses of sexism on psychoanalytic views that are dependent on the Mahlerian tradition, but they broaden psychoanalysis with sociological analysis. As described by Mahler, the special need for and significance of primary caretakers, demonstrated in the child's dyadic relationship with the mother, usefully explains human alienation and brokenness. In this view, human identity and personality pivot around the sense of self developed in the state of dependent relationship to the giver of life, the mother. A relationship to a primary caretaker is so central to one's survival that either fear of loss of mother (whether perceived or real) before one is prepared to be autonomous, or the reverse, a fear that she will control one forever, is what makes humans essentially human.[31] We require others for attachment. We also need space from them in moments of disengagement.

The girl's experience.   Given the significance of the underlying vision of people inherent in these psychological perspectives, we have yet to address the question of how girls negotiate the processes of separation-individuation. Mahler describes the infant as moving through four stages:

1. Differentiation and the initial development of body image, that is, from symbiosis to hatching, which is usually complete by ten months of age.
2. Practicing, which is marked by the development of an obvious bond to mother and physical movement away from her, between ten months and eighteen months.
3. Rapprochement, with increasing mobility and greater awareness of the importance of the mother's mediating presence, diminishing after twenty-one months.
4. Consolidation of individuality and the beginning of emotional object constancy, which is achieved between twenty-one months and three years of age.[32]

At a point somewhere at the end of the practicing (stage 2) or the beginning of the rapprochement subphase (stage 3), the toddler becomes aware of her or his genitals. Being male or female, however, colors the experience significantly. During the rapprochement stage, the child becomes both more mobile and more anxious about the presence or absence of the mother. Even though the child glories in and anguishes over the fearful discovery of her ultimate separateness, the girl realizes she is like her mother sexually while the boy realizes he is unlike her. This discovery seems to have two meanings for the child.

First, as the attachment takes on a differentiated and sexual flavor, a girl apprehends in a way different from the boy that she is not destined to be her mother or any other woman's special love.[33] The boy is able to sustain a sense of his fantasied liaison and hence his own connection to his mother and his feeling of his delightfulness to her for a longer period of time. Perhaps a girl is disappointed in the discovery of her femininity, not because she sees femininity as inferior, but because she has the concurrent experience of giving up mother as an unattainable prize and identifying with her. We see in girls this age (16 months) a slight but clinically observable depression. Stoller, among others, has linked these clinical observations to theories of penis envy.[34] Just as likely, from an object-relations perspective, is that one internal meaning of core gender identity for the girl is the loss of the profoundly important partnership and the fantasied continuation of her partnership with the adored mother. She is depressed because she grieves, but through her grief she internalizes her mother in an important way. A boy, in contrast, can be more blithely omnipotent in the oedipal situation, at least for a while.

A second and corollary issue for the girl has to do with the dilemma that is raised for her on the separation side of the separation-attachment equation. The push away from mother is also a strong one, and, however much the child needs a mother, both boys and girls are eager to be independent of her. The boy, who discovers he is unlike his mother, may have an easier time of it.[35] He can assume he is different from his mother without the need to prove it. The girl sees she is like her mother, but this identification and felt similarity may intensify the struggle to determine who she uniquely is as separate from mother. The girl has a need to sharpen the sense of mother-daughter difference and may do so in heightened rivalry. Still, if she proceeds too far in that direction, she may feel threatened by isolation or abandonment. Adaptively, the girl becomes more attentive to the nuances of interpersonal relationships and to the impact of her assertiveness, and more focused on taking care (cautious, in a watchful sense, lest she be abandoned) and on caring (through identification with the person who has been her caring mother).

Adult implications of identification.   Both Gilligan and Belenky and associates[36] describe the adult outcomes of what has occurred in the early developmental period. Women proceed from a different frame of reference than men. They work first from a position of concerned involvement and caring rather than from evaluating truth and weighing justice. Their frame of reference includes sensitivity unique to them (which may have been protective in its origins) and includes deepened empathy (an ability to comprehend another's experience).

Gilligan identifies the consequences of this distinct developmental sequence for women as it is worked out in the processes of ethical decision-making. Boys focus on justice and ultimately may be able to incorporate care; girls and women focus on care and ultimately may incorporate justice for themselves into the equation of caring. Belenky and associates describe the effects of this process on the methods and modes of feminine learning and knowing. Women, they have found, are initially awed by authority but, unlike the men of an earlier study by Perry,[37] do not identify with it. Although men in this developmental stage assume they possess authority, women do not. Some women may next evolve into a phase of highly subjective knowing. These women know by intuition or by an inner sense of the meaning of experience and are less intimidated by authority. Fifty percent of the Belenky group's sample can be described as subjective knowers who ascribe to a theory of individual-subjective truth.[38] Many women who enter this epistemological position do so as a result of becoming mothers—a developmental task that draws them into counting on themselves and their own experience to care for their young. Fewer of the same sample afterward enter into a more rational examination of experience, called *procedural knowledge*. Having discovered themselves as possessors of knowledge, they now hold personal truth in tension and conversation with other points of view and use knowledge in a more dialogical process. The opinions of others are again considered and weighed; not all individual truth is equally credible, but the knower's own awareness is used, not slighted, in discerning truth. Unlike men, women at the stage of procedural knowledge are more apt to focus on connections, on understanding, and on discerning through conversation what others are trying to describe. Men who are procedural knowers are apt to be more focused on separateness and on defining distinctions than on sharpening comparisons. These male-female differences may be modified by educational experience, which generally advocates masculine procedural knowledge. Finally, a few women evolve a capacity to construct knowledge, put information and awareness together in a way that is uniquely theirs, and yet allow this work to be informed by the methods and procedures of their disciplines (or by evolving methods consistent with their disciplines). These women are able to draw on their own insights and work by making connections, by seeing similarities, and by discerning what feels to them to be essentially true. In this final epistemological position, women are articulate, reflective, and intensely self-conscious in the best sense. At the same time, they are able to be more fully involved with others in describing and organizing and to view knowledge as a profound way of caring for others and for the world. What they know is vital and alive, but it is essentially created and no less valid because they recognize themselves as active in the creation of knowledge.

The unique developmental crises of women can create or shape feminine personality in other ways. Given what we have described, competition may become for some women an acutely powerful, although perhaps underground, issue. Men compete and may do so more or less openly—in fact, all too openly. Women may compete but withdraw from overt competition or directly aggressive forms of competition while being highly motivated to distinguish themselves.[39] If not demonstrating too clearly her own distinctiveness at the same time she is inwardly compelled to experience uniqueness is paramount for a girl, she may be very ambivalent about getting into a position where she is the apparent success, the winner. The current paragon of feminine virtues is not the virgin Mary. The idealization of relational qualities is a potential trap for women, however, if this converging definition of feminine perfection begins to dictate behavior. Must women be noncompetitive, supportive, egalitarian, equal, and so on? What was descriptive is prescribed, and a new cultural norm extends the sometimes but not always valuable dilemma of the girl into her womanhood. The apparent lack of competitiveness may not be what it seems, but it may be a protective demonstration of an unresolved and inherently difficult aspect of being female. Whereas social-psychological and cultural reinforcement of inhibitions against competition is probably more significant for most mature women than the internal psychological dilemma I have just described,[40] for some women unresolved feelings about the status and security of their mother's affection (the internalized object) are powerful motivators to fail. These feelings, of course, will be all the more likely if her mother has been either depressed or narcissistic and, hence, unavailable.

Rhythmicity

The third aspect of feminine experience begins with puberty and is related to development of secondary sexual characteristics, that is, menstruation, pregnancy, delivery, and lactation. Mary Dean and Mary Louise Cullen write at length about the psychological tasks and theological consequences of the specifically biological aspects of femininity in Chapter 4. While also dependent on the resolution of earlier developmental issues, biological developments create universal stresses or pressures in feminine experience. The developing girl must adapt to significant changes in body image and in functioning. Each of these processes involves the girl in reexamination of body awareness and in assimilation of the ebb and flow of hormonal wash. Two particular outcomes are worth noting. First, menses can create feelings of physical discomfort, even pain, and has special connotations because it represents the absence of control over body fluids. Thus menstruation can promote considerable frustration in women and may rekindle feelings of shame or humiliation. Particularly if one's female sexuality has already been the source of humiliation, whether by actual abuse or by psychological depreciation,[41] menstruation may be interpreted through the sense of helplessness, acquiescence, and passivity that already presides over self-concept. Ernest Becker, for example, suggests that a woman's sheer physicalness becomes the focus of the child's obsession to avoid the limits of our bodies.[42] Yet, menstruation, pregnancy, delivery, and lactation all press the young woman to be involved in more thoughtful personal planning and self-care. Practically speaking, women are required to deal with the absence of control over their physical bodies on a continuing and regular basis. What is mastered thereby is the recognition and acknowledgment of the reality of human helplessness, and women learn this fact in the safest way possible, that is, in regular, small doses. What they can learn is that what cannot be changed must be lived with gracefully, that is, self-acceptance. Such experience, however taxing—and it may be very taxing to the woman whose life experience has been marked by sexualization[43]—also can enhance ego development.

Maternal Identification

The significance of maternal identification is a fourth aspect of a unique feminine psychology. Whether or not a woman has children, motherhood represents the capacity for loving perseverance (*hesed:* steadfast love) and the fostering of development in the service of the maternal ego ideal. In this chapter, I am particularly concerned to dissociate the psychology of mothering from the notion of masochism. (In Chapters 3 and 8, respectively, Bonnie Miller-McLemore and Priscilla Denham describe in greater detail issues of mothering and changes in life-styles.)

Mature mothering, when it is accomplished, requires remarkable sublimation of the adult and promotes sublimation and mastery in the child. Harold Blum, who has described a new feminine psychology, writes,

> Masochism is a residue of unresolved infantile conflict, and is neither essentially feminine nor a valuable component of mature female function and character . . . it is important to distinguish between masochistic suffering as a goal in itself, and tolerance for a discomfort or deprivation in service of the ego or ego ideal. . . . it is impossible to derive maternal devotion and empathy from masochism, narcissism, and penis envy.[44]

At times mothers may experience pain, sadness, or suffering as a consequence of the important attachment to the child, but these feelings are not necessary prerequisites or organizing realities of mothering or of the feminine character.

THEOLOGICAL REFLECTION ON
DEVELOPMENTAL THEMES

The four developmental themes identified above—intrusion anxiety, the continuity of identity with the primary parent (customarily mother), rhythmicity, and maternal identification—suggest areas for theological reflection and new approaches to pastoral care. Recognition of these motifs emphasizes distortions of pastoral practice which are not helpful in our work with women. Each of these four elements in women's experience deserves much greater consideration than can be developed in the remainder of this chapter, but the following outline suggests directions for further thought.[45]

Intrusion Anxiety and Invasive Conduct

Whereas castration anxiety in men can be assimilated to foster male identification with the weak and helpless and thus enable them to extend themselves toward others, their normal defenses shift toward aggressive adaptation. Men may be less inclined to avoid conflict than women, who live with the threat of intrusion. Men may be more likely to behave in a contentious, blustery fashion. In places where men gather, this behavior may be seen in too little respect for interpersonal boundaries, too great a readiness for confrontation, and a too knowing posture. Male defenses focus on the subordination of those over whom they have authority. Power-hungry males reflect an underlying fear of smallness and the masculine struggle with threat.

Feminine intrusion anxiety serves to push women in the direction of concern for the threatened or threatening other and to a positive identification with the weak, the poor, and the vulnerable. Women prioritize toward "the least of these" (Matt. 25:40, 45), toward the young and the vulnerable. What is most natural to women is in keeping with the strong thrust of the Judeo-Christian tradition to do justice and walk humbly, to express and use one's energy for those who suffer economic and personal hardship.

Implicit in the notion of intrusion anxiety, as in castration anxiety, is the underlying threat of physical harm and uncomfortable feelings attendant to overstimulation. In early childhood, as sexual and gender awareness develops, a youngster is particularly vulnerable to intrusion. The threat, however, need not assume a purely physical form. The parent who is too much—too needy, too loud, too involved, too honest, too demanding, or even too helpful—creates psychic dissonance. The intrusive parent, whether physically abusive or not, generates neurologic discomfort.

Amid the theological reflections of Dietrich Bonhoeffer are accounts of his life in prison and of his relationships with other prisoners.[46] Through the solitude and anxiety of waiting, Bonhoeffer generally maintained a quiet calm. Toward those inmates who described their own fear during the air raids, however, Bonhoeffer says, "There are people who feel themselves called upon to 'tell the truth,' as they put it, to everyone who crosses their path."[47] He writes further,

> Many things in man are to remain concealed, and that if it is too late to eradicate evil, it is at least to be kept hidden. Exposure is cynical; and even if the cynic appears to himself to be specially honest, or if he sets himself up to be a fanatical devotee of truth, he nevertheless fails to achieve the truth which is of decisive importance, namely the truth that since the Fall there has been a need also for concealment and secrecy. . . . In my view "telling the truth" means saying how something is in reality, i.e., respect for secrecy, confidence, and concealment.[48]

Humans modulate relationship with others in a movement between seeking attention and seeking solitude. Both qualities of experience— the ability to become focused and engaged and the paired opposite, the ability to disengage and be self-contained—enhance a sense of self.[49] As receivers of pastoral care, we need to be as assured of our ability to avert attention, to remove ourselves, as we are to gain it. We are not always interested in making ourselves or our inner experience available. We become psychologically disorganized in the absence of attention and psychologically disorganized with overstimulation.

The crucial question about what can be said or told and what should be left unsaid is central to how we demonstrate respect for others, a little addressed but foundational dilemma for pastoral theology and practice. Although we begin to learn of the potential destructiveness of secrets in women's lives (particularly concerning sexual abuse) and in pathological family structures,[50] we should avoid the suggestion that full disclosure is necessarily healthy. Equal concern for reserve, the avoidance of misunderstanding, and the avoidance of sensationalism are pivotal to "saying how something is in reality."[51]

Intrusive pastoral acts fall on the side of too much interaction. Pastors who command attention by overinvolvement, vivacity, or bossiness are intrusive. Ministers who insinuate themselves into the projects, plans, or situations (especially personal ones) of others' lives against their wishes, expressed or not, may like to think of themselves as helpful, but may in fact be experienced as an additional trauma to be endured.

Invasion also occurs when we mistake the need for comforting with the need for intimacy. Pastoral care does not require that we impose ourselves (any more than we would impose Scripture or proclamation) on our parishioners and clients. Pastors can identify and respect interpersonal boundaries. As a minister, I might inquire, "Would it make sense for us to schedule a time to talk?" To ask is far less upsetting than to imply "You need help on this or that issue. . . ." There are also times not to ask questions, to give advice, or even to offer reflective listening. We can avoid the temptation, promoted by popular psychological wisdom, to become soothsayers who are too knowing and too ready to confront. "How blest are those of a gentle spirit; they shall have the earth for their possession" (Matt. 5:5 NEV). We need not speak all we feel, even though it may be "the truth."

Identification with the Mother

A woman's internalization of her mother and her essential sense of continuity with her mother as the primary caretaker is intrinsic to the woman's sense of self. Feminine identity comes naturally through relatedness. Identity formation does not require of women the early leap to separate from the image of the mother, as is required of men. But, a woman also needs to be guaranteed her individuality and may dread enmeshment. Although a sense of self-in-connection comes easily, the demonstration of individuality may be conflicted or require effort to achieve, particularly in a sexist culture that reinforces feminine dependency. When required, the heroic stance can be attained through self-conscious efforts. Yet, the feminine route to heroism is essentially a woman's path; heroic women stand for and with others against the demonic powers of destruction. They do not demonstrate courage in the masculine fashion by standing apart in order to stand for and attain identity; they stand with the mother, hence for others, and can, therefore, stand apart.

The mystic, inward "oceanic," feeling may be inherent to femininity, and it is an essential ingredient in the accomplishment of woman's heroism. Faith, synthesized in trust and love of God, allows a woman to turn away from pursuits or standards that are not her own, while she can preserve relationships. The spiritual traditions of Christianity and the discipline of theological study may help women uphold connected individuation. If the woman knows herself to be a participant and not just an adjunct to a historic tradition, "the mighty cloud of witnesses," she is enabled to take a moral position when it is needed.

This heroic position is neither mere individualism nor religiously fla-vored self-aggrandizement but an authentic expression of her most profound attachment to parent and child, as representationally sym-bolized within the family of faith.

Through the internalization of the primary object, women's gender identity is made secure. On the one hand, although I am in accord with the feminist movement to describe God as female, mother, and nurturer, I believe there are psychological reasons why, until recently, women have not felt an urgent need for a Mother-God. In the unconscious depths, we already know her. In her ecstatic episodes, Julian of Norwich,[52] in the late fourteenth and early fifteenth centuries, describes the mystery of God as mother, intimating every woman's potential vision of the divine.

On the other hand, as males relinquish attachment to the omnipotent maternal object and ground their personal identity in a lesser known male, the need for the image of a male God surfaces. The image of a male God also serves to reestablish the egotistical position of the child who has been wounded by the realization that he (that is, the child) is not like the one who held him enthralled. Assumptions about God's gender, therefore, may be more significant as a psychological marker of early parenting arrangements within a culture than as a theological principle.

Another way feminine connectedness may be demonstrated is through women's way of perceiving ethical responsibilities. Giving, understanding, and being in relationship are the moral expressions of her identity as opposed to analyzing and evaluating right and wrong. In fact, women may be distressed by critiques of behavior whereas they readily respond to moral conversation or dialogue that is nourished in deeper processes of identification. Narratives and parables are more apt to engage women than efforts to deduce principles or establish codes of conduct. What separates them from others is experienced as foreign; what connects them to another's circumstance informs and guides their own living.

Rhythmicity

Menstruation is women's secret. Pregnancy and lactation also suggest the quiet and private harboring of potential and future life. In them, a woman feels the fullness of being: "My soul doth magnify the Lord," suggests the early christological hymn. Her body also celebrates the ones who are to come. These separate but inseparable aspects of being female locate an indescribable and primary faith: hope is never distinguished from being. The fullness of time is known bodily. I am given life. I bring life. I am not all, but I am life.

Yet, with menstruation comes wounding. I bleed. I endure loss but I am not diminished. Finitude is repeated in cyclical processes of renewal and loss. These biologic events prepare women to deal with the routine exigencies of life through participation of self in suffering and salvation. A woman imparts herself in caring, in cleaning, and in touching wounds, not simply in deciding about good and evil. The first time she washes her own menses she may recoil inwardly, but it prepares her to clean up a baby's vomitus and excrement. Her dismay over the soiling is apt to be transitory to her sense of satisfaction in providing relief and in comforting another. Furthermore, these actions bond her to others; she is not diminished by them. She is loved and is united with those for whom she cares. Yet, these are private acts of love; she does not go into the street to perform them but to her closet.

Ministry can be a silent act. Through the private solace of those in despair and the keeping of confidences, we are promised reward. "When you do some act of charity, do not let your left hand know what your right hand is doing; your good deed must be secret, and your Father who sees what is done in secret will reward you" (Matt 6:3-4 NEV).

Maternal Identification

Finally, maternal identification suggests aspects of ministry best expressed through the metaphor of parenting. Of course, women have much to contribute here both out of our being—our distinct psychological makeup that is different from that of men—and out of our understanding of the experience of being like our mothers. A practical theology of care can be organized around an understanding of the religious and psychological significance of parenting. We can identify, describe, and practice the moral dimensions of parent-child relationships with specific attention to the rights and responsibilities of being parents.

A passionate concern for the relationship of elders to the young is a central understanding of pastoral theology, even though mothering is not all. Such concern is the way God is involved in and revealed in the life of the world. This concern is not dependent on religious persuasion or theological party. It is fundamental to a universal theology and intrinsic ethic. How one nurtures, guides, and educates the young, the vulnerable, the poorest, and the most troubled to fuller self-understanding and participation in human social life—this is what matters. Our world is desperately in need of adults to behave as parents, in a parental, not patronizing (whether patriarchal or matriarchal) way. Moreover, as adults we equally need to know what it is to parent, although not necessarily in a biological sense. We parent for our own salvation; it is essential to human nature. According to Paul Lehmann, the first and fourth commandments are central to Luther's doctrinal understanding of the decalogue.[53] The injunction to honor parents includes and is informed by the covenantal relationship of parent to child. Because we are introduced to these rights and responsibilities through the experience of being a child, and that relationship is always crucial to our experience of life, the fourth commandment states simply, "Honor your father and your mother." The first commandment is connected to the fourth and provides a preeminent framework for an interpretation of the meaning of being a parent.[54] We parent in response to the love and worship of God and in keeping the covenant as gospel.

The same relationship of parent to the young is intrinsic to all pastoral authority, to teaching, to pastoral ministry in all its dimensions, and to counseling. The relationship requires of the parental figure appropriate human behavior: to know the one who is served and to know oneself as an adult. It has a corresponding ethic: to maintain parent-child boundaries. The parent does not use the child. Intrinsic to the covenantal relationship for the child is the capacity and safety to be a child. The most profound human task and theological conduct is to behave as good parents in those places where as adults we are required to act in the stead of parents. Discipline of the self and the sublimation of one's own ego needs in order to nurture another's ego are not reserved for mothers or for women. They require the fullest and most thoughtful use of the self on behalf of those who are not yet mature. Whether in the lives of pastors, believers, the church, or society, our efforts will not be amiss if we focus on this redemptive task—the exposition of God's steadfast love for people, as exhibited in the passionate shouldering of concern for others.

NOTES

1. See pp. 1–5.

2. See pp. 50–54.

3. Carol Gilligan, *In a Different Voice* (Cambridge: Harvard University Press, 1977).

4. Allison Stokes, *Ministry After Freud* (New York: Pilgrim Press, 1982).

5. Don S. Browning, *Religious Ethics and Pastoral Care* (Philadelphia: Fortress Press, 1983), and *Religious Thought and the Modern Psychologies*

(Philadelphia: Fortress Press, 1987); Donald Capps, *Deadly Sins and Saving Virtues* (Philadelphia: Fortress Press, 1987), and *Life Cycle Theory and Pastoral Care* (Philadelphia: Fortress Press, 1983); Charles Gerkin, *The Living Human Document: Revisioning Pastoral Counseling in a Hermeneutical Mode* (Nashville: Abingdon Press, 1984); Thomas Oden, *Care of Souls in the Classic Tradition* (Philadelphia: Fortress Press, 1984), and *Pastoral Theology: Essentials of Ministry* (San Francisco: Harper & Row, 1982).

6. Browning, *Religious Thought*, 5–6, 29–31.

7. I am suspicious that pastoral theologians have not been as purely motivated to restore Christianity to its roots as is claimed. Just as when blacks began to drive Cadillacs, whites discovered a new status symbol in Volkswagens, perhaps some of the move away from the discussion of psychology in pastoral theology includes the impetus to avoid issues of gender. Do we remove ourselves at the point of challenge in order to maintain an established position?

8. Fred Pine, "The Four Psychologies of Psychoanalysis and Their Place in Clinical Work," *Journal of the American Psychoanalytic Association* 36, no. 3 (1988): 571–96.

9. Joseph D. Lichtenberg, *Psychoanalysis and Motivation* (Hillsdale, N.J.: The Analytic Press, 1989); Steven A. Mitchell, *Relational Concepts in Psychoanalysis* (Cambridge: Harvard University Press, 1988). These syntheses represent significant advances over what Browning has described as "many schools and specialties dotting the landscape," (*Religious Thought*, 34).

10. Joseph D. Lichtenberg, *Psychoanalysis and Infant Research* (Hillsdale, N.J.: The Analytic Press, 1983); Margaret S. Mahler, Fred Pine, and Anni Bergman, *The Psychological Birth of the Human Infant: Symbiosis and Individuation* (New York: Basic Books, 1975); Daniel N. Stern, *The Interpersonal World of the Infant: A View from Psychoanalysis and Developmental Psychology* (New York: Basic Books, 1985).

11. See pp. 48, 59 nn.66–69.

12. See, for example, Capps, *Life Cycle*, 11, 37–60; Gerkin, *Human Document*, 19–35.

13. See Erwin Wallace, "A One-Sided Image of Science," *Journal of the American Psychoanalytic Society* 37, no. 2 (1989): 493–529, for a discussion of psychoanalysis as a science. Wallace argues that personal meaning and motivation, that is, self-interpretation, are essential to understanding personality but that arguments for a strictly hermeneutical view of personality or psychotherapy reduce the notion of preexistent reality to absurdity.

14. Following Mitchell's understanding of the unconscious, *Relational Concepts*, 261–62. Rather than a clean distinction between what is conscious and unconscious, the boundary between them is permeable, shifting, and indistinct. We construct understanding outside our own awareness and oblivious to all the meanings of our actions and experience because mental activity is far too complex on any other basis.

15. See pp. 69 n.10; 85.

16. D. W. Winnicot, *Babies and Their Mothers* (Reading, Mass.: Addison Wesley, 1987).

17. Virginia Clower, "A Developmental Approach to Understanding Femininity," 1982.

18. Ibid.

19. Robert Stoller, "Primary Femininity," *Journal of the American Psychoanalytic Association* 24 (1976): 59–77; and *Sex and Gender* (New York: Aaronson, 1974).

20. Karen Horney, "On the Genesis of the Castration Complex in Women," *International Journal of Psychoanalysis* 5 (1924): 50–65.

21. Castration anxiety might be understood as sexualized anxiety about threatened aggression. Core gender identity seems to become an identifiable developmental concern of the child at about the same time she or he recognizes separation from mother as inevitable. The inherent threat of real physical harm is attendant to that acknowledgment; hence gender awareness and the new sense of physical vulnerability coincide developmentally and may converge into fear formulated in the child's concretized thinking as "penis loss," or, as I am arguing, the fear of invasion. In addition the child in the practicing subphase of separation-individuation is more physically active and will likely behave in ways that cause pain.

22. Mary Field Belenky, Blythe McVicker Clincher, Nancy Rule Goldberger, and Jill Mattuch Tarule, eds. *Women's Ways of Knowing: The Development of Self, Voice, and Mind* (New York: Basic Books, 1986), 58–60.

23. Ibid.

24. Mahler and others, *Psychological Birth.*

25. Ibid. 123–209.

26. Don Browning (*Religious Thought*, 5, 32–60) associates Freud with the culture of detachment. This culture is dominated by "deep metaphors and views of human nature which push people toward pessimism about the range of beneficence that can be reasonably expected from one another," 5.

27. Joseph D. Lichtenberg, "A Theory of Motivational-Functional Systems as Psychic Structures," *Journal of the American Psychoanalytic Association* 36 (1988): 57–72.

28. Although Stern describes this stance in *Interpersonal World of the Infant* (10), in public lectures in Denver in the spring of 1987, he stated that he had overemphasized his differences with Mahler in order to provoke discussion. He does see the stages of separation-individuation as a portrayal of what occurs for the child in normal development, although he does not see the child as enmeshed or undifferentiated from birth.

29. Browning, *Religious Thought*, 5.

30. Nancy Chodorow, *The Reproduction of Mothering: Psychoanalysis and the Sociology of Gender* (Berkeley: University of California Press, 1978); Dorothy Dinnerstein, *Mermaid and Minotaur: Sexual Arrangements and Human Malaise* (New York: Harper & Row, 1976).

31. For an interesting and humorous description of identity formation as focused by threat, see James Gorman, "Light Elements," *Discover*, May (1987): 22–24. Gorman argues that hatchery-born salmon lack self-understanding as fish because they have no opportunity to develop a "fear of Cod."

32. Mahler et al., *Psychological Birth*, 41–120.

33. I believe that the daughter herself has a reaction to the recognition of her gender that does not presuppose a mother's imposition of gender constraints. It is to be distinguished from the position taken by Louise Eichenbaum and Susie Orbach, *What Do Women Want? Exploding the Myth of Dependency* (New York: Berkley Books, 1983). Eichenbaum and Orbach argue that a mother communicates to her daughter that women must not expect to get their needs met; they must learn to meet others' needs and make others feel especially loved. Hence, identification entails early object loss because of the mother's withdrawal from caretaking functions.

Mothers may or may not withdraw from their rapprochement-aged daughters. Nevertheless, I would argue that in either case the normal girl does undergo a developmental crisis around feminine identification.

34. Stoller, "Primary Femininity," 70–75.

35. My male analyst friends take exception and point to the inherent difficulties in male identity formation because of the mother's importance and the need to break free of her. Their view underscores the apparent fragility of males and the obvious hatred of women that is evident in the too numerous rapes and murders of women.

36. Belenky et al., *Women's Ways;* Gilligan, *Different Voice.*

37. N. G. Perry, *Forms of Intellectual and Ethical Development in the College Years* (New York: Holt, Rinehart, and Winston, 1970).

38. Belenky et al., *Women's Ways*, 55.

39. B. Bunker and L. Bender, "Dare Women Compete: A Guide for Managers," *Management Review* August (1980).

40. Marcia Westkott, *The Feminist Legacy of Karen Horney* (New Haven: Yale University Press, 1986), 66–87, 145–83.

41. Ibid.

42. Ernest Becker, *The Denial of Death* (New York: The Free Press, 1973).

43. Westkott, *Karen Horney.*

44. Harold Blum, "Masochism, Ego Ideal, and the Psychology of Women," *Journal of the American Psychoanalytic Association* 24 (1976): 188–89.

45. My initial effort to address these questions was "Gender Issues in Pastoral Theology," presented at the meeting of the Society for Pastoral Theology in June 1987. I will expand those ideas and others based on the four elements of women's experience in a later manuscript.

46. Dietrich Bonhoeffer, *Letters and Papers From Prison* (New York: Macmillan, 1953).

47. Dietrich Bonhoeffer, *Ethics* (New York: Macmillan, 1964), 334.

48. Bonhoeffer, *Letters*, 158.

49. Lichtenberg, "The Attachment-Affiliation Motivational System," in *Psychoanalysis and Motivation*, 69–94.

50. James Lechan, *Pastoral Care for Survivors of Family Abuse* (Louisville: Westminster/John Knox, 1989), 91–94, 122–25.

51. Bonhoeffer, *Letters*, 158.

52. Julian of Norwich, *Showings*, ed. Edmund Colledge and James Walsh (New York: Paulist Press, 1978).

53. Paul Lehmann, "The Decalogue and Parameters of the Common Life," delivered at the annual conference for the Association for Clinical Pastoral Education, October 1981.

54. Ibid.

• • • • • • • • • • •

CHAPTER 2

The Psychology
of Women and
Pastoral Care

JEANNE STEVENSON MOESSNER AND
MAXINE GLAZ

• • • • • • • • • • •

WOMEN ON THE PSYCHOLOGY
OF WOMEN • J.S.M.

Pastoral care texts rarely mention contributions to the field from women.
Men such as Carl Gustav Jung, Sigmund Freud, Anton Boisen, and
Seward Hiltner have stood in the limelight; women have remained in
the shadows. Here, three women are brought to the foreground as
representatives in analytical psychology, psychoanalysis, and Clinical
Pastoral Education: Frances Gillespy Wickes (1875-1967), Karen
Horney (1885-1952), and Helen Flanders Dunbar (1902-59). Selections
from their research that have particular significance for the pastoral
care of women are highlighted: Frances Wickes's emphasis on a woman's
power of choice and her internal authority, Karen Horney's exposition
of the role of culture in development, and Helen Flanders Dunbar's
focus on psychosomatic unity and her connection between religious
symbolism and mental health.

Frances Gillespy Wickes: Choice and Authority

Because of the gift of choice, according to Hebraic legend, humankind
is higher than the angels.[1] Women traditionally have not utilized the
extent of their power of choice; they have not perceived themselves as
in control of their lives and their options. They have not intimately
known the authority within. The church participates in this socialization
when it fosters women's dependence on male, external authority figures

and when it uses predominantly male images in ritual, hymns, and theology.

When Frances Gillespy Wickes wrote *The Inner World of Choice*, she meant by the title that inner reality or inner experience. For women, entering "the inner world of choice" is precipitated by a rebirth that includes befriending the masculine principle (the animus) within her.

Wickes, an American analytical psychologist, utilized the theory of the psyche developed by her teacher, Carl Gustav Jung.[2] In Jungian theory, each person has both a dominant, conscious, sexual ego-identity, either male or female, and an element of the opposite sex, referred to as the *anima* (the feminine principle) in the male personality or the *animus* (the masculine principle) in the female personality. The interplay of contrasexual elements makes a balanced individual.

Women and men can consciously allow the contrasexual element to express itself. When women let their animus develop and express itself, they empower themselves in the subsequent exercise of choice and authority. The animus is the power to will and to act, the capacity to take charge, the ability to separate, and the spirit that searches out meaning and that clothes ideas in words.

Pastoral ministry can be enhanced by an understanding of the contrasexual elements of the human personality. In the pastoral care of women, this approach can be utilized as a woman looks at "the man" within and emboldens herself with her newfound power of choice and authority. In general pastoral care, this approach generates inclusiveness and decreases gender exclusiveness. "The male pastor in touch with his anima and the female pastor in touch with her animus will be better able to do pastoral ministry because they can affirm femininity along with maleness and masculinity along with femaleness respectively."[3]

Seven Wickian themes have significance for the pastoral care of women. First, women can realize their power of choice. For example, a woman may consciously choose to stay in an unhappy marriage until the children are grown or until she is financially able to sustain herself; a pastor might help her acknowledge this choice to remain in an undesirable situation as a practical or even moral option. Second, women can realize that completeness or wholeness is not perfection. They can be encouraged to say and believe, "I did the best I could under the circumstances." This attitude counters the ideal of perfection under which so many well-meaning women have suffered.

Women's acceptance of the interplay of opposites is based on an awareness of good and evil as continuing forces both in the world and in her own psyche. She knows that she is both good and bad, and she knows that as long as she lives she is going to be both good and bad. She knows that the same forces are existent in every human being whom she encounters.[4]

Third, women can be helped to see their lives as connected to, yet separate from, others. Wickes suggested dispelling the participation mystique; a woman who came to Jung for analysis felt "dismembered by the demands of conflicting relationships which drew her into such *participation mystique* that she hardly knew whose life she was living."[5] A pastor can remind a woman that "you cannot please everyone." Women who have been socialized to be pleasing and who are symbiotically connected to others are at risk for this type of dysfunction and dismemberment, which is to lose one's life and not find it. Fourth, women who discern and discriminate in helping others can avoid "help" that becomes incapacitating or crippling. A woman needs encouragement for separation to allow healthy growth in relationships: "she must be alert to perceive the moment when giving can impoverish the spirit of both giver and recipient so that even her withholding may serve life."[6] Wickes's suggestion is followed by a clinical example of a woman, overanxious to assist a young man in a difficult professional position. She dreamed of standing in a room with the naked youth in front of her and a gleaming, double-edged sword at her feet. As she looked at him, a voice stated, "You can cut off his testicles if you want to."[7] With discernment and mature discrimination, a woman can avoid such psychic castration and offer instead genuine care. Fifth, women benefit by relating to both the image of Earth Mother and the image of Wise Woman within the psyche. Wickes rightly differentiates between a woman's development vis-a-vis her mother and that of a man.

> Woman cannot and should not separate herself from the Mother, as man must; her freedom lies in her increasing consciousness of how this image lives itself within her own psyche. . . . The relation to the image of Earth Mother is the fundamental determinant of the feminine principle. . . . The spirit form of the Earth Mother is the "Wise Woman," who knows the secrets of the heart.[8]

Before a woman can locate these images within herself, she will often locate a representation of these images outside herself. One cancer patient found a model for the Wise Woman in her counseling sessions with a female hospital chaplain. From the chaplain she received advice and direction amid listening and empathy. At the conclusion of their pastoral visits, the chaplain gave the patient an embrace at the door as she departed. To the patient this act represented the Earth Mother and was as instrumental in her recovery as the wise counsel that represented the Wise Woman. The patient may one day find both the Earth Mother and the Wise Woman within herself. Sixth, a woman may choose to be free of regrets and avoid the morose refrain, "it could have been." In this book, the blame, guilt, and shame that have encumbered women in their development are frequently mentioned. As pastoral care providers, our sensitization to these feelings equips us for the moments when a woman makes peace with her regrets. Wickes describes this process:

> Her daily life demands this heroism of woman. She learns to love, to hold and to let go. She discovers it is not that which has lived and gone from her that she secretly mourns, but the unborn potential, the unlived experience, the demand of life that she refused. Yet, even when she feels drained by regrets, she must make peace with them if she would keep them from stopping up the wellsprings whose waters must flow again and once more give life to the seeds of her spirit.[9]

Seventh, a woman can choose to be true to her central purpose and not lose herself in drudgery and diffuseness which are the enemies of creative choice. These enemies surface in perfunctory activities, busyness unrelated to a woman's life goal, and multitudinous works.

Wickes maintained that women with underdeveloped animuses are attracted by external authority figures. Male authority figures such as pastors and priests appeal to a woman's undeveloped animus and offer a pseudo-psychic balance with the woman's anima. As pastoral care providers, we might be cautioned of the danger of placing long-term authority in spiritual leadership.

> When the authority image is placed upon the man of intellectual attainment or spiritual leadership—teacher, philosopher, priest—woman may appropriate the words and the husks of thought without letting the seed, the spirit contained within the word, enter and be born within her. . . . Thereby her ego is inflated but not nourished.[10]

Because their animuses are not developed, women also too easily identify with their husbands. In acquiring the husband, his accomplishments and advancements become hers. Thus, upon relating her husband's promotion, she can be heard to say, "We have just been made vice-president."[11]

A woman may instead consciously choose to allow the animus to express itself. She can do so while retaining her central attitude as woman. The animus can express itself in a number of ways, among which are thinking and clothing ideas in words. The anima expresses itself in feeling and in demonstrating tenderness and sensitivity. Wickes gives an example of a female physician who allowed the animus to serve the anima; her thinking was used in the service of feeling.

Devoted to research on occupational hazards, she was fighting for the passage of a more humane labor law. She had to face a group of approximately fifty antagonistic men and speak scientifically, persuasively, and clearly. She did this without arousing their hostility, which normally occurs among men when a woman exercises her animus. When asked how she was able to do this, the female physician replied, "I keep before my inner vision a scene I once witnessed—a thin tired bewildered child sitting with loving patience beside a father who was dying of lead poisoning. Then I remember the meaning of my research in terms of human life."[12] Thus, Wickes remarked, this physician held steadfast to her feminine center; she spoke as a woman but made use of characteristics of her animus. She spoke with scientific facts; she presented lucid arguments; she appealed to common fairness and humaneness. She knew her subject thoroughly. All of these attributes were used to serve her passion, her feelings, and her inner vision. This inner world of choice can catapult a woman to a position of interpersonal influence and power that is higher than the angels.

Karen Horney: The Anatomy of a Culture

Karen Horney's vivisection of Western culture exposed the view that woman's every thought should center exclusively on the male or motherhood, in much the same manner expressed in Marlene Dietrich's famous song, "I know only love, and nothing else."[13] Concerned with the observation that a woman's efforts to be independent and to enlarge her interests and activities were met with resistance, Karen Horney revised psychoanalytic theory to incorporate the impact of culture. She argued that biologic drive and its aberrations do not manifest themselves directly in neurosis but are mediated by tradition, environment, and society.[14] Her modification of the Freudian presupposition that "anatomy is destiny" was, in fact, a proposal to alter an essential theoretical underpinning of psychoanalysis as originally conceived. Freud maintained the crucial importance of biology to personality. Horney's position served as a counterpoint: biology modified by culture is destiny. As a woman trained in psychoanalytic thought in Berlin, analyzed by Karl Abraham and Hanns Sachs, and admitted to the prestigious Berlin Psychoanalytic Institute, Horney's reformulation of Freud's position on biologic determinism was seen as a daring, if not dangerous, move.

Furthermore, her explicit attention to female psychology and to the correction of male views of female psychology put her at odds with the psychoanalytic establishment in the United States. "Psychoanalysis is the creation of a male genius, and almost all those who have developed his [Freud's] ideas have been men. It is only right and reasonable that they should evolve more easily a masculine psychology and understand more of the development of men than of women."[15] In her critique of culture, Horney utilized the work of the German sociologist Georg Simmel, who depicted Western civilization as a masculine civilization.[16] Simmel proposed that the state, the laws, morality, religion, and the sciences are all the creation of men. Thus, the "objective" in our society has been equated with the masculine.[17]

Horney described in *Feminine Psychology* three additional changes of Freudian theory essential to a pastoral care of women that moves away from a masculine psychology: First, the oedipus complex occurs only under certain cultural conditions, and female masochism also is a product of a culture and not a biologic given or a psychological necessity.[18] Second, whereas Freud depicted male and female sexuality as determinative or decisive, Horney annotated the way in which gender identification as male or female is unnecessarily divisive. Her work on the distrust between the sexes highlights man's dread of woman. Male fear and anxiety is provoked by the mystery of motherhood, which serves as a menace to man's self-respect and also by his envy of woman's essential creativity and centeredness in being. A woman does not have to prove her womanhood through performance; in the sexual act, for example, she proves her part by merely being, without any doing. This contrast alone is cause for jealousy. Third, rather than focus on sex and aggression as the biologic underpinnings of all behavior, Horney directed her work toward an understanding of anxiety, which she believed underlies the neurotic need for love as represented in Dietrich's song. Unraveling the biblical injunction to love God, self, and neighbor in such a way that is not neurotic for women is surely a theological task.

Although Horney acknowledged diversity among women, she exposed a traditional tendency in her study of morbid dependency in *Self-Analysis*. In her case study of Clare, Horney exposed the neurotic need for dependency and the compulsive need to depend on a partner. "Its main feature was an entirely repressed parasitic attitude, an unconscious wish to feed on the partner, to expect him to supply the content of her life, to take responsibility for her, to solve all her difficulties and to make her a great person without her having to make efforts of her own."[19] This parasitic attitude can be described as learned helplessness. (Psychiatry labels it dependent personality disorder.[20]) Horney described the antithesis of this parasitic helplessness as the neurotic need for self-sufficiency and independence.[21] Horney was ahead of her time here. Only recently has the traditional developmental schema with autonomy and individuation as the goal of maturation come under scrutiny as a male theory. One researcher has unofficially created a new diagnostic category, the independent personality disorder, a disorder more prevalent among self-sufficient males.[22]

We are only beginning to see how gender roles contribute to disorders. For example, an overemphasis of the female stereotype contributes not only to depression (chap. 7) but also to phobic and eating disorders.

> In depression, women feel inadequate, worthless, and helpless; they blame themselves too much for failures. In phobic disorders, women have excessive fears; in agoraphobia, women are overly feminine and dependent. Women with eating disorders are excessively concerned with being slim.[23]

A review of Horney's counterpoint position to Freudian presuppositions—biology modified by culture is destiny—is therefore appropriate.

As pastoral caregivers, Horney's legacy pushes us to theological considerations. How does the church participate in biologic and cultural determinism? Does God portrayed as "Determiner of Destiny" have any impact through our lives on this determinism?[24] How do our spiritual understandings or religious assumptions penetrate the interaction of the biologic and cultural as described by Horney? As we move beyond the oedipus complex to theories of the family of origin, what is the role of the family of faith in the life of an individual? Whether male and female sexuality is seen as decisive or divisive, what difference does the church's vision of gender inclusiveness make in actuality and practice? They are the questions of this volume, a volume offering the anatomy of a culture that includes the church.

Helen Flanders Dunbar: Mind-Body Dualism

A woman's relationship to her body has ramifications in her sense of self. A theology that does not take into account the interplay of mind and body is a type of doctrinal decapitation. This can only result in a destructive process as seen in Helen Flanders Dunbar's analogy of the headless horseman. "Once the mind has abdicated its responsibility, the personality becomes a headless horseman galloping crazily to destruction."[25] Her understanding of the connectedness of spirit, mind, and body, as well as the interplay of psychic and somatic forces, was reinforced by her interdisciplinary training at Union Theological Seminary (B.D.), Columbia (Ph.D. in comparative literature), and Yale (M.D.). Under the supervision of Anton Boisen, Dunbar had clinical pastoral training at Worcester State Hospital in 1925. In addition to Boisen's early influence, she underwent psychotherapy with the prominent Freudian Helene Deutsch, met with Carl Gustav Jung on several occasions in Zurich, and visited the shrine at Lourdes, France. Of that shrine, which to her demonstrated the connectedness of spirit, mind, and body, she wrote: "Much more dramatic evidence of this therapeutic quality of the emotions may be seen at Lourdes, and anyone interested in the psychosomatic ideas of illness and health would do well to ponder the curious phenomena which takes place in this French shrine of miracles."[26] Disagreeing with the French medical bureau that counted only organic cures, she maintained that many more changes in personality and in improved health occurred among pilgrims than would ever satisfy the mechanistic tests of the Lourdes medical bureau.[27]

In September 1930, Helen Flanders Dunbar became the director of the Council for the Clinical Training of Theological Students. In April 1931, she also became the director of the Joint Committee on Religion and Medicine, a group of religious and medical professionals who sought the relationship between religion and health. In addition to her pivotal role in the religion and health movement, she was a link between the work of Anton Boisen, who promoted her career, and the work of Seward Hiltner, whose work she promoted.[28]

Dunbar described the relationship between mental health and religious teachings.[29] Because religion sets standards, influences emotions, and provides adherents with a worldview, religion teachers can contribute to states of mental illness. Dunbar's attention to religious damage of the emotions contributes to our thinking about the pastoral care of women.

Helen Flanders Dunbar identified these aspects of religion as problematic: an anthropomorphic God; authority images; and a suffering God. She suggested that God portrayed as Father may awaken a deep and hidden resentment against the tyranny of earthly fathers. An inadequate handling of the symbol "dear heavenly Father," therefore, can evoke either fear or resentment as the church becomes a continuation of parental authority. The Father as a symbol can also stimulate our longing for the avoidance of responsibility. Some theistic teachings portray God as a sort of monitor, a projected superego, shaped by actual experiences with a father. The father symbol can evoke the expectation of punishment and rewards; when anticipated punishments to others or rewards to self are not forthcoming, faith in this God is easily lost.[30] Equally as deleterious as the father symbol is the portrayal of the God of the New Testament as a suffering God. Personalities shaped by belief in this understanding of God "have found equal encouragement for any tendency they might have toward self-depreciation and self-torture (masochism)."[31] The way of the cross may lead to the mental hospital.[32] Dunbar summarized her observations:

> Each teacher of religion, however, should study the development of the emotional life (not merely the learning process) sufficiently so that in his [or her] teaching of religion those elements in its symbolism and concepts which are consistent with adult living are emphasized, rather than those which encourage the persistence of infantile patterns.[33]

Religion deals in the realm of ideas we have not yet mastered. The language of religion is that of symbolism.[34] Lest symbols such as God the Father contribute to neurotic mechanisms, Dunbar challenged teachers of religion to stress the dynamic meaning of symbols. Dynamic symbolism points to the infinite and comprehensible; the use of multiple symbols can prevent an overbearing focus on or concretization of any one of them. The effect of religious symbolism, like religion itself, is on the whole person, mind and body.

Dunbar's writings sought to dispel the mind-body dualism that was and is prevalent in medical as well as theological circles. Even today, in some pastoral training, one is encouraged to speak from the heart and not the head, as if the two can be separated. To Dunbar, the meaning of *psychosomatic* was that your mind is your body and your body is your mind.[35] She published a number of books on this theme. Her *Psychosomatic Diagnosis* (1943), a study of sixteen hundred unselected, consecutive patients admitted to Columbia Presbyterian Hospital, was later condensed into a more popular version, *Mind and Body* (1947). Although her work on preventive medicine and mental health has equal value for men and women, her comments on environmental and cultural contributors to illness have special relevance to women who seek to understand their "dis-ease" in our society.

Illustrating the effect of culture on illness, Dunbar cited chlorosis (anemia) as an ailment of adolescent girls in the late Victorian era. She saw beneath constricting Victorian apparel to constricting social influence.[36] Connecting the physical and the psychic, she noted: "The constricting garments of our grandmothers can be no more damaging to our own health today than the constricting ideas of our grandfathers."[37] She regarded penis envy as a product of a society that values possession of the male organ over the female and remarked that children of both sexes are equally shocked by the discovery of anatomic differences. Thus, vagina envy surfaces for some males. "For in fact, penis envy is not a spontaneous reaction. Much more truly spontaneous was the remark of a little girl who, seeing her baby brother in the nude for the first time, said optimistically, 'Isn't it lucky that he hasn't got that on his face.' "[38]

Dunbar traced the interplay of psychic and somatic forces in a wide variety of illnesses such as allergy, ulcers, heart attacks, diabetes, and tuberculosis. Her unique suggestions about the underlying emotional causes of accident-proneness are included as well. Dunbar's treatment of illnesses met with resistance from medical skeptics who contended that "a germ or a peculiar condition of body cells is the sum and substance of disease."[39] Her view of illnesses can be illustrated in her position on tuberculosis; she adopted the view of Sir William Osler that the fate of the tubercular was more a matter of the head than the chest. She substantiated her position with the following observation:

> Victorian novelists were more realistic than these skeptics. Their prim and prissy heroines succumbed in droves to an epidemic of ladylike behavior. Disappointed in love or deprived by the malignity of fate of some adored object, they went into gentle declines and perished with immense propriety. They never seemed to suffer symptoms any more distressing to themselves or their attendants than a becoming pallor, a flutter of the heart or lovely dark shadows under the eyes. They died of simple excess of emotion and sensibility.[40]

Many pastoral theologians have maintained a biblical connectedness of body, soul, and spirit. The implications of this connectedness in a pastoral ministry with women, however, has yet to be adequately explored.

Frances Gillespy Wickes, Karen Horney, and Helen Flanders Dunbar have been presented in silhouette; they are among the predecessors to this volume. Their work illuminates some of the themes in Part Two: the power of woman's inner world of choice and the external ramifications in work and love, in lifestyles; the role of culture in sexual abuse, battering, dependency, and depression; the significance of religious images, symbolism, and language to women; the connection between women and their bodies. As we call forth new pastoral perspectives in this volume, our work can only be enhanced by spotlighting these and other women in the shadows.

DEBATES IN THE PSYCHOLOGY OF WOMEN AND PASTORAL CARE • M.G.

Controversy about women and their psychology has centered around the theories of Sigmund Freud. The power of psychoanalysis as a personality theory pervades our culture and supports the popularization of Freud's understanding (read here, misunderstanding) of women.[41]

Explorations in the psychology of women within psychoanalysis describe the constitutional or biological givens of personality rather than socially imposed qualities or feminine characteristics derived from cultural conditioning.

In contrast, feminist critiques of Freud's sexual theories focus on the causal influence of cultural values on the formation of feminine personality, especially in comparison with the notion of "anatomy as destiny." The feminist response proposes reform in order to create a more equitable society, eliminate sexist attitudes toward women, and underscore the erroneous favoritism toward men. Discussions of inherent differences between the sexes or even of divergent developmental sequelae have been avoided in the fear that admission of gender differences could result in political concession.

More recently, later second-wave feminist writers such as Jean Baker Miller, Nancy Chodorow, Carol Gilligan, and Nel Noddings develop the notion of women's relational identity as a positive feature of feminine personality and as a value to be understood, upheld, or even emulated within a male-ordered culture.[42] This latter position, although appealing, is inherently dangerous if used to infer an idealized or mysterious feminine temperament, especially given the prior efforts of feminist scholarship to identify what is contingent in gender patterns.[43]

The debate over women's psychology centers around three focal points: (1) that "biology is destiny," (2) that feminine personality is a byproduct of social experience, or (3) that gender experience (whatever the etiology) makes for a distinct feminine personality with predispositions that serve as assets in social organization. Freud and the analysts who model their theory after him developed an understanding of women's personalities based on a biological view of development. As the discussion has evolved since Freud, the debate within the field of the psychology of women asserts two alternative opinions concerning the development of feminine character: (1) that it is a byproduct of history and culture and can be changed by constructive change in the social environment; and (2) that it is a byproduct of a particular developmental experience within the Western, postindustrial family and that the organization of feminine personality, although different from the organization of male personality, is at least as valuable as that of men's. The stages of the debate and its arguments are detailed below.

The Debate within Psychoanalysis

Freud's early effort to construct an understanding of women's psychology was organized around a biological core, just as the general theory of psychoanalysis was conceived as a physical-biological model.[44] Although I argue that a retrievable and useful psychology of women based on current analytic thought is still possible (see chap. 1), such a move may seem controversial to the many women who endure the psychoanalytic tradition with skepticism and disdain.[45]

Who can blame them? After all, Freud wrote that young girls think of themselves as little boys until they observe anatomic differences and become envious of a boy's penis and of his superiority.[46] Furthermore, Freud thought that a girl avoids the horror of castration anxiety by turning away from her defective mother, who is similarly deprived of a penis, toward relationship with her father, who possesses one. Entry into the oedipal phase was viewed, therefore, as an effort by girls to avoid the terror of castration anxiety. This perception of the psychological conflict of the girl led Freud to the unfortunate conclusion that females—inherently less frightened of the father—are condemned to the vicissitudes of a weak superego and to a future of poor critical judgment. That women are morally inferior to men was not Freud's innovation but a perspective about women long grounded within the Judeo-Christian culture. After nineteenth-century religion and capitalism shifted toward understanding women as the moral guardians of the home,[47] Freud's scientific argument protected the domestic position of women (against the tide of feminism) from the ethical demands of the workplace.

Freud also described female drives as passively aimed, "entirely based on the primary, erotogenic masochism, on pleasure in pain."[48] Sandor Rado and Helene Deutsch, building on the theories of Freud, posit feminine masochism as the psychological consequence of anatomic sex differences.[49] Because she perceives herself as damaged and inherently inferior, the girl is apt, according to Rado and Deutsch, to assume the stance of a wounded, victimized being whose primary satisfaction derives from having a man.

The writings of women who pioneered in psychoanalysis and contributed to thinking about the psychology of women varied in their response to Freud. Many did little more than reiterate his views and strengthen his theories with their support. Helene Deutsch, Marie Bonaparte, Joan Riviere, and Jeanne Lamp De Groot did not depart significantly from Freud's original concept of women's psychology.[50] Their efforts to understand women were overshadowed, if not determined, by the dominant male-oriented psychology of their teacher.

Other psychoanalytic approaches to the psychology of women modified the basic Freudian stance. These writers—Melanie Klein and Karen Horney, in particular—modified Freud's view of the oedipal situation of the woman (the emerging identification with the parent of the opposite sex and the triadic relationship between child and the parental couple) and of the outcomes of oedipal strivings in feminine development. Analysts who represent these views became prominent in reworking and reconstructing interpretations of feminine experience and of feminine psychology. These women in particular were able to contribute a fresh perspective to the field of psychoanalysis, often at great professional cost.[51]

Melanie Klein, a child analyst and a key figure in the English psychoanalytic movement, became the center of controversy because she contradicted a major tenet of Freudian thought with her focus on the developmental significance of the pre-oedipal situation.[52] The young child, in its tenuous existence, experiences intense feelings of rage and deprivation and develops an urgent object-seeking (relational) envy.[53] Klein refocused drive theory on the experience of the infant and more primitive levels of socialization and survival. This notion undercut the importance Freud placed on the biologic differences between women and men. If essential psychological development begins in earliest infancy in relationship to one's need for a primary caretaker, then later developmental crises would be of secondary importance for the individual's emerging personality. Moreover, Klein asserted that the resolution of the oedipus complex was largely determined by the flavor of pre-oedipal attachments and conflicts. She was convinced that, if girls do envy a male's penis, it is not because of their distinctly female feeling of inferiority. Oedipal-aged girls and boys both may view their parent's genitals with a concretized, ambivalent mixture of jealous envy and adoration, especially if the relationship to either parent was askew in an earlier developmental phase.[54]

Anna Freud, also a prominent child analyst, took strong exception to Klein's views. Understandably, Anna Freud sided with her father that the oedipus complex is a determinative component of the neurotic outcome for both sexes.[55] Both Freuds sought less to promote a sexist view of women than to defend the organizing importance of the notion of instincts, the centrality of the oedipus, and the belief that important aspects of human behavior were organized around physiologic arousal and discharge. In addition, Anna Freud's understanding of a child's personality organized around the real-life experience of the child. Accordingly, she viewed development as a combination of the effects of the family constellation and maturational and psychological developmental issues. She was less interested in very early life events than Melanie Klein. Therefore, the debate between Melanie Klein and Anna

Freud was vigorous if not contentious—Klein arguing for the importance of pre-oedipal development (before three years) and Freud supporting her father's conviction that the later-occurring oedipal crisis (three to six years) was central to an understanding of human development and the child's psychological behavior.

Karen Horney, in comparison to Klein, represents a significant and more obvious modification of biologic drive theory as the essence of psychoanalysis. She is known for her attention to the repercussions of cultural values and social relationships on feminine personality development.[56] Because she first suggested how problematic the male effort to construct a psychology of women is, she has been viewed alternately as merely reactive in her stance toward Freud[57] or as formative for an authentic feminist position of personality development.[58] In either case, Horney aptly regarded Freud's interpretation of female psychology as an extension of his own male psychology or, as I suggest, as male projection.[59]

Although Horney's early work highlights her disagreement with Freud over the issue of the female oedipus complex, her later work shifts toward greater comprehension of cultural values as determinative of the adult neurotic conflict. What was implicit in the earlier controversy over sexual theory (the impact of cultural reinforcement through parental management of the child) was more specifically described in her later writings.[60] Furthermore, awareness of the significance of culture in the formation of neurosis was generalized so that a gender-specific portrait became a minor note in the elaboration of her theory. Marcia Westkott currently uses both components of Horney's theoretical work to describe and elaborate the feminine psychology implicit in Horney's writings.[61]

Karen Horney, in contrast to Klein, was more directly critical of Freud's implicit sexism and focused theoretical challenges around the impact of culture on development, especially on later personality development. Her work represents a significant adaption, perhaps a deviation, from predominant psychoanalytic perspectives. Horney's thought is highly compatible with feminist theory yet maintains a psychodynamic perspective that is of considerable clinical use and interest. Klein, rather differently, attempts to push the sexual theory back toward its earlier social origins and to understand penis envy and castration anxiety as symptoms of perversion in primary relationships. Klein contends with the psychoanalytic understanding of the oedipal crisis in such a way as to push psychoanalysis in a new relational direction.

W. R. D. Fairbairn and D. W. Winnicott, two prominent English analysts indebted to Klein, further developed object-relations theory.

The object-relations perspective, now including Otto Kernberg, focuses on the impact of the dyadic (social) relationship on human personality within theories of psychoanalysis.[62] This perspective—far more adroitly than the strict Freudian view of the oedipal crisis will allow—creates foundations for understanding character formation, including the problems in object constancy that occur in certain personality disorders. From a clinical point of view, the notions of castration anxiety and penis envy might be usefully regarded as derivative of problematic relational issues but not as normal for human development. Object-relations theory also makes the works of feminist writers such as Dorothy Dinnerstein and Nancy Chodorow possible. Once psychoanalysis is freed from a rigid drive theory model, it more readily functions as a potent source for hypotheses about the sociopolitical situation of patriarchy.[63]

Feminist Critique and Change

After the early years of psychoanalysis (1930s), the debate about the psychology of women lay dormant until the beginning of the second wave of the feminist movement (1963). The clinical studies of Margaret Mahler (see chap. 1) began during this thirty-year period. However significant Mahler has been for our understanding of early childhood development (her interest was to discern causes of autistic psychosis in children),[64] her writing was not intended to be part of the discussion of female psychology. A few women in the field studied, wrote, and revised, but they were mostly ignored. As if by some silent conspiracy, the dominant worldview of women's inferiority reigned. Although early feminists had won the vote, their power had been diffused. The "science" of psychology had participated in muzzling women's voices. Women were thought to be weaker intellectually, psychologically, and morally and to be inherently masochistic. Middle-class women were counseled to accept their dependency, envy, masochism, and inadequacy and to find self-respect in being women!

The women's movement was not significantly rekindled until 1963 when, on the heels of the civil rights movement, Betty Friedan's *The Feminine Mystique*[65] reawakened concerns with women's social roles and economic positions. Discussion of women's experience and psychological makeup again became prominent in the mounting dissent. Established psychoanalytic views were rightly under assault. By the end of the 1960s and through the 1970s, women's research confirmed that "science," for all its supposed objectivity, was as Karen Horney had thought—male science. The evidence grew that sexual discrimination limited feminine potential far more than any inherent predisposition toward masochism.

Controlled studies in social psychology demonstrated the impact of gender preference on patterns of graduate school admissions, hiring, and career advancement.[66] Studies in group process suggested significant differences and more positive responses of group members to men than to women leaders.[67] Even studies of clinical diagnosis confirmed how differently clinicians saw the same behavior when observed or described in women than when ascribed to a man.[68] In contrast, controlled comparisons of actual trait differences of men and women suggested that, whereas our perceptions of men and women were different, in reality women were not so different from men in the way they performed and responded to task requirements.[69] Repeatedly, scientific studies tended to support the feminist critique.

The Journal of the American Psychoanalytic Association in 1976 published a supplementary volume on female psychology. Harold Blum's introduction suggests that the feminist debate over the psychology of women has had an important impact on psychoanalysis.

> Advances and innovations within psychoanalysis as well as scholarly critiques from both within and outside of psychoanalysis have highlighted unresolved theoretical questions and have inspired challenge, controversy, and re-evaluation. . . . Expanding knowledge has spurred our efforts to clarify theoretical assumptions and formulations; to detect and correct our inconsistencies, oversights, and errors; and to propose extensions and modifications of our initial developmental models.[70]

Although not all of the articles within the volume depart completely from the language or presuppositions of Freud, the debate over female psychology undoubtedly had been revised on new grounds. The American Psychoanalytic Association, which at one time had removed Karen Horney from its membership, was now reconsidering presuppositions about female psychology that had risen to doctrinal status: female penis envy, masochism, and the assumption of female dependency. They were no longer regarded as the normal consequence of feminine development.

A comparable evolution of the field of the psychology of women can be traced within the American Psychological Association.[71] Helen Thompson of the University of Chicago and Leta Stetter Hollingworth, later at Columbia University, were two pioneers in the area of the psychology of women within academic psychology. Their research on the skills and intellectual ability of women suggested a correspondence between the sexes as early as 1903 and 1906, respectively.[72] The Freudian controversy over the psychology of women and the resulting hardening of position within the American Psychoanalytic Association, however, had daunting repercussions within academic psychology.

Women, although one third of the membership of the American Psychological Association, had little influence outside academic circles. A special committee, the National Council of Women Psychologists, was created in 1941 to change the status of women within the APA but had minimal success.[73] Only after the civil rights movement and the later feminist movement of the late 1960s did the APA recognize the psychology of women as an official division for study. Finally, the status of women in psychology was challenged by the establishment of an APA task force on the position of women within the organization in 1972.[74] From that time until now, women's studies in psychology has burgeoned.

Current discussions in the psychology of women demonstrate the misgiving that the political gains of feminism might unwittingly be lost if they are supported by a science whose methodological premises are not yet proven to be free of gender bias.[75] Given how dangerous psychology has already been for women, such continuing discussion is warranted. At the same time, the field of the psychology of women can be confusing even for an insider. Yesterday's exciting new discovery about women and their psychology becomes today's hot debate. For example, Matina Horner's suggestion that women suffer from achievement-related conflicts is challenged by a further look at her underlying assumptions and repeated use of her scientific measures.[76] Carol Gilligan's *In a Different Voice*, which won her the *Ms.* magazine woman-of-the-year award in 1984, raises a concern for some that a theory built in part on the responses of women to the question of abortion is inherently doomed to sexual bias.[77] Nancy Chodorow's *The Reproduction of Mothering* is criticized for locating our motives for mothering in a psychodynamic source when a biologic explanation would be more adequate. These feminist critics worry that Chodorow presents a psychic rationale for sexism, when privilege or economic advantage is its own justification.[78] Thus the debate has come full circle.

Debates That Impact Pastoral Care

We have not found final answers to the debates in the psychology of women. The discussion, however, has deepened our understanding of women's behavior and of men's behavior in relationship to women. By considering these issues, their ideological underpinnings, and theological connections, we hope to reopen religious and moral questions about gender which can benefit pastoral theology.

To what extent is sexual and gender psychology biologically or socially determined? Since the onset of the second wave of the feminist movement in the early 1960s, crucial questions have been advanced about the possibility of a psychology of women.[79] Two strands of feminist thinking about the psychology of women have emerged. The first stream of feminist critique of women's psychology was antagonistic to the existing tradition in psychoanalysis and psychology—a history of thought that left many women feeling misunderstood and inalterably inferior. Psychological theory (with the possible exception of Jung's analytic psychology)[80] had perpetuated the sense that women themselves were accountable for their inevitable problem with low self-esteem. Early second-wave feminists' critique focused on analysis of the feminine mystique and argued that concepts of gender are acquired through culture. This scholarship established that historically created patterns of gender relationship are contingent and subject to change, rather than inherent.

A second strand of feminist scholarship has moderated its criticism of the effort to forge a psychology of women. Nancy Chodorow, Carol Gilligan, Jean Baker Miller, and Nel Noddings have each described a cluster of personal characteristics identified with women.[81] These traits converge around an increasingly popular notion of women as relational and as disposed to viewing relationships and the care of others as primary to a sense of self. Moreover, freed from the sexist perception that a caring nature dictates patterns of hierarchical social relationships, the writings suggest the positive value of women's relational qualities.

Feminist interest in what is constitutionally versus socially determined behavior in feminine personality raises important problems for the minister who deals with these ideas at the popular level. If women's conduct is understood to be biologically determined or constitutionally given, then we might simply identify those givens and moderate our pastoral care of women on the basis of them. That alone might be of some value in our work as pastoral caregivers. If we also believe that at least some of the injustice in women's experience is created by sexist culture, however, then we need to think critically about our participation in social structures and integrate our awareness into alternative methods in the ministry of pastoral care.

Moreover, as the feminist debate is assimilated by the church, we are required to nourish the concern for continuing theological integrity. The church's ministry has two fundamental poles: raise theological concern for justice and keep the formative values of the Christian tradition in an ongoing tension with new ways of thinking about human experience (within both the social sciences and politics). The pastoral task, then, is continued by thinking theologically about practical concerns, as discussed later.

The position that women's self-understanding has been contingent on history and social circumstance, which was emphasized by the first strand of feminist revision of psychology, frees us from the view that feminine behavior is biologically determined. It provides a welcome insight and relief for many women stalemated by custom and restricted options. Other women have reacted with mixed feelings to the feminist critique, as they struggle to adapt their lives to the many changes in social roles engendered by the feminist movement. For them, feminism has created conflict rather than resolved it.

In either case, the feminist perspective on women's psychology is that sexism creates unnecessary problems for women's development and undue constriction of feminine personality. These constrictions are social, systemic, and external to the individual woman. Self-concept is, in large measure, dependent upon social views, cultural experience, and cultural reinforcement. As a result, feminism generally advocates a reformation of the community's understanding of gender and an alternate political and social strategy.

At the early stages of the present feminist discussion that began in the 1960s, the analysis outlined previously, along with a corresponding conviction about the necessity of social reform, helped to extricate many women from immobilizing guilt. Impoverished by gender restrictions, by male-dominated psychology, and by an understanding of themselves as less valuable than men, women are left self-doubting and inhibited. Feminist scholarship modifies both self-perceptions and agendas: a good offense replaces poor defenses against sexist descriptions of women and a sexist self-concept.

This thrust of feminist scholarship has served as a needed corrective to prevalent notions of women's psychological destiny as originating in anatomy. In the extreme, however, a woman may come to understand herself as essentially at the mercy of the social system. Although no longer believing she is restricted by biology or internal psychological organization, she may come to feel she is primarily the victim of cultural circumstance. Male-dominated society is then seen as the villainous, self-serving defender of the sexist status quo. All things patriarchal are viewed as suspicious, perhaps even evil. Such a radical interpretation of women's experience stops being helpful if an understanding of social behavior is reified and becomes doctrinaire. What appeared to offer greater freedom can be inverted to a manifesto of social determinism. A belief that provided some relief of responsibility for one's prescribed circumstance may be reconstrued as the inevitable source of impotence in realizing one's destiny.

Seeing behavior as determined by others moves the conversation toward an ideological battleground. Ultimately, a view of life as either fixed by biologic drive or ordered by sexist culture may shift a woman away from the sense of personal responsibility and choice that is inherent to the Christian understanding of will. Although we may regard God as "author of our portion," however unfairly, we are helped most by theology when it supports our conviction that we remain free to make moral decisions that shape but cannot control existence.

Sexism, like other human problems, is an ugly reality, but in the midst of injustice the belief that God knows and abides with us in our rejection provides comfort. We can come to understand our parcel of experience, identify injustice and suffering, and identify with suffering, and yet we can make good on the only life that has been given to us, according to God's purpose.[82] God stands with us in injustice, grief, and even agony. Our sorrow is known, can be endured, and can be transformed and used to a new end. Nancy Ramsay's chapter on incest demonstrates just how difficult coming to terms with sexual injustice may be for the victims of abuse, and, as she suggests, it becomes even more difficult when God is variously experienced as perpetrator and/ or savior. Nevertheless, the process of coming to terms with the life that is ours is essential to personal and cultural restoration. For example, the concluding chapter of Marcia Westkott's *The Feminist Legacy of Karen Horney* proposes that being aware of sexualization and injustice is crucial to recovery and to a heroic response because only as reabsorption of the meaning of experience occurs can the pain be absorbed for personal and social transformation.[83] Little is accomplished by mere fury or self-pity except insofar as it serves the transition to an assimilation of experience. Through the assimilation of injustice, the intention of a person's life—however paltry it may seem to others, however choked by suffering—becomes clearer. We are relieved from the full sense of having been deprived and damaged, and as this occurs we experience for ourselves what has been called sanctification.[84] Our lives assume new meaning and fullness even to us! The ensuing restoration of the self is not an act of narcissism but recovery from it.

An ideological view that construes experience through the lens of victimization does offer psychological relief and the hope for lasting political benefits for the oppressed. It should not be summarily dismissed by those who cannot appreciate the value of its social program. Yet the argument of social determinism in common with the politics of male domination can be demoralizing, rob individuals of alternatives, and forge experience in bitterness if it is framed without an eschatological vision.[85]

In a similar way, the new stream of feminist scholarship that sees women as particularly relational by nature raises both psychological and anthropological questions. As Marcia Westkott writes, "I was concerned that, in the absence of contextual understanding, the traits would be mystified and unselectively idealized as an inherent female essence."[86] Westkott's interpretation of Karen Horney suggests that female altruism might have an underside, an overwhelming sense of responsibility that is based on culturally reinforced dependency.[87] If so, the purpose of such behavior is to do, care, and be for others in order to win approval, help, and affection (the psychological equivalent of works-righteousness). The real psychological goal of this stylized form of feminine virtue lies in "living up to the dictates of the idealized self."[88] However, living out of the false self is at best merely undifferentiated compliance. Dependence masquerades as responsibility for others. Moreover, when a charade of femininity is sustained by any political ideology that places the woman on a pedestal, whatever the social program, it puts at risk the possibility of both feminine heroism and conversion; one is tempted to live falsely.

Thus each strand of feminist critique adds to our understanding of women and their psychology. Nevertheless, neither is without its dangers. Biologic determinism and biologic influence need to be further distinguished. Social determinism and social influence might also be further distinguished. Both biologic determinism (metaphorically conceived) and social determinism (practically understood) raise serious problems for Christian understandings of will and for Christian notions of God's ultimate say over meaning and purpose. As ministers we cannot afford to collapse questions of the meaning and purpose of experience (as in the problem of living within sexist culture) on either side of the eschatological question (whether realized or future). The unfolding of an adequate pastoral theology, however, depends in part on an assessment of one's anthropological views in relation to ends beyond immediate experience or, traditionally stated, to divine activity or purpose. Thus, whether current psychoanalytic thought may be a valid way of interpreting women's experience is a question to be thoughtfully considered by the pastoral theologian. If one is a feminist as well, the question is doubly interesting.

Practical and perhaps more immediate concerns for pastors are implicit in the controversies described previously. If, for example, mothering behavior contributes to the devaluing of women, clergy can help a congregation to think carefully about who is to be involved in child-rearing. As Christie Cozad Neuger will suggest in Chapter 7, to what extent women are more susceptible to mental illness and depression and how they become so are everyday concerns for the pastoral minister. The list continues: Do women speak in a different moral voice? What are the ramifications of women's moral positions for the church's thinking? Should mothers stay at home with their young children? Should fathers stay at home? Can they? What can the minister rightfully say about childcare? When should she or he remain silent? Does abortion cause psychological harm to women? Do women fear success? Is lesbianism a sickness? Is pornography harmful to women?[89]

Current issues under debate have important ramifications for the lives of women and hence for our culture. Each begs for theological reflection. Every question that has been argued about women's psychological experience is of concern to the minister, the pastoral caregiver, and the pastoral theologian.

Conclusion

The overview of women's thinking about psychological development and experience, as illustrated in the works cited previously, describes the result of critical and constructive work on gender presuppositions. These works view women positively and develop theoretical understandings that evaluate women's lives without prejudice. The misconception that women's second-class standing is an outgrowth of a basic psychological flaw is repudiated. With few exceptions, contributors to the psychology of women are suspicious of the notion of women's inferiority, their innate envy, or their propensity to masochism.

In general, the theorists suggest that the question of the relationship of biology to culture is, indeed, complicated. We are now certain of social influences in the construction of psychological phenomena. This influence occurs both when experience is mediated through the relationship of parent and child and by a larger cultural experience. Although individual women contributors treat the problem of internal experience and social circumstance differently, we presume that these realities are not easily extricated. We are equally certain of the influence of societal movements on theory building.

The feminist movement within psychology, in particular, provides considerable evidence that perceptions of women are social constructs. This research has also confirmed what many women have known, that perceptions of them were negative even when negative perceptions were not warranted. These prejudicial views become embedded in the relationship of parent to child, of child to family, and of child to the world beyond home. Such misconceptions are predictive of women's social recognition in the world external to herself. They are also formative for aspects of self-concept and worth in her internal (inner) world. Even so, we do not believe social discrimination is decisive for human character. It certainly does not determine personal value.

Although women have a developmental pilgrimage that is different from that for men (at least in part due to cultural reinforcement), the consequences for personality formation contribute special strengths to culture through feminine ways of organizing experience. Women are relationally oriented caregivers and predisposed, whether biologically or culturally, to preserve community. Indeed, feminine experience may be more congruent with traditional religious values than the dominant male-normed psychology we have known. Furthermore, women's psychology shares many continuities with the psychology of men. Our awareness of what is distinctive about feminine experience deepens our thinking about all human experience and about aspects of male psychology that we have not yet understood.

Every concern addressed through these works becomes a question of subtle but real importance to ministers. Issues of justice are perhaps most obvious. We are reminded of the presumptuousness that is inherent in classifying others and of the damage we may thereby do to them. However, perception is also determinative of functioning in ministry. It will highlight whom we view as needing care and determine how we approach them. In addition, we are disquieted by the recognition that every thinker develops his or her thought within the context of a system of beliefs that is common to the age. Thus we underscore the need for continual critiques of these systems.

Now, we return to the point of view with which we began Part One. As a field, pastoral theology has been strongly influenced by psychology. The introduction of women's experience to our discipline will demonstrate that pastoral care has been overly informed by a male-normed psychology. Current pastoral theologians raise questions about the underlying assumptions and values of psychology that may be in conflict with a theological approach. The perspective of women's experience also confirms that an indiscriminate psychology is a poor basis for pastoral theology. At points, the fact that it has been male-biased psychology contributes to it being at odds with fundamental values of inclusivity in the Christian tradition.

Our conviction is that on practical grounds as well, correction within pastoral care through the development of an understanding of women's perspectives is much-needed. In the pages that follow the themes developed within Part One are explored and expanded. By reading carefully, each particular pastoral problem will be seen as organized by the existential and anthropological position of the author. Each writer's dilemma shapes both the theological questions that are raised and the answers that are offered. Each, in addition, employs a somewhat unique method for arriving at her solution. Are all the chapters pastoral theology? Does each inform pastoral care? We think so, and we think that even with their differences, each strengthens our comprehension of how we think theologically about pastoral questions.

NOTES

1. Frances Wickes, *The Inner World of Choice* (New York: Harper & Row, 1963.

2. In recent years, women psychotherapists have offered a growing critique of Jungian theory that is important to note and credit. For example, Ursula Baumgardt draws attention to Jung's depiction of the anima as an extension of the animus. Thus, the animus becomes the primary polarity for Jung. The anima is characterized by attention to relationships, feelings, and Eros, which to Baumgardt carries a "negative imprint." Her provocative conclusion is that the animus is not an archetype but a complex developed by patriarchy. "Zwischen Idealiserung und Entwertung: C. G. Jungs Frauenbild," in *Frauen Verlassen die Couch: Feministische Psychotherapie* (Zurich: Kreuz Verlag AG, 1989), 54.

3. Edward Morgan III, "Implications of the Masculine and the Feminine in Pastoral Ministry," *Journal of Pastoral Care* 34 (December 1980):277.

4. Wickes, *Inner World*, 210.

5. Ibid., 177.

6. Ibid., 205.

7. Ibid.

8. Ibid., 215.

9. Ibid., 226.

10. Ibid., 243.

11. Ibid., 242.

12. Ibid., 238.

13. Karen Horney, *Feminine Psychology*, ed. Harold Kelman (New York: W. W. Norton, 1967), 182.

14. Ibid., 182

15. Ibid., 54.

16. Ibid., 55.

17. Throughout this book, we will be stimulated to reconsider the objective approach to Western civilization and the impact of this approach on pastoral care.

18. Horney, *Feminine Psychology,* 223.

19. Ibid., 82.

20. *Diagnostic and Statistical Manual of Mental Disorders,* 3d ed. (Washington, D.C.: American Psychiatric Association, 1987), 353.

21. Horney, *Feminine Psychology,* 59.

22. Marcie Kaplan, "A Woman's View of DSM III," *American Psychologist,* 38 (1983):786–92. Among the criteria for this unofficial diagnostic category are (1) putting work and career above relationships and (2) reluctantly taking into account significant others when making major and minor decisions.

23. Margaret W. Matlin, *The Psychology of Women* (New York: Holt, Rinehart and Winston, 1987), 418.

24. This nomenclature was used of God by H. Richard Niebuhr in *The Responsible Self: An Essay in Christian Moral Philosophy* (San Francisco: Harper & Row, 1963), 175–76. This concept, Determiner of Destiny, was not used in a fatalistic context but rather incarnationally: "When the Christian addresses the Determiner of Destiny actually, not merely verbally, as Father, he [she] knows he [she] does it in the name, because of the presence in him, of Jesus Christ" (176). This at-homeness in the universe and freedom to be responsive is actualized by Jesus Christ.

25. Helen Flanders Dunbar, *Mind and Body: Psychosomatic Medicine* (New York: Random House, 1947), 214.

26. Ibid., 89.

27. Ibid., 95.

28. Allison Stokes, *Ministry After Freud* (New York: Pilgrim Press, 1985), 87. Stokes's Chapter 4 has more biographical data on Dunbar. See as primary source for the beginnings of the clinical training of theological students the pamphlet by Dunbar, *A New Opportunity in Theological Education: A Description of the Policy and Program of the Council for the Clinical Training of Theological Students, Inc.,* October 1933.

29. Helen Flanders Dunbar, "Mental Hygiene and Religious Teaching," reprinted from *Mental Hygiene* 19 (July 1935):353–72.

30. Ibid., reprint p. 11.

31. Ibid., 10.

32. Ibid., 12.

33. Ibid., 20.

34. H. F. Dunbar, "The Faith and the New Psychology," *The Living Church,* 13 Jan. 1934, 11.

35. Dunbar, *Mind and Body,* 260.

36. Ibid., 161.

37. Ibid., 245.

38. Ibid., 259.

39. Ibid., 216.

40. Ibid., 16.

41. Hannah Lerman, "From Freud to Feminist Personality Theory: Getting Here From There," in *The Psychology of Women: Ongoing Debates,* ed. Mary Roth Walsh (New Haven: Yale University Press, 1987), 39–45.

42. Nancy Chodorow, *The Reproduction of Mothering: Psychoanalysis and the Sociology of Gender* (Berkeley: University of California Press, 1978); Carol Gilligan, *In a Different Voice: Psychological Theory and Women's Psychology,* (Cambridge: Harvard University Press, 1982); Jean Baker Miller, *Toward a New Psychology of Women* (Boston: Beacon, 1976); Nel Noddings, *Caring: A Feminine Approach to Ethics and Moral Education* (Berkeley: University of California Press, 1984).

43. Marcia Westkott, *The Feminist Legacy of Karen Horney* (New Haven: Yale University Press, 1986), 1–3.

44. For a current book that describes the correlation of Freud's theory to scientific metaphor, read Stephen A. Mitchell, *Relational Concepts in Psychoanalysis: An Integration* (Cambridge: Harvard University Press, 1988), 67, 94–126, 145, 243, 251.

45. Lerman, "From Freud," 39–58.

46. Sigmund Freud, "Some Psychical Consequences of the Anatomical Differences Between the Sexes," *SE* 19 (1925):248–58; "Female Sexuality," *SE* 21 (1931):225–43; and "Femininity," *SE* (1933):112–35.

47. Westkott, *Feminist Legacy,* 20–52.

48. Freud, "Some Psychical Consequences," 162.

49. Helene Deutsch, "The Psychology of Women in Relation to the Functions of Reproduction," *International Journal of Psychoanalysis* 6 (1925):405–18; and *The Psychology of Women* (New York: Grune & Stratton, 1944–45); Sandor Rado, "Fear of Castration in Women," *Psychoanalytic Quarterly* 3, no. 4 (1933).

50. Marie Bonaparte, "Passivity, Masochism, and Femininity," *International Journal of Psychoanalysis* 16 (1935). Deutsch, "Psychology of Women"; Jeanne Lamp de Groot, "The Evolution of the Oedipus Complex in Women," in *The Psychoanalytic Reader,* ed. R. Fliess (New York: International Universities Press, 1950), 207–22; and "Thoughts on Psychoanalytic Views of Female Psychology," *Psychoanalysis* 51:1–18; Joan Riviere, "On the Genesis of Psychical Conflict in Earliest Infancy," in *Developments in Psychoanalysis,* ed. Melanie Klein et al. (London: Hogarth, 1952).

51. Walsh, ed. *Psychology of Women,* 20.

52. Paul Roazen, "Melanie Klein: The English School," in *Freud and His Followers* (New York: Alfred A. Knopf, 1976), 478–88.

53. Hanna Segal, *Introduction to the Work of Melanie Klein* (New York: Basic Books, 1974), 39–66.

54. Ibid., 103–16.

55. Sigmund Freud, "Female Sexuality," *International Journal of Psychoanalysis* 13 (1932):297; Roazen, "Melanie Klein," 436–59.

56. Karen Horney, "The Flight from Womanhood: The Masculinity Complex in Women as Viewed by Men and by Women," in *Feminine Psychology* (New York: W. W. Norton, 1967), 54–70.

57. Lamp de Groot.

58. Westkott, *Feminist Legacy.*

59. Horney, "Flight from Womanhood"; and "The Dread of Women," in *Feminine Psychology* (New York: W. W. Norton, 1967), 133–46.

60. Westkott, *Feminist Legacy*, 10–13.

61. Ibid.

62. Mitchell, *Relational Concepts*, 95–109.

63. Chodorow, *Reproduction of Mothering;* Dorothy Dinnerstein, *Mermaid and Minotaur: Sexual Arrangements and Human Malaise* (New York: Harper & Row, 1976).

64. Margaret Mahler, *Symbiosis and Individuation: The Psychological Birth of the Human Infant* (New Haven: Yale University Press, 1974), ix–xii.

65. Betty Friedan, *The Feminine Mystique* (New York: W. W. Norton, 1963).

66. R. L. Dipboye, H. L. Fromkin, and J. K. Wiback, "Relative Importance of Applicant Sex, Attractiveness, and Scholastic Standing in Evaluation of Job Applicant Resources," *Journal of Applied Psychology* 60 (1975):39–43; J. E. Haefner, "Sources of Discrimination Among Employees: A Survey Investigation," *Journal of Applied Psychology* 59 (1974):9–14; E. A. Shaw, "Differential Impact of Negative Stereotypes in Employee Selection," *Personnel Psychology* 25 (1972):333–58.

67. G. W. Bowman, N. B. Worthy, and S. A. Greyser, "Are Women Executives People?" *Harvard Business Review* 43 (1965):14–17; V. E. Schein, "Relationship Between Sex-Role Stereotypes and Requisite Management Characteristics Among Female Managers," *Journal of Applied Psychology* 60 (1975):240–344.

68. I. K. Broverman, D. M. Broverman, F. E. Clarkson, P. S. Rosenkrantz, and S. R. Vogel, "Sex-Role Stereotypes and Clinical Judgments of Mental Health," *Journal of Counseling and Clinical Psychology* 34 (1970):1–7.

69. K. M. Bartol, *Male and Female Leaders of Small Groups* (East Lansing: Michigan State University, Bureau of Economic and Business Research, 1973); D. R. Day and R. M. Stogdill, "Leader Behavior of Male and Female Supervisors: A Comparative Study," *Personnel Psychology* 25 (1972):353–60.

70. Harold Blum, "Introduction," *Journal of the American Psychoanalytic Association* 24 (1976):1.

71. This review of academic psychology and women's psychology is adapted from Walsh, ed., *Psychology of Women*, 1–5.

72. Leta Stoller Hollingworth, "Variability Related to Sex Differences in Achievement," *American Journal of Sociology* 19 (1914):510–30; Helen Thompson, *The Mental Traits of Sex: An Experimental Investigation of the Normal Mind in Men and Women* (Chicago: University of Chicago Press, 1903).

73. Walsh, ed., *Psychology of Women*, 3.

74. Ibid., 4.

75. This discussion is again adapted from *Psychology of Women*.

76. Walsh, "Do Women Fear Success?" in *Psychology of Women*, 165–202.

77. Walsh, "Do Women Speak in a Different Moral Voice?" in *Psychology of Women*, 274–332.

78. Walsh, "Does Mothering Behavior Contribute to Devaluation of Women?" in *Psychology of Women*, 246–73.

79. See, for example, Walsh, "Introduction," in *Psychology of Women*, 1–21. Walsh includes as the first debate, "Part I: Psychoanalytic Theory and the

Psychology of Women." From my perspective, Shala Chehrazi's article in the same book, "Female Psychology," 22–38, presents a revision of psychoanalytic theory but does not offer a critical discussion of biologic drive theory and hence cannot revise enough to be satisfactory. Hannah Lerman's rebuttal, "From Freud to Feminist Personality Theory: Getting Here from There," 39–58, presents useful criteria for the evaluation of psychological theories yet discounts any potential value of the psychoanalytic model.

80. The description of anima and animus within Jungian psychology tends to give equal weight to feminine and masculine dimensions of experience and thus, in the minds of many women, is exempt from criticism as a sexist theory. Jungian theory, however interesting, may be unsatisfactory on other theoretical grounds. See Demaris Wehr, *Jung & Feminism: Liberating Archetypes* (Boston: Beacon Press, 1987), for a balanced feminist critique of Jung. In addition, see Don S. Browning, *Religious Thought and the Modern Psychologies* (Philadelphia: Fortress Press, 1987), 161–203, for a critique of the harmonistic metaphor implicit in Jungian thought.

81. See n. 39.

82. I do not mean to suggest that God's purpose is that we should suffer but rather that each of us has a unique life experience that may require us to come to terms with a harsh reality.

83. Westkott, *Feminist Legacy,* 199–214.

84. Sanctification is understood as a kind of continuing conversion or transformation that increases the sense of living within God's mercy and with gratitude toward God. Thus processes of recovery from a sense of having been damaged by oppression or abuse that has crippled, deprived, or broken one's spirit might be included as a means of purification. The term *sanctification* is ordinarily construed within a nineteenth-century framework of personality and rationality. Removed from that historical context, however, *sanctification* captures the essence of Westkott's description.

85. In this case, the term *eschatology* is used to suggest that some ultimate end and/or meaning exists beyond what can be derived from immediate experience.

86. Westkott, *Feminist Legacy,* 2.

87. Ibid., 145–65.

88. Ibid., 146.

89. Walsh, ed., *Psychology of Women.*

. . . .

PART TWO

Travail

. . . .

CHAPTER 3

Women Who Work and Love: Caught Between Cultures

BONNIE J. MILLER-MCLEMORE

• • • • • • • • • • •

It is especially unpleasant irony to discern the depths of co-optation circulating through the apparent channels of liberation.

Catherine Keller, *From a Broken Web*

Theologian Catherine Keller's words inspire me. She captures the core of my struggle to sit happily in my professional job as seminary professor and pastoral therapist *and* to live and love as wife and mother. This tension reflects a radical transfiguration of an ancient conflict of loyalties not unlike that faced by the three women, Naomi, Ruth, and Orpah, in the hills of Moab. Traditionally, however, the church has idealized and admired Ruth's decision to follow Naomi, her late husband's mother, and virtually ignored the courage of Orpah in her painful choice "to return to her mother's house" (Ruth 1:8). More significantly, it has passed quickly over the cries of anguish of all three women as they tried to reconceive themselves in a world suddenly bereft of men. Cultural mores that made women dependent upon men divided them from one another and sent them searching.

The story of Naomi, Ruth, and Orpah paradigmatically raises questions that continue to plague humankind, women in particular. These three women suddenly found themselves adrift, outside the classical social mores that defined the position of men and women. They were no man's property. To whom were they bound? Where were their loyalties? What should they become? Today many such social norms no longer hold. Women face the dilemma of "being pulled between two poles," as Berenice Fisher remarks: "the biological and psychological nurturing of the mothers who bore us and the moral and political nurturing of the women we, so often, hope to be." We each need to "make a life that is different from that of our mothers, perhaps also at odds with that of many of our contemporaries."[1] Yet, we need lives that do not deny the inherent value of our connections to both.

Finding images of support and validation that do not feel like betrayals of either original nurturance or forthcoming aspirations is painfully difficult. Many working women face the same questions of child care, work schedule, housework, and marital arrangements. Few resolve them in the same way. The variation in domestic and vocational patterns among women stands in contrast to the more formulaic career patterns of most men.[2] As with Naomi, Ruth, and Orpah, each woman finds her way. Perhaps the significant moment comes with the blessing in the wilderness—the embrace between Orpah, her mother-in-law, and Ruth and the affirmation of all three amidst the grief and loss.

Women have, of course, traveled a long way from the absolute requirement of men for self-definition and well-being of Naomi's time. Yet contemporary, American, middle-class, white women[3] stand before a troubling turning point in gender role definitions: We no longer know what being a woman means.[4] Feminist criticism rests squarely on dismantling conventional images of women's lives. Because we stand in the very midst of this meltdown, we overlook the revolutionary transformations in relations between the sexes that have occurred in the past two decades. Old ways of relating and of becoming a self as defined in the patriarchal society of Naomi hold considerably less sway.

Yet a new sense of self that moves beyond dependence upon men and the restricting patriarchal definitions of adulthood has only begun to take shape. Thanks to women who have gone before them, white, middle-class, "late second wave" women in the 1990s[5] who have choices far beyond following Naomi or returning to the "mother's house" face this conflict in their search for self. Although freed from some oppressive models of femininity, they face a "new form of seduction," as Keller describes it—the danger of co-optation that infiltrates the apparent channels of liberation.[6] Patriarchy, although crumbling, still stands. Women who enter its structures in pursuit of new freedoms may find themselves restricted in subtle ways.

Resolution of the conflicts between work, family, and self leads inevitably to contradictions, frustrations, ambiguous solutions, and hard choices. My efforts here reflect my own beleaguered answer to the very questions of working and loving that I have raised: As I revise for publication between the nursery school schedule of my first son and the naps of my second, I feel torn between my desire for total unin-terrupted silence and my horror at my fantasy that a capricious god might grant me my perverted wish and I would lose both children forever. My situation illustrates the dilemma I seek to portray: the difficulties of "conceiving" in professional and familial ways at the same time. One moment I want to drop my whole project to turn to household matters of great importance; the next I want to see it through for its own value and for the love of my work. No matter how a woman designs her life, whether she chooses to stay home, work at home, or work outside the home, conflicts plague her resolution to questions of working and loving.

Beyond battles over inclusive language and ordination of women, however, most mainline churches have all but ignored these struggles and the deeper implications of the women's movement. A wide gulf separates the raised consciousness of women and a typical Sunday morn-ing service. Many women, I believe, seriously question their current engagement with church; they come wanting nourishment and leave empty. In a letter to the editor of the *Journal of Feminist Studies in Religion,* one woman expresses her concern about the co-optation that "is nowhere more poignantly experienced than in the institutional churches." She wrestles constantly with whether "it is even worth it to attempt to work from the inside."[7] Whereas more conservative churches adopt a clear stance that demands a return to the "traditional" family concept, mainline churches remain aloof, caught in the crossfire between feminism and conservative trends. When all is said and done, they have paid little attention to the transformations brought about by the former and to the retrenchment of the latter.

Yet to ignore the radical changes in models of adulthood and family and the intense role strain for both men and women is to miss the cries of anguish in the midst of their congregations. Most women under fifty now work; most continue to take the major responsibility for their families. Yet church expectations of women have not adapted to the changes in women's and men's lives. Women still fix the funeral meals, staff the nursery, cook the potlucks, clean up, teach Sunday school, run rummage sales, and now, in addition, take on new roles of lead-ership.[8] Women struggle to realize what they value. Men absent them-selves. When will these traditional arrangements and, more importantly, the undergirding dynamic receive fresh consideration by mainline churches?

This chapter remains at a different level of abstraction than others in this section, and for specific reasons. These problems of work and love stand at a distinct point in history: Like the conflicts that Priscilla

L. Denham portrays in her chapter on the new woman on her own ("divorced/never married/widowed/lesbian"), the problem here of many white, middle-class, North American women is peculiar to our era and our era alone. Mainline churches have yet to respond in any clear way. Whereas depression, incest, and abuse have existed for a very long time, the struggle of so many women to work and love is relatively new. Like the intense strain of labor, time stands still; we attend a birth that will have a radical impact in the next few decades. At such a juncture, I have no concrete steps, no strategies of intervention, no new support group to suggest. Instead, I call for closer listening and more critical reflection, and I demand careful, thoughtful response. Without this, churches have much to lose in both vitality and members.

Caught Between Cultures

The conflict has moved from its initial form as a *debate about* radical ideologies and principles that inevitably remained ideals to *an enactment* of these dreams—an embodied, lived state. Women today avoid some of the basic restrictions and political battles over equal rights that faced the first feminist wave. In a way distinct from their forerunners, nevertheless, they must find ways to work out personal and professional identities with integrity in the midst of two explicit models—the standards and images of a patriarchal society that continue to control social structures *and* the standards and images of the liberated first wave that have begun to exert new kinds of pressures.

Women influenced by the second feminist wave can no longer simply talk about the necessary transformations; they must live and breathe them, sometimes without explicitly espousing feminist beliefs and hopes. The options are no longer simply ideals; they are known, stated, and popularized. We see them, albeit trivialized and stereotyped, in the plethora of articles in women's magazines that declare a standoff between working mothers and those who stay at home. Today even the woman who chooses the so-called traditional role of housekeeper and childraiser knows her role is in tension with other possibilities and implications.

Women in the late second wave tend not to demand social justice and equality with the fervor of the first or early second wave. Naively forgetting history, women now take these notions for granted and reap the benefits while they bear the consequences. Yet as a further result of where they stand in history, late-second-wave feminists almost unavoidably live out justice in their own lives in a slightly different way than their senior feminist sisters. They may refuse to prepare all the meals or to bear sole responsibility for toilet training the children.

Simultaneously more willing to reembody their mothers' characteristics, they may find themselves less willing to meet some of the patriarchal standards of the work world and its definitions of success: Long work hours deprive one of time with family and time for oneself; the demand for productivity and upward mobility ignores the different rhythms of a life that includes childbirth or simply more abundant daily existence. Yet women struggle to do so in a materialistic, product-oriented public world still unsympathetic to such values.

At the same time the conflicts have become more explicit, sexism has become more subtle. A few examples from the popular culture illustrate this situation. By 1978 the feminist movement had exerted enough pressure on Breck hair products to force them to suspend their "Breck *girl*" competition and magazine portraits. A decade later, by popular demand—"in response to hundreds of requests . . . and the public's desire for nostalgia," said Breck product manager Gerard Matthews—Breck brought back the beauty campaign but now with the cosmetic concession of a new name, "Breck *woman*."[9] The heroine of the recent movie *Baby Boom* portrays the comic side of the struggle to integrate corporate success with alternative home and family values. In a scene over dinner to discuss the time-honored invitation to become a partner, her senior in the firm must finally recognize the problem that her womanhood still poses for him and for patriarchy: "Do you understand the sacrifices you're going to have to make?" he asks her. "What if you get married and he expects a wife?" He draws an intriguing distinction: "A man can be a success and *still have a personal life, a full personal life*" (even though he clearly does not have one and doesn't even know how many grandchildren he has); a man has a wife who "takes care of things . . . raises the children, decorates." In essence, he cannot think of her "as a woman" and as a capable adult at the same time, at least not according to traditional definitions. He does not know how to integrate the full meaning of "woman/partner." He never questions his ideal of "success." Nor does a much ballyhooed article in a recent issue of *Harvard Business Review*. While feigning a concern for "career-and-family women," and advocating their suitability for middle management positions—now dubbed the "mommy track"—author and corporate manager Felice Schwartz never challenges the "masculine rules of career development." Maximum productivity and the bottom line remain the chief criteria for measuring worth and success.[10] In a culture with such values, children and "family women" do not count.

These examples demonstrate the dangers of believing that women have made progress just because we use inclusive language, hire women without certain discriminating practices, or let women occupy roles previously guarded by men. Despite the importance of such ideological and structural changes, people deceive themselves when they believe these changes suffice. The problems run deeper. In contrast to the blatant sex discrimination and harassment that led to court cases filed since Title VII of the Civil Rights Act in 1964, sexism now wears a screen of sensitivity and even deference, making it harder to recognize and name when it does occur.

Voices in the Wilderness

The decade of the 1980s, with its superficial solutions to serious problems and its nostalgic desire to return to the good old days, challenged the stability of the women's movement. In the midst of change, women now face the danger of compromise from within and subversion from without. Psychotherapist Anne Wilson Schaef and theologian Catherine Keller exemplify two prominent voices in the wilderness.[11] Both struggle to keep women on the proper path toward greater selfhood and depict the temptations and dangers of our times.

"Queen Bee" and the "Supercompetent Woman."   The popularity of Schaef's book *Women's Reality* invites reflection. Her appeal lies in her ability to voice the elusive problems of what being a woman means today. According to Schaef, women grow up in a culture dominated by the "White Male System": White men hold all essential power and influence. Within this system women see themselves as "tainted." Schaef calls this the "original sin of being born female" or innately inferior.[12] When women find their perceptions at odds with those of men, they discount their own as "sick, bad, crazy, stupid, ugly, or incompetent."[13] As an extension, women project their loathing for themselves and for femaleness onto other women, view them with distrust, and view men as godlike.

Schaef refers to the conflicts of late-second-wave women only indirectly. She warns us of the "Queen Bee" syndrome: Fearful that the room at the top is limited, "successful 'token' women" dissociate themselves from the women's movement. They neither give credit to the women who have gone before them nor feel empathy for those who come after. They then can claim a superiority to women who have not made it and absolve the sin of femaleness. Schaef also talks about the "supercompetent woman" who uses competence as a weapon to rise above other women and similarly detaches herself from the women's movement.[14]

The feminist movement itself can become a "house divided against itself." The distrust of women is simply more abstruse and hidden.[15] When the ideals of liberation are used against women as new standards for condemnation, they are worse than the dogmas of the White Male System. To be told "You are not a true feminist," as radical feminist and theologian Mary Daly, among others, tends to tell women, can debilitate a woman just beginning to voice her own perceptions.[16]

Complicity and "Co-optation."   Using the classical dyad from the Greek myth of Odysseus and Penelope as a model for depicting the dilemmas of the modern woman's search for self, Keller spins out a thesis that threatens to change the way people construe themselves.[17] The dynamic of the warrior-hero and the woman-in-waiting repeats itself in religious story, popular culture (for example, Daniel Boone, the Lone Ranger), and every particular relationship between man and woman. Odysseus represents the dominant Western image of being a man—as psychologist Jean Baker Miller puts it, the "totally strong, self-sufficient person . . . freed forever from weakness or neediness, and, most of all, *from the effects of other people.*"[18] Penelope exists solely because she complements Odysseus. In contrast to his "separative self"—Keller's replacement for the term *separate self* to indicate the fallacy of the latter[19]—she becomes a "soluble self" or what developmental psychologist Daniel J. Levinson and his colleagues call a "transitional figure" or a mere "component" of the man's self-structure.[20] Like Naomi without her husband and sons, she is artist Shel Silverstein's "missing piece"—not much by herself, useful only as she resolves the man's incompletion, and dependent upon the selfhood of man (husband or son) for her very being.[21] Her work in maintaining the web of relation permits men the illusion that people can actually develop "separate" selves. Keller suggests that hidden within this insistence on the ideal of a purely separate, monolithic ego lurks a profound fear and hatred of the chaotic connections that women embody.[22]

Recognizing how these mythic dimensions subtly pervade life, Keller gains greater insight than Schaef into the problems of late-second-wave women. Modern women fall prey to two impulses: not only collusion with limited definitions of womanhood but also imitation of the patriarchal ideals of adulthood. Complicity with male dominance has been a key aspect of women's struggles since Ruth and Naomi. It results from the threat of covert and overt violence if resisted and even from the very commitment of women "to the value of relation itself."[23]

The danger for late-second-wave women is not purely that of complying with patriarchal definitions of what being a woman means. Today we face a more complicated temptation toward co-optation into patri-archal definitions of what being a fulfilled person means—separative selfhood. We must now ask not only the old question of female com-plicity but also the new question of co-optation—a "new form of se-duction by the sovereign structures."[24]

The path to mature adulthood and the male-defined workplace as well seem to require the path of separation. Women deceive themselves if they believe that they can enter these worlds without both obvious and subtle co-optation. As middle-class, white career women find them-selves achieving a new level of economic self-sufficiency, the separative urge becomes harder to resist.[25] If they wish "success," the only avenue seems to be further imitation of the oppressor and the values of the dominant system. Moving into roles once occupied only by men, the knot tightens: To the problems of their already restrictive, self-denying feminine selves, women add the anxieties of the traditionally masculine separative self.[26]

Like Athena who disdains her female origins, working women quick-ly learn to repress qualities that threaten their advancement. Many messages about what it means to be a woman, subtly conveyed by mothers and society—to consider the needs of others, to take care of men, to care for children, and so forth—threaten to paralyze "success" in the public realm, as the *Harvard Business Review* article indicates. Even the conventional male-dominated education that women endure to acquire a job requires a similar sacrifice.[27] The skills of care and nurture may possess more integrity and promise for human survival, but, as Miller notes, they "will not . . . 'get you to the top at General Motors.'" Indeed, these characteristics are "*the* very characteristics that are specifically dysfunctional for success in the world as it is."[28] In defense we turn against other women and usually against ourselves; we become our own accomplices to matricide. In the workplace still defined by male values and in homes run almost solely on women's energies and ingenuity, how can we then truly both work and love?

The Search for Self

How then do late-second-wave women move, as Miller says, from "out-side the 'real world'" to inside without succumbing to its misogynistic infrastructures? Schaef and Keller offer similar suggestions. Both rec-ognize the dangers of a self that remains secondary and symbiotically submerged in a primary, dominant self—Schaef's "tainted self," de-pendent upon men for self-definition, and Keller's "soluble self," dis-solving into the other. Both bear the onus of rescuing a female system.

In spite of these apparent affinities, important distinctions exist. Schaef sees the problem as one in which the self stands over against oppressive culture; her solution entrusts women with the task of claiming a divergent system. For Keller, the problem is woven into the very fabric of society, and the remedy requires transforming basic definitions of self and even our metaphysics. At least two identifiable options for dealing with the dangers of the wilderness stand before us then: the singular self against patriarchal culture and the connective self transforming patriarchal culture. Both suggest far more than a simple exchange of roles, but they are radically different. The self against culture opts out of the White Male System. The self transforming culture dives deeper to alter the very metaphysics and anthropology of sexism. I will argue that the option of self transforming culture, although at times more difficult and more likely to bring suffering and failure, is a more worthy response to our modern-day version of the ancient decision in the wilderness.

Singular self against patriarchal culture.   Schaef's solution remains at the level of consciousness-raising. Many people found in her book a radically new way of seeing reality; women saw their own reality as being as valid as men's, perhaps for the first time. Schaef concludes that women must come to recognize and believe that the White Male System is *"only a system. It is not reality. It is not the way the world is."* [29] We can see the superiority of men and their system as sheer nonsense; then we can live within the Female System, which means trusting the perceptions of women. This attitude shift—a confirmation of " 'female experience,' whatever that may be"—will finally save us. [30]

Schaef offers rudimentary steps for such a shift, each of which entails emoting or facilitating feelings—blame, pity, rage, love of self, and femaleness—and leads to increased self-reliance and eventually a "humanistic" concern for men as well as women. [31] She describes a movement from "childlike innocence" to a turning point of rage and bitterness and on to " 'innocence with wisdom' "—that is, an anger and awareness that does not turn to cynicism or diminish personal happiness. [32] She acknowledges that we have to "pass through the stage of having to 'make it' in the White Male System" to get beyond it. [33] True liberation then requires a three-step movement from (1) oppression in the White Male System to (2) success within it to (3) the Female System.

Schaef calls this progression a theological transformation. Theology itself supports a male-dominated hierarchy. Religion makes women dependent upon omnipotent male godheads—men and a masculine God both. Only a religious change can break the bonds of perhaps the most powerful ideology of dominance and submission in the White Male System. In her last few pages, she suggests that living according to the Female System means "living in tune" with a god internal to oneself. Sin then means a denial of one's own "internal process."[34] Nothing should undercut personal growth and change. Women must take care of themselves; care for others flows naturally from self-care.

These contentions reflect problems akin to the problems of a group of humanistic psychologies that practical theologian Don S. Browning classifies as promoting the "culture of joy."[35] Once again, psychology becomes culture: Prominent psychologists, intending to remain value-free descriptive scientists, implicitly and sometimes explicitly begin to suggest values and promote orienting metaphors for how people should live. Schaef's theological reflection shows little awareness of the differences between her work as psychologist and the work of theology. She claims in her scientific voice that "all I do here is to describe"[36] and that she makes no value judgments, yet at the same time she wants to present "philosophical, . . . political, and theological" concepts.[37]

Like many of the psychologists in the culture of joy, Schaef advocates an individualistic, situational ethic that is insufficient for the problems of late-second-wave women and at odds with Christian ethics. She assumes a covert ethic of ethical egoism—that one ought to act so as to promote one's own welfare and advantage.[38] Rules make sense only when they "facilitate personal growth"; rules must serve the needs of the individual, not those of the system.[39] A woman's success depends upon a strong, albeit implicit, moral imperative toward individuation and preservation of the separative self. She makes the dubious assumption that, as each woman realizes her own individual good, she will have a congenial social balance of needs met and desires gratified.

Humanistic psychologists, such as Fritz Perls, Carl Rogers, Abraham Maslow, and others, locate problems outside the individual in the social system. They contend that given a warm, accepting environment, an individual quite naturally obtains the joy of a deep sense of personal fulfillment. Schaef narrows the boundaries of the oppressive environment from society as a whole to male-dominated society. She also assumes an inherent goodness in human nature but limits this quality to the nature of women. With such faith in the Female System, she does not believe that women who gain power will misuse it as men have or in other ways. The problem of external control and dominance has no place in this system. Should women oust the male system and the traditional reactive female system, they will naturally and effortlessly evolve healthier, more satisfactory ways of living and working. The "solar plexus experience"—the experience of inferiority that women feel—is not a basic characteristic of essential human nature. Rather, were it not for the White Male System, women would feel good about themselves.

This premise rings shallow and ignores the complex dynamics of human duplicity. Schaef ignores, I believe, the depth and complexity of human nature and its capacity for both greatness and corruption, goodness and evil. The "solar plexus experience" possesses a certain universality that reaches beyond the oppressions of gender discrimination. As psychoanalytic theory and much of traditional theology reveal and as our own conflictual experience confirms, we are almost unavoidably divided against ourselves and against others. We ought not allow ourselves the presumptuous, even prideful temptation of blaming the subtle divisiveness of human nature on men alone. Problems of inappropriate control and dominance would and do creep into the Female System.

Although Schaef outlines steps toward change, in the end she fails to construct a new model for selfhood. Despite her awareness of the inappropriate blame placed on mothers as women move beyond the sphere of their mothers, she perpetuates it rather than reclaiming the best of what women have gained from their "mother's house." She warns us of our self-hatred, but does she finally offer us an image to love? Ironically, her model of development remains covertly male-identified—shaped by dominant images of the life cycle defined primarily from the perspective of men.

According to Levinson and his colleagues in *Seasons of a Man's Life,* the typical pattern of development for "normal" people, that is, for men, involves "becoming one's own man," climbing the "ladder" of success in the hierarchical public world of labor and productivity.[40] Maturity means productivity and has "individuation" as the ultimate goal.[41] Although Schaef challenges much in the White Male System, she does not ultimately question this ideal. Not much in the original or traditional female system that might undercut the male model of development merits salvaging. Women's desire to be empathic, their dislike of aggression, their "peacekeeping talk," their fear of breaking away from mother and fear of abandonment and isolation—she names all these "stoppers."[42] They all hinder genuine development and success in the work world. Similarly, connections to mothers contain almost entirely negative elements: They confer a state of inferiority; they breed resentment, depression, suffering, and conflict. Given the choice between, on the one hand, a relationship with mother that may bring depression and, on the other hand, personal gratification that requires a forfeiture of "the life-sustaining bond," she encourages the latter—

destroying the bond to save oneself.[43] The traditional female system and her new Female System—which "emerges when women . . . feel free to express their values"[44]—mutually oppose each other. From Schaef's perspective, we can move from one to the other with few strings attached to our mothers, sisters, friends, and even those parts of ourselves so strongly formed by the White Male System. Mature women who wish to succeed must depart from home and traditional mothers.

Schaef ignores the experience of many women: the ambiguities of making work and self the vehicle for fulfillment; the strong affinities with mothers; the emotional desire and moral commitment to care for others. As women struggle to find places in the public domain, they cannot so easily discount such formative emotional and moral factors of selfhood, but Schaef gives few suggestions about how to reintegrate them into a professional self and world. For her, the desire to preserve them signals compliance with the White Male System and, ultimately, denial of a woman's autonomous power of self-definition. Her writing implicitly stirs up animosity toward women who try in any way to return to their mother's house or follow Naomi and who, in her view, remain caught up in the addictive system of men as a result.

In addition, Schaef assumes that the White Male System and the Female System form cohesive, singular wholes, completely separate and at odds with one another. She fails to address how these two systems come together or how to integrate one's Female System qualities into a world still ruled by the White Male System. In a society that continues to sanction, protect, and prioritize the White Male System, what ultimate rationale will finally tempt men and, indeed, even liberated working women away from the White Male System? To honor the Female System still means forsaking security, status, and significance. How can we weather such trials?

Can we move in and out of systems this way without peril? In a real sense, we must live in both, no matter how radical our ideologies of separatism. Professional women, in particular, must move from "outside the 'real world'" to inside, crossing and moving the strict boundaries of male and female systems. Merely exchanging systems or, perhaps more accurately, venturing off into the wilderness of Moab on our own does not adequately resolve our struggles. "To promote independence and autonomy, with no ontological interconnectedness," argues Keller, "risks co-optation by masculine models of separatism."[45] We cannot so easily discount our connections with our mothers. We cannot discount traits that we have acquired—giving and meeting others' needs, participating in others' development, cooperating, being vulnerable, being emotional. In fact, we might consider the possibility that "male-led society" has "delegated to women not humanity's 'lowest needs' but its 'highest necessities.' "[46] A genuinely woman-identified model sees these traits as inherently valuable qualities of the total human experience.

Connective self transforming patriarchal culture. "The crisis," Keller contends, "demands more than a few considerate shifts of rhetoric and lifestyle. What is required is nothing less than our lives."[47] The logical escape route—"achievement of the separate individuality heretofore expected only of men"—ultimately disappoints.[48] Women who have reached the top of the corporate ladder quit; others do so after childbirth. Knowing what we know about the meaningfulness of conversation, of intimacy, of caring for children, and of bonds that do not bind, do we really want what men fashion for themselves? I think not. Indeed, as Keller claims, women must not "emulate the . . . style of the traditional male."[49] The implications of emulation extend far beyond the individual.

What is required is nothing less than a realignment of perceptions at the deepest level. Keller challenges the assumption that "selfhood requires separation" and argues that it is inextricably linked to another fallacious sexist assumption, "that men, by nature and by right, exercise the primary prerogatives of civilization."[50] In her constructive response, she states that we must (1) deconstruct the structures of the separative self that hold us so tightly within their grip; (2) reclaim the power of our mothers, femininity, and women—the repressed "monsters of the Deep" that mark the repression of connection itself—and (3) ultimately begin to live out a new kind of selfhood. Selfhood must not become entrapped in the dichotomy of self versus relation or the divisive complementarities of Odysseus and Penelope. Instead, by moving toward a "connective" selfhood for women and for men, we may begin to mend the web broken by the deification of a separative self that depends upon the web of connection yet ignores its care.

Keller's idea of a connective self reweaving the web comes as a relief to many women who have intuited its moral and psychological appropriateness. "I had never before heard a challenge to the notion that separation and independence are the primary developmental tasks for all persons," wrote one of my students. "I certainly had internalized the primacy of separation; and yet, in my shadowself had struggled quite painfully to at least appear well differentiated and deny and resist my own needs for nurturing. To hear from Keller a call back to the pre-Oedipal stage and a valuing of the experience of the oceanic was like hearing permission to seek and find that which I had been missing in my life, but that which I had been led to believe was regressive, not o.k., and bad." Keller's ideas speak directly to the struggles of women wanting both to salvage something from their mother's house and yet to venture into new territory, both by Naomi's side and on their own. Only a fluid, interpermeable self can travel in these many directions with any sense of cohesion and assurance.

Others have glimpsed the repression of this vision of selfhood but more successfully articulated the psychological and moral components of its recovery than Keller. Psychoanalyst Heinz Kohut, founder of the American movement of self-psychology, departs from Freudian interpretations of the self which sanction separation; he proposes a second line of development that respects attachments. Healthy persons not only develop from a narcissistic love of self to a mature object love or love of others as Freud contends. They also develop from a primitive love of self to a mature narcissism.[51] As part of the latter, attachments to and dependencies upon others are not necessarily unhealthy infantile addictions that people must outgrow. Rather, in order to retain a cohesive sense of self, people depend on others—what he calls "mature self-objects"—for empathy and idealization throughout life. Based upon observations of children, psychiatrist Daniel N. Stern disputes the pervasive interpretation that the child develops from an undifferentiated, hazardous enmeshment with the mother through separation to ever-increasing heights of individuation. Infants differentiate themselves from birth. Growth then entails learning more and more sophisticated modes of relating. Development, in Stern's words, "is not primarily devoted to . . . independence or autonomy or individuation—that is, getting away and free from the primary caregiver. It is equally devoted to the seeking and creating of intersubjective union with another."[52] Attachment and dependency are issues throughout life.

Despite their theoretical emphasis on connection and on alternative models of maturity, however, Kohut, Stern, and those who use their theories still have trouble breaking free from the values of "separative man." Kohut and Stern ignore gender issues. Their focus on early intrapsychic changes prevents them from exploring adult concerns or social implications. Granted, they affirm that we have ignored a particularly critical line of development, the development of intimacy, relationships, and care. However, perhaps the heart of the problem lies in masculine perceptions of success and a devaluation of women's development. Whereas men's moral understandings parallel a development from aggression to separation through achievements, as Carol Gilligan has established, women's moral reasoning reflects growth from differentiation to interdependence through attachments.[53] Women's immature and mature moral understandings of success center around intimacy, relationships, and care and not around individuation and actualization of increasingly objective, universal, and distant material results. When a sense of self distinct from others appears in the most mature phase of development, this separateness stands in necessary relationship to others. Maturity now means an awareness of the web of interconnection at all stages and an increasing ability over time to negotiate ever more complex relationships.

These theories force us to stop and think. For far too long we have taken for granted the ideal of success in the public workaday world as an increase in self-sufficiency and productivity. These theories represent an underside of human nature which has surfaced as women feel, think, and talk. The truth as we have known it is unsettled once again, and the assumptions that undergird our world stand before us for review.

Nevertheless, the social sciences alone do not have the resources to begin to construct a fully adequate conception of selfhood. We need a theoretical foundation wider than psychology can provide to answer moral and religious questions. We need to move beyond an examination of the models of psychology to a metaphysic that as Keller says, "drives beyond the sphere of the interpersonal" and seeks "a broader context" in which to ground its argument.[54] This necessarily entails uncovering the deeper metaphors that shape culture and the self.

Next to Keller, Schaef's ethic of joy and faith in the goodness of the Female System seem misplaced and naive. From a broader vantage point, Keller recognizes the complexities of human fallibility and perversion. She more self-consciously asserts the necessity of an ethic of reciprocity between self and other in an ongoing chain of multiple events and actions. Her position has affinities with what Browning describes as an ethic of care that promotes a positive attitude of "active care and concern . . . not only for oneself and one's progeny but for the wider community," even "possible future communities which may extend beyond the limits of one's individual life."[55] Keller backs this ethical position with a metaphysic. Not only should we consider such connections imperative but also essential, in spite of our intense fears of what such connections might mean for us. Our choices and actions are interconnected in the very process of being. We cannot avoid considering the larger web of relationships with the communities and societies to which people belong.[56]

Keller further supports such an ethic by attempting to transform certain grounding images of God. Religion has heretofore persisted in upholding misogynist presuppositions about separation: The God of classical Western Christian theology embodies the supreme case of an ultimately separate, self-sufficient object, safe from change and influence in his ("this God could only take the pronoun *he*") complete omnipotence.[57] Religion and a God "true to its name," argues Keller, "activates connection." A God who cares for communal and cross-cultural webs contrasts sharply with a corporate godhead who models climbing ladders to success. Is not our God a God of work and love in quite a different sense?

We must avoid a danger in Keller's position. She acknowledges superficially but does not fully comprehend the developmental dangers of merger, symbiosis, and collapse of boundaries between self and other that Kohut, Stern, and others point out. Her ethic of multiple commitments in an ever-widening circle of connections threatens to demand of women more than they can or should contribute. To return to a connective self may lead only to less clarity and self-definition than ever. Valerie Saiving has talked about women's particular sin of self-dispersion. Men have traditionally defined *sin* as pride or self-assertion, which is not generally the problem for women; women struggle with a contrasting tendency toward self-abnegation or loss of self in distractibility, diffuseness, and "dependence upon others for one's own self-definition."[58] Where does a woman's commitment and connection to others begin and end? Women have struggled with this question, and, as Saiving and others demonstrate, they have sacrificed themselves and their needs in their efforts to remain connected to others for too long.

Our intellectual triumphs and even the increase of women in professional occupations lure us into false optimism. Keller speaks for an upper strata of white women and alludes only casually to the blights of racism and classism.[59] She avoids the pragmatic questions of how structural, institutional, socioeconomic change might occur, given her new constructions of the self. Enormous changes in current social structures must occur if women and men are to work and love humanely.[60] Society's work institutions function as if workers have no domestic needs. Indeed, women stand at risk in a society that does not reward affiliations and interconnections but instead sanctions separation and material achievements. Over and over, society communicates its disregard for all helping professions that do take care of the interconnected family of humanity (for example, nurse, mental health worker, nursing home aide, school-teacher). By comparison with other jobs and considering the value of their work, these and other caregivers receive less monetary reward, security, or status; local and state government and private employers continue to ignore the crying need for adequate childcare; criteria for promotion seldom build in, much less honor, maternal and paternal time off for children, flexible work time, and equal perquisites. Given these current conditions and the large proportion of wage-earning women who continue to carry the major load of household tasks, how much longer can we expect women to make the sacrifices necessary to maintain connections and sustain family life?

A more inclusive enactment of connection means new language to describe maturity—language other than "autonomy," for example, to describe the growing capacity for self-assertion that comes with "a fuller not less ability to encompass relationships to others."[61] We need words that describe an ability to function independently and responsibly that is intricately linked to an ability to sustain healthy dependence upon others.

If we cannot find new language, we may want to reconsider the limiting definitions of the words we do use, such as *autonomy, altruism,* and *dependence.* Why do we automatically suppose that autonomy and self-concern stand opposite concern for others? Might mature autonomy include a free state of being concerned for oneself *as one is concerned for others?* Similarly, the word *altruism* assumes an overt disregard for oneself; yet when we adopt this term for all forms of doing good for others, we imply that we can do good for others only at our own expense. Should we begin to admit that mature altruism—authentic giving to others—remains inextricably linked to the capacity to take care of oneself or else risks disintegration into a well-disguised form of manipulation?[62] When we say someone is "dependent," we instantly perceive this as a negative comment. Yet Gilligan has shown that for many women dependence can sometimes mean a healthy reliance upon others. "Being dependent, then, no longer means being helpless, powerless, and without control; rather, it signifies a conviction that one is able to have an effect on others. . . . In this active construction, dependence, rather than signifying a failure of individuation, denotes a decision on the part of the individual to enact a vision of love."[63] Keller talks about interdependence;[64] Miller describes a mature affiliation,[65] and Kohut names the ability to sustain contact with "mature self-objects," not greater ego control, as the essence of successful psychoanalytic cure.[66] As of yet, none of these depictions of maturity carries the same weight as claims to autonomy and independence. Rethinking these words or finding new language that actually compels us will not happen easily.

Ultimately, a more adequate enactment of connection will require new social structures that honor alternative values. Among other things, we must find better ways to allow people to work and to care for children and home—to work and love. We now need to reevaluate society's ideals of success and personal qualities in light of values that women have long upheld. Our social structures and our church institutions need to support these values. Only by revisioning the structural possibilities and responsibilities for a more inclusive enactment of connection for women and men can we reach satisfying solutions to the many current dilemmas that make it difficult for all of us to work and to love.

BIBLIOGRAPHY

Andolsen, Barbara Hilbert, Christine E. Gudorf, and Mary D. Pellauer, eds. *Women's Consciousness, Woman's Conscience: A Reader in Feminist Ethics*. San Francisco: Harper & Row, 1985.

Belenky, Mary Field, et al. *Women's Ways of Knowing: The Development of Self, Voice, and Mind*. New York: Basic Books, 1986.

Bolen, Jean Shinoda. *Goddesses in Everywoman*. San Francisco: Harper & Row, 1984.

Browning, Don S. *Pluralism and Personality: William James and Some Contemporary Cultures of Psychology*. Lewisburg, Pa.: Bucknell University Press, 1980.

———. *Religious Thought and the Modern Psychologies*. Philadelphia: Fortress Press, 1987.

Chernin, Kim. *Reinventing Eve: Modern Woman in Search of Herself*. San Francisco: Harper & Row, 1987.

Dittes, James E. *The Male Predicament: On Being a Man Today*. San Francisco: Harper & Row, 1985.

Downing, Christine. "Gender Anxiety." *Journal of Pastoral Care* 43 (Summer 1989):152-61.

———. *Journey Through Menopause: A Personal Rite of Passage*. New York: Crossroad, 1987.

Fisher, Berenice. "Wandering in the Wilderness: The Search for Women Role Models." *Signs: Journal of Women in Culture and Society* 13, no. 2 (1988), 211–33.

Frankena, William K. *Ethics*. Englewood Cliffs, N.J.: Prentice-Hall, 1973.

Gennuso, Mary J. "Letter to the Editors." *Journal of Feminist Studies in Religion* 5, no. 1 (Spring 1989):101–2.

Gilligan, Carol. *In a Different Voice: Psychological Theory and Women's Development*. Cambridge: Harvard University Press, 1982.

———. "Why Should a Woman Be More Like a Man?" *Psychology Today*, June 1982.

———. "Women's Place in Man's Life Cycle," *Harvard Educational Review* 49 (1979):431–36.

———, et al., eds. *Mapping the Moral Domain: A Contribution of Women's Thinking to Psychology and Education*. Cambridge: Harvard University Press, 1988.

Gould, Carol C., and Marx W. Wartofsky, eds. *Women and Philosophy: Toward a Theory of Liberation*. New York: G. P. Putnam's Sons, 1976.

Hahn, Celia Allison. "Sexual Paradox: Pride and Hiding." In *Spice*, Washington D.C.: The Alban Institute, 9–11.

Halper, Jan. *Quiet Desperation: The Truth About Successful Men*. New York: Warner Books, 1988.

Keller, Catherine. *From a Broken Web: Separation, Sexism, and Self*. Boston: Beacon Press, 1986.

Kemper, Robert G. "Where Have All the Assumptions Gone?" *Chicago Theological Seminary Register* 77, no. 1 (Winter 1987):1–11.

Kohut, Heinz. *The Analysis of the Self*. New York: International Universities Press, 1971.

———. *How Does Analysis Cure?* Chicago: University of Chicago Press, 1984.

———. "Introspection, Empathy, and the Semi-Circle of Mental Health." In *International Journal of Psycho-Analysis* 63 (1982): 395–407.

Lear, Martha Weinman. "The Second Feminist Wave." *New York Times Magazine*, 10 March 1968.

Levinson, Daniel J., et al. *Seasons of a Man's Life*. New York: Ballantine, 1978.

Miller, Jean Baker. *Toward a New Psychology of Women*. Boston: Beacon Press, 1976.

Plaskow, Judith. *Sex, Sin and Grace: Women's Experience and the Theologies of Reinhold Niebuhr and Paul Tillich*. Lanham, Md.: University Press of America, 1980.

Saiving, Valerie. "The Human Situation: A Feminine View." In *Journal of Religion* 40 (April 1960): 100–12.

Schaef, Anne Wilson. *Co-Dependence*. San Francisco: Harper & Row, 1986.

———. *When Society Becomes an Addict*. San Francisco: Harper & Row, 1987.

———. *Women's Reality: An Emerging Female System in the White Male Society*. Minneapolis: Winston, 1981.

Schwartz, Felice N. "Management Women and the New Facts of Life." *Harvard Business Review* (January-February 1989): 65–76.

Silverstein, Shel. *The Missing Piece*. New York: Harper & Row, 1976.

Soelle, Dorothee. "Sin Is When Life Freezes." *Christian Century*, 12 May 1982, 558–59.

Stern, Daniel N. *The Interpersonal World of the Infant: A View from Psychoanalysis and Developmental Psychology*. New York: Basic Books, 1985.

Thistlethwaite, Susan B. *Sex, Racism and God: Christian Feminism in Black and White*. New York: Crossroad, 1989.

Washbourne, Penelope. *Becoming Woman: The Quest for Wholeness in Female Experience*. New York: Harper & Row, 1977.

Weisstein, Naomi. "Psychology Constructs the Female." In *Women in Sexist Society*, ed. V. Gornick and B. K. Moran. New York: Signet/New American Library, 1971.

NOTES

1. Berenice Fisher, "Wandering in the Wilderness: The Search for Women Role Models," *Signs: Journal of Women in Culture and Society* 13 (1988):216.

2. See, for example, the details of men's life stages in Daniel J. Levinson, with Charlotte N. Darrow, Edward B. Klein, Maria H. Levinson, and Braxton McKee, *Seasons of a Man's Life* (New York: Ballantine, 1978). There is some indication that men have begun to experience the strain of their career paths. Levinson talks about a midlife crisis when men abruptly question the emptiness of the path they have chosen. Others such as James E. Dittes (*The Male Predicament: On Being a Man Today* [San Francisco: Harper & Row, 1985]) and Jan Halper (*Quiet Desperation: The Truth About Successful Men* [New York: Warner Books, 1988]) reveal that men are questioning their roles, disillusioned by the "fruits" of their "success."

3. I write from the perspective of a white, middle-class, professional woman. Throughout, when I use the term *women*, I refer primarily to this specific population. Much more could and needs to be said about the particular problems of work and love of other populations—women of color, blue-collar women, third-world women—that I do not presume to touch upon here.

4. Christine Downing developed this idea in a lecture presented to the American Association of Pastoral Counselors in New Orleans, Spring 1987. A version of this appears under the title "Gender Anxiety," *Journal of Pastoral Care* 43 (Summer 1989): 152. See also her book, *Journey Through Menopause: A Personal Rite of Passage* (New York: Crossroad, 1987).

5. Martha Weinman Lear coined the term *second wave* in reference to the period of feminism dating from approximately 1966 ("The Second Feminist Wave," *New York Times Magazine*, 10 March 1968). When I say "late" second wave, I mean primarily the experience of white, middle-class women beginning careers in the 1980s after years of education shaped in part by both patriarchy and feminism. Rather than restricting it chronologically, I leave the term open to include any person who experiences a conflict between at least two explicit images of womanhood, adulthood, and their related value systems.

6. Catherine Keller, *From a Broken Web: Separation, Sexism, and Self* (Boston: Beacon Press, 1986), 16.

7. Mary J. Gennuso, "Letter to the Editors," *Journal of Feminist Studies in Religion* 5, no. 1 (Spring 1989):101.

8. One minister reporting the changes in his suburban upper-middle-class congregation in the last thirteen years notes that feminism has had little impact on liturgical language or women's groups but that the women's movement has dramatically eroded the amount of "volunteer participation" and made church attendance on Sundays difficult for families. Indeed, he uses "the changing role of women" as his "point of entry" into his discussion of the significant changes in parish life (Robert G. Kemper, "Where Have All the Assumptions Gone?" *The Chicago Theological Seminary Register* 77, no. 1 (Winter 1987):5.

9. *Chicago Tribune*, 17 July 1988, Tempo Woman.

10. Felice N. Schwartz, "Management Women and the New Facts of Life," *Harvard Business Review* (Jan.-Feb. 1989):66.

11. Anne Wilson Schaef, *Women's Reality: An Emerging Female System in the White Male Society* (Minneapolis: Winston Press, 1981) and Keller, *Broken Web*.

Schaef has also written *Co-Dependence* (San Francisco: Harper & Row, 1986) and *When Society Becomes an Addict* (San Francisco: Harper & Row, 1987). Both books mark a shift in her original theses or at least a sharp development; she emphasizes the addictive society as the enemy against which women and men struggle. Here, I restrict my remarks to *Women's Reality*.

12. Schaef, *Women's Reality*, 27.

13. Ibid., 38.

14. Ibid., 44.

15. Ibid., 23.

16. Ibid., 77.

17. Schaef also acknowledges the metaphor of women's responsive "waiting"; she calls men "gypsies" and women "nesters" (*Women's Reality*, 64).

18. Jean Baker Miller, *Toward a New Psychology of Women* (Boston: Beacon Press, 1976), 103; see also p. 23.

19. Keller, *Broken Web*, 13.

20. Levinson, *Seasons*, 109.

21. Shel Silverstein, *The Missing Piece* (New York: Harper & Row, 1976). Schaef talks about this in graphic terms: When a man swallows a woman, like an amoeba absorbs its food, "he literally does not perceive that she is separate being" (*Women's Reality*, 56–62).

22. Keller, *Broken Web*, 3.

23. Ibid., 17.

24. Ibid., 16.

25. Ibid., 11.

26. Ibid., 16.

27. Jean Shinoda Bolen, *Goddesses in Everywoman* (San Francisco: Harper & Row, 1984), 82 (cited by Keller, *Broken Web*, 57).

28. Miller, *Toward a New Psychology*, 124.

29. Schaef, *Women's Reality*, 7. Emphasis added. See also pp. 19, 145.

30. Ibid., 89.

31. Ibid., 91f.

32. Ibid., 79.

33. Ibid., 58; see also p. 111.

34. Ibid., 168.

35. Don S. Browning, *Pluralism and Personality: William James and Some Contemporary Cultures of Psychology* (Lewisburg, Pa.: Bucknell University Press, 1980), 20–22, 195; see also idem, *Religious Thought and the Modern Psychologies* (Philadelphia: Fortress Press, 1987), 5–6, 29–31. Browning's general theory here is that psychology, narrowly conceived as a science that merely charts material causes and consequences of human actions and feelings, easily becomes inflated into a broadly conceived project that shapes culture.

36. Schaef, *Women's Reality*, xvi.

37. Ibid., xx.

38. William K. Frankena, *Ethics* (Englewood Cliffs, N.J.: Prentice-Hall, 1973), 14–16.

39. Schaef, *Women's Reality,* 129.

40. Levinson, *Seasons,* 9, 59, 60, 144.

41. Ibid., 239. It is "separation" that "fosters growth"; attachments hinder it. Growth through dependence seems fraught with danger. As Carol Gilligan, author of the pivotal study of women's moral development, verifies, for men ambivalence about intimacy prevails (*In a Different Voice: Psychological Theory and Women's Development* [Cambridge: Harvard University Press, 1982], 8, 42, 62).

42. Schaef, *Women's Reality,* 71–80, 99.

43. Ibid., 80–85.

44. Ibid., xix. She deems the system that challenges the White Male System "*The* Female System" (xix). By so naming it, she gives it an exclusivity that she earlier protested in the White Male System. To claim that it includes "women from other ethnic systems" defines their reality for them from a *white* female perspective (3, 145). This "reality" hierarchically rates racial discrimination as secondary to the oppressions of gender and ignores important differences within the respective "systems" themselves.

45. Keller, *Broken Web,* 209.

46. Miller, *Toward a New Psychology,* 22–23, 25–26.

47. Keller, *Broken Web,* 4.

48. Ibid., 3–4.

49. Ibid., 8, 22, 46.

50. Ibid., 2.

51. Heinz Kohut, *The Analysis of the Self* (New York: International Universities Press, 1971), 220; idem, "Introspection, Empathy, and the Semi-Circle of Mental Health," *International Journal of Psycho-Analysis* 63 (1982):402; idem, *How Does Analysis Cure?* (Chicago: University of Chicago Press, 1984), 65–66.

52. Daniel N. Stern, *The Interpersonal World of the Infant: A View from Psychoanalysis and Developmental Psychology* (New York: Basic Books, 1985), 10.

53. Gilligan, *In a Different Voice;* see also Carol Gilligan, "Why Should a Woman Be More Like a Man?" *Psychology Today,* June 1982, 68–77; and "Women's Place in Man's Life Cycle," *Harvard Educational Review* 49 (1979):431–36.

54. Keller, *Broken Web,* 155, 158.

55. Browning, *Pluralism and Personality,* 41.

56. Gilligan, *Different Voice,* 149.

57. Keller, *Broken Web,* 35.

58. Valerie Saiving, "The Human Situation: A Feminine View," *Journal of Religion* 40 (April 1960):109. See also Judith Plaskow, *Sex, Sin and Grace: Women's Experience and the Theologies of Reinhold Niebuhr and Paul Tillich* (Lanham, Md.: University Press of America, 1980); Celia Allison Hahn, "Sexual Paradox: Pride and Hiding," *Spice* (Washington, D.C.: The Alban Institute), 9–11; Dorothee Soelle, "Sin Is When Life Freezes," *Christian Century,* (12 May 1982).

59. See Susan B. Thistlethwaite, *Sex, Racism and God: Christian Feminism in Black and White* (New York: Crossroad, 1989). She argues that white feminist attention to connection overlooks the different struggles of women of color and ignores racial differences.

60. See Barbara Hilkert Andolsen, "A Woman's Work is Never Done." In *Women's Consciousness, Women's Conscience: A Reader in Feminist Ethics,* ed. Barbara Hilkert Andolsen, Christine E. Gudorf, and Mary D. Pellauer (San Francisco: Harper & Row, 1985), 3–18.

61. Miller, *Toward a New Psychology,* 94.

62. Larry Blum, et al. "Altruism and Women's Oppression." In *Women and Philosophy: Toward a Theory of Liberation,* ed. Carol C. Gould and Marx W. Wartofsky (New York: G. P. Putnam's Sons, 1976), 223–24.

63. Carol Gilligan, "Remapping the Moral Domain: New Images of Self in Relationship." In *Mapping the Moral Domain: A Contribution of Women's Thinking to Psychological Theory and Education,* ed. Carol Gilligan, Janie Victoria Ward, and Jill McLean Taylor with Betty Bardige (Cambridge: Harvard University Press, 1988), 15.

64. Keller, *Broken Web,* 154.

65. Miller, *Toward a New Psychology,* 95–96.

66. Kohut, *How Does Analysis Cure?* 66, 77.

CHAPTER 4

Woman's Body: Spiritual Needs and Theological Presence

MARY JAMES DEAN AND MARY LOUISE CULLEN

· · · · · · · · · · · ·

Women deal with the travail and transition of the physiologic issues of menstruation, birth, menopause, and gynecologic diseases. Women's identification with body and its reproductive functions is a source of primary identity that is inherent in our experience. For good or ill, much of women's existential life is oriented toward the body and the physical, psychological, emotional, and spiritual aspects of reproduction. Corresponding to bodily issues, women deal with the theological realities of identity, embodiment, generativity, rhythmicity, guilt and shame, limitation, and loss and grieving. The pastoral care needs around the gynecologic issues of contemporary women are great, but the task of breaking through our learned defenses and creating a viable language and a credible theological presence is difficult, given a patriarchal history and cultural assumptions.

History and cultural learning have trained us—male and female, clergy and layperson—to identify women with reproduction, to describe reproductive functions as illness and pathology, and to interpret women's roles in gynecologic treatment as passive, narcissistic, and masochistic. Historically, women have not been in charge of their health care because they have not been truly informed consumers; rather, typically, they have been submissive to male physicians who, in too many instances, have "worked to maintain women's ignorance, believing women too child-like and capricious to understand the complexity of drugs, treatment, and choices."[1] With the reproductive system seen as pathological, we can easily understand how women have tended either to be enmeshed in reproductive functioning or in denial of its full impact on our lives.

This enmeshment or denial presents a central dilemma when we are faced with mourning the loss of some gynecologic functioning. We may have been consumed, limited by, or enmeshed with roles, so that we felt *defined* by the functioning. In this case, the loss of that functioning can be devastating because we lose our very identity. In an effort to neutralize and minimize the masculine-judged weakness of the female experience, however, we may have *denied* and ignored our real feelings about these processes. In so doing, we have cut ourselves off from the power of their creativity, and we cannot grieve for the loss of the function.

The purpose of this chapter is to help clergy understand the integration of gynecologic experiences as a part of our humanness, a part of the whole and not an ultimate definition or an irrelevance to be ignored. We integrate by standing in relation to something, by confronting it and calling it by name, and by rejoicing in its power and mourning its loss. Out of interviews with twenty women, plus five pastoral counselors, doctors, and nurses, we will listen to women's composite voices as they tell their stories about the following gynecologic life issues: premenstrual syndrome, menopause, infertility, miscarriage, infant death, breast cancer, and other gynecologic cancers. From the theological and personal identity issues expressed in the interviews, we can learn more about a new pastoral care for women in transition. We may then bravely put aside our learned defenses of embarrassment, minimization, and silence around these female concerns and confront the essential need to become an active, involved theological presence with women who are dealing with these crucial life problems. A credible theological presence goes with a person on a journey, shares the burden, listens to the anguish, finds the strengths, and holds out for hope in the midst of desolation.

Natural Gynecologic Processes

Premenstrual syndrome.   Premenstrual syndrome implies several conditions that recur month after month at the same time in the cycle. Cycle changes are thought to account for somatic symptoms (fluid retention, abdominal bloating, back and abdominal cramps, breast tenderness) and mood fluctuations (irritability, anxiety, depression, anger). Most women are aware of some changing symptoms through the cycle. For some, this is merely an awareness; for others, these changes can be uncomfortable and disruptive. Despite various hormonal explanations, no consensus has been reached as to the rationale for premenstrual syndrome. Most theories identify maximal symptoms with the fall of estrogen and progesterone to low levels. Medical management of premenstrual syndrome is available; however, the self-charting of data, combined with loving support and reassurance from significant others, is of utmost value to the woman suffering from premenstrual syndrome.

> Five days before my period, I am really depressed, down in the dumps, thinking about my mother's death, just sad. Then I have all the classic symptoms of bloating, backache, and cramps, which I deal with by withdrawing for safety. I don't offend other people, but I can't do anything for myself. I walk alone, clear my mind, and collect my thoughts. I have to talk about it. I do have male friends who talk with me, and it is really beautiful the way they understand. My hormones are changing every month, and there is nothing weak about that. I would never want anyone to judge or define me by this physiological change.

> Premenstrual syndrome is not something that can be counseled. It affects everyone differently. Meditation helps. Being able to relax helps. Vitamins, exercise, and diet (no caffeine, chocolate, or sugar) help. Removing myself from stress and being able to meditate and relax is probably the most helpful thing for me. I try to do something every day that is quieting, focusing, to relax in the goodness of God. Just take yourself to that place every day for a time, be away from the world, and you will come out refreshed. With premenstrual syndrome, this is enormously helpful. I do this one week prior to my period.

Most women would not go to clergy for issues of premenstrual syndrome, but they did agree that they would like clergy to read more and understand premenstrual syndrome as a real physiological, emotional reality for women. Some women may still feel unconscious or even conscious self-depreciation, shame, and inferiority stemming from the historical, Hebraic interpretation of menstruation as a state of uncleanliness. Therefore, to help women put away these myths, pastors must not minimize, depreciate, or laugh at premenstrual syndrome and instead should openly explore new interpretations for its meaning. Menstruation can be very positively understood as an embodiment of a powerful rhythmicity indicative of the generative cycles of life itself. From clergy, women want empathy, understanding, and acceptance during this time—permission to feel anger and irritability, not judgment for these real feelings.

Spiritual leaders who know about meditation and/or relaxation techniques can offer help with imaging, letting go, and focused relaxation. Many women find a direct connection between a focused spiritual center—a belief in something beyond immediate sensation, which involves pulling back from the stress of the external world—and how they deal with premenstrual syndrome. The experience of the uncontrolled flow of blood, then, is seen as an essential part of a spiritual embodiment of focus and meditation. As pastoral counselors can accept and integrate the idea of rhythmicity and the creative cycles of menstruation, we can find innovative ways to help women appreciate the link between the "letting go" of menstrual fluid and the spiritual "letting go" so necessary for spiritual oneness and release of energy. In this way, paradoxically, the inability to control bodily fluids is the same release that enhances focus in the spiritual process.

Menopause.   The climacteric is the transition from the reproductive years to the nonreproductive years in the woman. The physiological events of the climacteric can be divided into three phases: premenopausal, perimenopausal, and postmenopausal. During the premenopausal phase, the woman is still menstruating; however, estrogen changes may occur years before the interruption of periods begins and perhaps create feelings of loneliness, insecurity, and depression before any physical symptoms of menopause are present. With the change in regularity of menses during the perimenopausal phase, fertility decreases. This decreased fertility is a possible result of the progressive disappearance of egg maturation activity that ultimately results in ovarian follicle degeneration. Menopause is a result of the ovaries' inability to respond to pituitary hormones. Because of the declining ovarian hormone production, estrogen and progesterone levels drop. Other compensating hormones secreted by the hypothalamus and the pituitary complicate the already complex hormonal cycle and can increase emotional disequilibrium.

The following signs can be directly related to changes in estrogen production: (1) changes in the menstrual cycle, (2) hot flashes and sweats (vasomotor instability), (3) decreased vaginal moisture and elasticity, and (4) decreased elasticity of the skin, especially facial skin. Other physical and behavioral symptomatology may be attributed to declining estrogen levels, but menopausal symptoms and their severity vary from individual to individual.

Estrogen replacement therapy can be important in reducing the symptoms of menopause; however, it requires that the woman take a systematic, educated approach to decide if estrogen replacement therapy is best for her. Low dosages of estrogen with cyclic progesterone have the potential to emulate the normal cycle and thereby relieve many of the physical signs and symptoms of menopause, while not increasing the risk for uterine cancer. Significant use of unopposed estrogen increases the risk for endometrial cancer, whereas the combination of estrogen and progesterone can often offer benefits of fewer mood swings, better bones, better skin, and less drying of vaginal tissue.

Menopause raises real life issues of meaning. You realize you're not that old, but a big part of your life is over, and you're going on to the last part of life. I find myself saying, "What haven't I done that I really wanted to do with my life?"

I find my thinking is confused much of the time, and I forget simple things. I sometimes can't focus on cognitive tasks, but I find myself daydreaming and becoming extremely sexually stimulated by attractive men. It's like a return to adolescence, but I never experienced this strong sexual desire in adolescence. When you're married, it's frustrating because there is an overwhelming feeling of wanting to satisfy this sexual desire with affairs.

I'm not so accommodating anymore. I've learned I can be angry too, and it's a little scary because I see more and more people getting divorced after twenty-five years of marriage. I'm afraid of a separation between us when all the kids are gone, and the gap is just too wide emotionally between us. I'm out of the box for the first time; it's like I'm beginning to emerge as this new person—not a wife or mother—but myself. It scared the hell out of me to think that I came very, very close to leaving all that suburban stuff and my husband and just going on to something very different in my life. There is a freedom, a new energy, a new aggression. It's exciting, but scary.

A biopsychosocial model for menopause is needed, along with explicit spiritual help for the confusion of feelings that may be overwhelming during this crucial time in the life cycle. So many events are converging: empty nest, struggle over career, marital stress, illness and death of parents, disappointments of past and present, fear of future.[2] The depression often attributed to menopause can also be linked to the real-life events that seem to come in bundles during this phase of life; depression comes from experienced loss in relationship, in addition to overdependence and repressed anger.

"The crisis of menopause is felt much less keenly by women who have not staked everything on their femininity."[3] If too much identity is derived from reproductive functions, the menopausal process can be devastating, and the sense of generativity as a creativity beyond the reproductive function is lost. As Simone deBeauvoir says, "Whereas man grows old gradually, woman is suddenly deprived of her femininity; she is still relatively young when she loses the erotic attractiveness and the fertility which in the view of society and in her own, provide the justification for her existence and her opportunity for happiness."[4] For the woman who has defined her life by reproduction, this life cycle event can be filled with bitterness. Her husband, her environment, and her occupations can seem unworthy of her, and she may feel unappreciated. This woman probably suffers in silence, carries the secret in her heart, and calls it forth only when she reminisces about her lost opportunities and what might have been her past.[5]

Pastoral counselors can be in tune with women's generativity as derived from our spiritual origins and connections with community and as not ultimately a function of biology. Women whose basic identity is shaped around reproduction can experience extreme loss during menopause, and clergy should readily respond with affirmation of the generativity of the person as a child of God and a contributing member of the human community, apart from the reproductive role. Encouraging women to become engaged in activities not at all related to reproduction could be a helpful pastoral care function. Starting a small business, learning golf, and taking a writing course are examples of creative life beyond menopause.

In contrast, in an attempt not to be trapped by the emotional upheaval of menopause, some women deny the endocrine changes and try to sail through this period without feeling the waves. Despite a need to sort out life crises and hormonal changes, to deny the physiological, emotional process only tends to arrest development during this period, so that older age may be even more difficult to handle. Pastoral caregivers who can meet this denial with an open acceptance and willingness to discuss the physical and psychological issues of menopause can help women break through the denial so that "joyful grieving" can occur as an appropriate response to this significant transition. Perhaps the healthy response is ambivalence, as described in a recent study of menopause: "Women express both regret and hope, nostalgia and current reality, loss and gain, pride and disappointment, a longing and a relief as they try to deal with a life period that each person must negotiate."[6]

Most women believe clergy could be more sensitively educated about the complexity of women's physiological and emotional changes during menopause. Women are angry that the approach to dealing with menopause frequently has been either to dismiss it with laughter and jokes or to define mid-life women in a condescending way by the emotional upheaval that characterizes menopause. Women want more open and honest discussion about menopause, its physical and emotional symptoms, what it means in terms of personal, existential threat, and how it impacts intimacy and other interpersonal relationships, although they may need to be invited to discuss these issues openly, especially with male clergy.

We must update our understanding of menopause. It is a more significant issue now than in the past because life expectancy is now longer. In the late 1800s, the life expectancy for women in the United States was from forty to fifty, the time of menopause. Now it is truly a mid-life issue and must be seen in that context. Women deal with the theological and self-identity issues of loss of reproductive functioning and its impact on their identity, significant changes in marital and family relationships, and unsettling questions about defining creative existence beyond reproduction, perhaps for another fifty years.

Too few menopausal women benefit from shared group support in group therapy or support groups. Ministers, priests, and rabbis could be catalysts who empower women to address mid-life issues with honesty and openness. Whether clergy themselves lead groups or not, they could help in the creation of support groups within the church. Negative attitudes around menopause can be altered through group work focused on education and support to counter misinformation and myth through honest experiences and sharing in a supportive context. More open discussion of the reality of menopause as a significant issue for female identity is facilitated by seeing it as a normal mid-life cycle process and offering discussion about the experience.

Failure in the Reproductive System

Infertility. *Fertility* is a woman's ability to conceive and give birth to a living infant; *infertility* is the inability to conceive after a year or more of sexual intercourse. Primary infertility describes the woman who has never been able to conceive, with secondary infertility implying that a woman has conceived at least once previously. At least ten million couples in the United States are infertile, as many as one in five couples. In forty percent the infertility is a male factor, in forty percent the infertility is a female factor, and in twenty percent the cause is unknown. For many of these couples, this problem constitutes a life crisis. In the course of acknowledging and investigating her inability to conceive, the infertile woman experiences many feelings about control, self-image, self-esteem and sexuality. Responses to infertility are usually surprise, denial, anger, depression (sadness, despair), guilt, and grief. Marital conflict often occurs, as one spouse quickly blames the other. Advances in medical technology offer the infertile couple opportunities for pregnancy, but this modern technology carries with it many emotionally charged procedures.

> The longer the infertility went on, the angrier with God I was. How can God be there and this be happening? Doesn't he know I love children and would be a good mother? How can I if I don't have a family? I was sobered by the thought of how little control I really had over these events in my life, and I blamed God.

Talk about stress! You don't know what stress is. With all those tests to complicate our relationship, I was saying things like, "My temperature's down, so *get up,* and I don't mean out of bed." Now that one's funny, but it put a strain on our sex life you wouldn't believe.

For seven years I put everything on hold while I was working on getting pregnant. I felt I needed to put full energy into it, and that was a mistake because now here I am at mid-life without a career.

I hated it when people said my emotions were leading to infertility. "If you'd relax more, you'd probably get pregnant." "Your mind is working against your body." "I'll let you borrow my children; then you won't want any." These were all comments that would send me into a rage. I don't think I ever accepted the infertility—that other people were fertile and I was not. I never gave up hoping to get pregnant, but I suffered in silence.

With infertility, the most common feelings are rage, loneliness, and depression. Women who closely identify with the desire to have children and who are unable to have them may experience intense anger toward God. The wail over infertility is a mourning of loss, and women react like Job. We want to curse God. Clergy need to be prepared for the intensity of anger and the irrational guilt that accompany infertility and actively accept the feelings and affirm the woman beyond the reproductive functioning. Clergy can support women during the crisis of infertility by a pro-active invitation to women to express whatever feelings they have. Ultimately some women may find solace in a shared grief perhaps in affirming their connection with biblical women who suffered infertility. When they recognize that they are similar to others and are reassured that infertility is not related to God's justice or punishment (God causes the rain to fall on the just and the unjust alike), women grow in faith toward an even more grace-filled life.

Women who were interviewed about the problem of infertility agreed that if they had been approached by sensitive clergy, they would have welcomed the opportunity to share their anguish. They do not want advice, but they would feel supported by a theological presence able to hear their pain and sadness. Clergy could help to network infertile couples to local support groups such as Resolve, as many women have valued the importance of sharing their stories with people who have a common experience. Clergy also need to be prepared for the emerging ethical dilemmas around infertility as seen through in vitro fertilization, surrogate mothers, and sperm banks, and give thought to interpreting the religious tradition in a manner that does not subordinate people to dogma.

Like infertility, pregnancy loss by miscarriage or infant death due to physiological defects can precipitate a crisis that cannot be readily resolved. Recent data support the fact that handling the dead infant, taking photographs for later viewing, and sharing feelings openly are some ways to help alleviate the stress, but many couples may require crisis intervention. Both miscarriage and infant death tend to increase marital conflict, with statistics of divorce following infant death approaching 85 percent.

Miscarriage.

After my miscarriage I refused to speak to God for a year. I had to go through a full year of events before I could make peace with God.

I was in denial right up until the actual process of miscarrying. There I was in the bathroom losing an incredible amount of blood and tissue, but I wanted to believe it was only spotting and that I would still be able to keep the baby. Then after I had to accept the miscarriage, I felt rage. We had worked for many years for this pregnancy; it all seemed like such a waste. I blamed God.

After my miscarriage, someone said, "Pull yourself together and do something else with your life." This was the worst advice anyone could give because I was not through with the mourning, and you do go through mourning and grief, along with the guilt. It's the guilt that is the worst part of miscarriage. You have to blame yourself, and I think everybody needs counseling around that.

I had three abortions before. We really wanted this pregnancy and baby, but I miscarried. I felt such guilt that I knew I had caused it because of the abortions. God was not going to let me have what I wanted now. I saw myself as a monster who had murdered babies, and now I would be forever deprived of having one. It was big-time guilt.

Women described having received significant help from clergy around miscarriage, but again they were not able to seek the help themselves. One young woman described a supportive priest who came to her house the night of the miscarriage and listened as she and her husband told their story.

He stayed a long time and just listened without giving advice or judgment or artificial sympathy. He worked with my husband on his grieving too, and that was good. He only came once, though, and I would have liked him to follow up after a few weeks and let me continue to talk with him about my mourning. I don't think I would have ever sought him out because back then people didn't see miscarriage as such a big deal. I knew there were people out there dying of cancer, and my priest needed to be with them. I didn't deserve to take up his time. But I would have liked to process more until the loss became real for me. It was helpful to hear him say he was sorry, as if he was participating with us in the sadness. He was there for us.

The grieving, anger, and guilt that accompany miscarriage clearly need spiritual processing. The core theodicy question ("If God is so good, why is this happening?") must be addressed at the clergy's initiative and in a manner that accepts the range of feelings experienced. Miscarriage is a time when few people are likely to reach out and ask for spiritual help because of their discomfort with their negative, hostile feelings about God. Ministers, priests, and rabbis can be pro-active during this life crisis and take a step toward the woman who has miscarried in order to be there to share the pain, give permission for the anger, and help interpret the experience.

Infant death.

Two years ago I had an abortion when I was five months pregnant. Then later, when I really wanted a baby, we had one, but she died. I thought God was punishing me with my baby's death. This was my one chance and God didn't let it happen.

My baby lived three days; then she died. At first I couldn't process the information. I needed to hear it directly, but I couldn't believe it. Then when it did sink in, I just sobbed and screamed. My children were so afraid they ran to their father for comfort. They couldn't stand to be in the room with me in so much pain. I went to the hospital and just held her after she died. I wanted to keep the memory. I didn't want to forget. I remember wanting to take her home with me after she died. That was the first reaction; I just wanted to take my baby home.

Some people don't want to talk about it because they don't know what to say. People want to protect me and help me move on, but I needed to talk and integrate the experience. I think some people can't hear because they haven't dealt with their own losses. One woman said to me, "Don't say another word; I can't hear any more."

My sister's baby died seven days after birth. He was on artificial supports when my sister and her husband decided to take the baby off support and take him home until he died. It was an intensely spiritual death. The baby had been with my sister's husband, but he got fussy. Her husband somehow knew the baby wanted to be with his mother. He gave the baby to my sister and left the room. My sister said the baby just looked at her lovingly, smiled, and died. It was a very profound moment of a communication beyond anyone's understanding. Then I had the strangest experience. I had been in almost constant telephone contact with my sister, who lived in another state, and I was very closely involved emotionally in the process. My breasts began to produce milk, but the doctors could find nothing physical to account for it. I believe I was so closely identifying with my sister's pain and the needs of this helpless infant that I began lactating sympathetically.

Women who have lost an infant feel massive grief, often mixed with guilt over the inability to control the situation and ensure life instead of death. At such a time, the physical support of family and friends is very important. Women describe the tremendous benefit of friends who just come and stay with them through the crazy times when they are not able to function. One such helpful support was a woman's friend who came every day for two weeks, did practical things to keep the house running, and was always there for the grieving mother when she wanted to talk. Primary support was felt most often by a friend or minister just being there, just "showing up." This "being with" was considered more valuable than any words spoken. The gift of time and presence and shared agony is the best support during this life crisis. Ministers, deacons, and church members could organize teams to provide supportive presence during this time of family grieving and to offer *themselves* in shared love.

Infant death raises the question of mortality. Women describe beginning to think about death and what happens after death in ways that they had never before considered. Out of this questioning of their own mortality, women want to address the spiritual dimension, but with theological options, not dogma. In the midst of anguish over her loss of a child, a woman does not want to hear "God's will for the design of one's life." This theological tack may deny the existential process of grieving and drive it underground, only to cause problems later. More than seeking simple answers, women want the church to affirm the baby's presence and memory and to help them reflect on their own spiritual questions. They want to be "invited to talk"—invited to think about the significance of the life that was lost.

Leading the entire family to talk and memorialize the experience could be a significant contribution of clergy. Ministers can take the lead in developing a service of memory that the entire family could help construct. Taking the time to help the family process the grieving, whenever it appears, is a most needed pastoral care task. In addition to initial rituals and ceremonies of mourning for the family, public acknowledgment of the family's loss can be made within the church through sermons focused on the meaning of death and the question of life after death, as well as with the dedication of flowers, physical property, scholarships, and the like, in grief and in memory of the loss of the infant child.

Also, clergy can be sensitive to anniversary dates of the death and be active in an overt remembrance of the family, particularly the mother, at significant intervals—one month, six months, one year. Clergy could plan to visit on an anniversary date to recall the memory of the infant who has died and be present with the continued grieving. Cemetery journeys with the family to renew the ritual of remembering can indeed help the grieving mother integrate the experience of loss.

Women also appreciate being linked to other families who have lost infants, and they receive positive help when family groups shared the painful experiences. In addition to making themselves available to listen and be present with grieving families, clergy could also learn more about available self-help support groups for infant death and be a resource for women to link them to this network of support.

Betrayal Through Disease

Breast Cancer.   Breast cancer, once the leading cancer in women and now second only to lung cancer, will affect one of nine women in their lifetimes. Because most breast lumps (90 percent) are found by the women themselves, self-examination is very important. Breast cancer is not a single disease; the term refers to a heterogeneous group of diseases with differing rates of growth and thus of potential malignancy.

Cancer of the breast has been the most extensively studied tumor site for its psychological and social impact. Although it is a stress that tests every woman's adaptive capacities, it is clearly more difficult for some than for others. Among the many factors that alter a woman's ability to cope with the loss of a breast are: (1) support of family and friends, especially her spouse, (2) the point in the life cycle at which the breast is lost, (3) what the woman brings to the situation, that is, her psychosocial parameters and coping abilities, (4) the psychological management of the patient by the health care team, (5) what the breast means to the woman herself, and (6) the extent of the disease.

> When the diagnosis was made that I had breast cancer, I denied it and thought even after the biopsy that they had made a mistake. Cancer happens to other women but not to me.

> My initial reaction was, "Oh, my God, my body will be mutilated." After the mammogram, I sobbed and screamed. Then I got silly and laughed and joked. There is such a sense of being out of control and trying to find a measure of control.

> I sat with my sister and listened to the radiologist explain in very basic terms what he saw. Now my sister heard what was said, but I, with two master's degrees and a reputation for logical thinking, totally blocked out the information and left the office thinking I could just rest and come back in six months and it would be gone.

These quotes are some initial reactions of women to the diagnosis of breast cancer. Most are at first shocked and then go into denial. How this denial is handled is extremely important, and clergy need to be prepared to help women negotiate a positive, affirming relationship with their medical doctors. Women with breast cancer report a wide range of treatment by doctors, from supportive intervention to almost cruel, abrupt condescension. Most women do not feel their emotional needs are adequately addressed; furthermore, they feel intimidated and brushed aside when they try to defend these needs. Some even find themselves put in the middle of clinical fights between doctors. Pastoral counselors must be "physicians of the soul" at this time and move into the arena in defense of the woman's right to full information, to multiple medical opinions, to access to a collaborative medical team, and to respectful treatment of the person.

The relationship between women and their physicians is extremely important during the time following the diagnosis and through the surgery. Even brilliant surgeons can lack interpersonal skills, and often they sound abrupt and harsh.

> When I was told a bilateral radical mastectomy was necessary, I was devastated. My surgeon said, "Honey, I'm saving your life here. What are your breasts compared to your life? They are nothing. You have no choices in the matter. Now let's get on with it. If you are going to cry and be a baby about it, I can't work with you."

Clergy need to know that women who feel harshly treated are angry when their feelings are not respected. Although they do not expect physicians to counsel them, they affirm that a few sentences stated differently would make a significant difference in how they are able to face the surgery. Just the permission to be sad and grieve and the identification of human feelings of sympathy are all that women want from their surgeons at this time. Because the medical profession is no longer oriented to family practice and holistic care but is more specialized and technological, however, we cannot depend on the technicians even to give these few sentences of emotional understanding. Pastors must step into this alarming emotional and spiritual gap in medical care and serve as resource, advocate, and caring friend to women facing surgery for breast cancer.

Although pastors cannot direct the treatment process, they can be advocates for the importance of a collaborative team of surgeon, internist, radiation oncologist, plastic surgeon, nurses, and clergy. This coordination of services increases the patient's knowledge of the options and creates the best treatment plan. Frequently, physicians have not taken the time to inform women of the various ways of handling the cancer; sometimes not all the pieces of information are given before the decision on the surgery. The sequence is too often a quick decision for mastectomy and then chemotherapy. Later, the woman is filled with many questions: Was this radical surgery really necessary? Did I have to have my breasts removed? Why didn't they tell me about lumpectomy?

Ministers can usefully function to help ensure that women participate in surgery decisions with full information about the stages of the process. Specific recurrent issues for clergy to be aware of include: the question of delay between biopsy and mastectomy and between mastectomy and breast reconstruction in order to grieve each loss and decisions of lumpectomy versus mastectomy and chemotherapy versus radiation, depending on the type and extent of cancer and on the woman's priorities in life.[7] These decisions need to be made with women having access to all the information and with caring clergy to help process the values and consequences involved.

Listening to the complex feelings of women during this life crisis is vitally important. Feelings run the gamut: shock, anger, grief, bereavement, depression, despair, hostility, sexual problems, loss of self-esteem, isolation, and fear of death.[8] If the woman has a significant other, clergy should involve this person in the grieving process as soon as possible. One physician works closely with husbands and requires them to participate in changing the surgical dressings immediately following mastectomy to encourage a partnership of caring. Husbands or significant others who say, "It doesn't matter. It's all right. I don't care" are not helpful. Rather, they need to be participants in the necessary mourning over losing this very significant body part. When spouses (or ministers) brush aside feelings of anger and loss, women are given the message to bypass these feelings, which may then resurface later in destructive ways.[9]

How women process their feelings about breast loss has a great deal to do with how they view their bodies. Again, women's identification with body image as a source of identity makes the loss of a breast a profound experience.

In my medical practice I have found that women are more affected by breast surgery than by hysterectomy. The body image is more mutilated by mastectomy than by internal hysterectomy. Loss of a breast regenerates deep feelings of losses in life, of deep pain. Hundreds of women have had hysterectomies, but they don't grieve about it like mastectomy. I believe it is easier to deal with the internal surgery, but when they have to look at that breast scar, it's bad.

Pastoral caregivers can overcome learned defenses and speak in a direct and intimate way with women about the loss of a breast and what this means for the woman. We need to provide a nurturing, holding environment that can embrace the full extent of a woman's rage and grief over this mutilation. The felt loss of a significant body part should be placed in the context of our absolute self-worth as creations of God with all our self-perceived imperfections. Until a woman is able to see her loss in this way, however, clergy should give implicit permission and encouragement for her to share all of her feelings and fears.

Along with feeling great loss and anger, women also report sensing a generativity beyond their physical appearance and finding increased self-integration.

> Cancer has changed my life. It has changed my priorities. I wake up in the morning and say, "If I die tomorrow, would I want to spend today the way I am going to?"

> I see a therapist, and we do a lot of imagery around my immune system, releasing old resentments. I am finding areas that I can have control with; this is very important to me. I'm separated from my husband now; he was so explosive that I held all my anger in—all my sadness and other feelings too. I believe there is a message in this. I don't think I caused it or can stop the cancer. But when you're sad or depressed for a long period of time, the immune system gets repressed.

What do women with breast cancer want from clergy? The consensus is that the spiritual needs evoked by breast cancer are monumental and that it is more complex emotionally than almost any other gynecologic issue. The following comments reflect women's needs:

> A whole large part of this is coming to grips with your own mortality. Everything before this was abstract.

> In my past, I had been treated by my minister in the same way that my surgeon treated me. "If you shut up and be good and do exactly as you're told, then you'll have a happy death." This was my image of clergy and religion from my past, and now my surgeon was acting the same way. The only way I would have been open to help from a minister is if he or she could prove to me that they could truly listen to all the feelings of my heart and be there with me without judgment or preaching.

> I had to get really angry with God. When I knew I would have the mastectomy, I ran out and screamed in the front yard: "God damn you, God, I've been such a good girl. I don't deserve this."

Women suffering from breast cancer have a range of complex responses. Perhaps the most important pastoral care need is an ongoing opportunity for the woman to talk and communicate feelings of fear, loss, anger, and grief, along with the complex feelings that accompany mutilation of the body. Most women feel a sense of guilt or sin, that they are being punished in some way. All feel their own mortality and an anger and grieving over the loss and limitation imposed by the cancer. Spiritual caregivers must first be human with women in this crisis and be willing to share the grieving. As the grief is shared, women can be guided toward a larger identification with humanity and an expanded generativity of spirit.

Another important help is to put the woman in touch with other women who have breast cancer. Women report that the single most important support was to receive the names, addresses, and phone numbers of people who had had breast cancer and to be assured that they could call them for information and support. Referral to Reach for Recovery, a national support group for women with breast cancer, provides the woman an opportunity for ongoing structured support. Women desperately need permission and encouragement to express their feelings and to be supported through this process. Isolation and suppression of feelings only frustrate the process of healing, but shared support for grieving and reshaping life can enhance the healing.

Other Gynecologic Malignancies.   Cancers of the reproductive tract—ovaries, uterus, cervix, vagina, and vulva—rank as the fifth cause of cancer deaths in women. These malignancies can affect a woman of any age, and often the diagnosis places stress unlike any other on the patient and family. The emotional impact, especially in relation to body image and sexuality, can often be overwhelming. The treatments or the disease itself may affect physical attractiveness, energy level, self-esteem, and the woman's role in her family and in society.

As with breast cancer, many factors alter a woman's ability to cope; perhaps the major factor is how the woman perceives the organ(s) involved. If she views the organ as major to her sense of self as a woman, then loss of the organ can often put her in a crisis. Of significant importance to the woman is the support system available to her. Allowing her to verbalize her feelings, educating, counseling, and providing for physical, psychological, and spiritual comfort are important goals. Providing adequate data—that is, enabling the woman to know the full range of options available, as well as the variable consequences—assures that she has the ability to make an informed decision.

With the gynecologic cancers, the more a woman identifies the organ as a "feminine" organ, the more difficulty she has in coping with its loss. If she views the organ as the center of her sexuality and she loses it, she sees herself as no longer being a complete person. Also, if the woman is young and wants children but must have gynecologic organs removed, the impact is traumatic.

> One of the most painful situations in my nursing experience was a very attractive, thirty-year-old woman who had been married for a couple of years. They had postponed pregnancy until they were more solid financially. She developed a carcinoma of the cervix and had to have her uterus, ovaries, cervix, and vagina removed. Not only was she dealing with the loss of the uterus, ovaries, cervix and some of the vagina, but she was dealing with the issue of not being able to have children. I can't say that she ever resolved that in her lifetime. I mean this woman went to her deathbed talking about the unfairness of it all and about adopting a child. She was afraid she would get grief from the adoption agency because she carried a diagnosis of malignancy. In her mind she was still going to live and was going to be able to take care of a child.

Women with gynecologic malignancies have trouble dealing with body image issues, self-esteem, hair loss, fatigue, loss of their role in the family, and the ability to be a mother, lover, and wife. For most women, body image, as it relates to the ability to fulfill the functions of a wife, lover, and mother, is very important. Men may be more detached from body image because of their historical, cultural identification as provider through external work, but for most women body image is tied to function as nurturer and caregiver. Gynecologic cancers wreak havoc with women's ability to continue as the caregiver. Women's cancers tend to be long, drawn-out illnesses, and a primary loss for most women is the loss of their role in the family. They don't feel good enough to be the nurturer anymore. When women have found their primary identity from their role as caregiver, whether to children or husband, this loss can be devastating. Clergy can be sensitive to the depth of this meaning for these women, while also attempting to promote a generativity and self-worth apart from gynecologic functioning.

Some women, particularly the elderly, who have surgery for gynecologic malignancy are usually so concerned about being cured that they do not mourn the loss of a reproductive organ as long as they are not going to die from the disease. Usually they tolerate the surgical procedures better than women who have mastectomies for breast cancer.

Other gynecologic surgeries can be much more difficult to process. Cancer of the vagina, vulva, or cervix may require major external surgeries. The young woman who has recurrent cervical cancer has a tough problem. In some women a potential for cure exists but only if she has a pelvic exenteration, which involves removal of the uterus, cervix, vagina, bladder, and often bowel.

> I have taken care of a number of young women who have what are called "posterior and anterior exenterations," meaning they take out everything. They wind up with two bags—one for their urine, one for their stool. These women go into surgery knowing what is going to be done. They shed a lot of tears, and they have to work through a lot of pain. When they wake up and start looking at a colostomy and a urostomy and having to deal with those bags, they have tough days and tough times.

These devastating gynecologic cancers create ultimate questions of life and death for women, which caregivers sometimes severely neglect. Although the physician may ask the woman for a sense of blind trust, the pastor may avoid dealing with the core issue of the woman's felt loss of identity as a woman.

Faith questions have to do with "Am I still a child of God? Am I still a woman? Am I still lovable? Can I love myself? Will other people, most often my husband or lover, still love me? What identity do I have apart from my body? If I survive this cancer, what meaning can my life have?" Whether the spiritual caregiver is male or female, the important thing is that the person is sensitive to the needs of the woman and is willing to sit on the bed and hold hands, to touch and communicate acceptance and caring. This need for human sensitivity is described by clergy and physicians:

> Clergy who are the most harmful are the ones who do not give permission for the woman to focus on the feelings that are so prevalent and so dominant, or those who persist to the person, "Do not feel this way; God will take care of you."

> Clergy should be aware that women frequently feel abandoned or punished because of some abortion or sexual affair from the past. They relate this to the cancer and tie it all to God's wrath or punishment. They have never forgiven themselves.

> Physicians are not comfortable with issues of sex, and neither are clergy. Clergy are not comfortable even using the words *breast, vagina, uterus, ovaries*. If they can't even use the words, how can they elicit the woman's feelings about these great losses?

We have explored many different gynecologic issues with consequences ranging from mild annoyance to suffering and death. With all of them, women's emotional and spiritual needs are amazingly consistent. Women want information in order to create a new understanding of their feminine identity, a context for sharing feelings and exploring spiritual questions, and a supportive theological presence to listen.

Women cannot be full participants in a partnership with professionals regarding health care without being given accurate and complete information. This goal requires an end to patronizing women with a condescending or joking attitude about gynecologic issues. It also implies that men and women talk more openly together and challenge the learned defenses that too often keep us silent and apart. Clergy need to use the words and talk about the gynecologic issues with respect. Underlying the ability to talk about gynecologic issues factually and experientially is the understanding that physicality and sexuality are a part of what being a woman means, but they are not definitive of being a woman. This knowledge implies a new understanding of embodiment and rhythmicity as women's issues that are also metaphors of a universal creativity. Information brings a new understanding of generativity as a creative identity as children of God beyond biological functioning.

A context of support for sharing and processing feelings is a significant spiritual and emotional need that is not met for most women. This dialogue forms the basis for a community of concern, whether it occurs in the family, the church, or a support group. Clergy need to know that most women want to process their experience with others, but they usually cannot reach out to make it happen for themselves. Feelings of grief and loss over miscarriage and infertility and feelings of anger, abandonment, and fear over breast and other gynecologic cancers need the support of shared understanding to help us transform them into a courageous stance of acceptance through God's grace.

Finally, a supportive theological presence is vitally important through emotional crises. Women speak repeatedly of the calming effect of a trusted person just "showing up," just being on hand as a listener, to hear the heartbeat and be with the person. As one physician stated, "It takes a lot of training not to do too much talking." This sentence seems to say it all. Women do not want advice or judgment, theological platitudes, or simplistic reassurances. The kind of presence women want from pastors has the potential for calling forth a fuller humanity for both the pastor and women congregants because it allows both to be in a faith process together. Women want a theological presence who takes the time to invite us to share our journey, with its joys and pains, and who really listens to our story, provides a hand to hold, and brings a promise of transforming hope.

BIBLIOGRAPHY

Barbar, Hugh. *Manual of Gynecologic Oncology.* Philadelphia: J. B. Lippincott, 1980.

Beauvoir, de, Simone. *The Second Sex.* New York: Alfred A. Knopf, 1961.

Bermosk, L., and S. Porter. *Women's Health and Human Wholeness.* New York: Appleton-Century Crofts, 1979.

Bernard, J. *The Female World.* New York: Free Press, 1981.

Boston Women's Health Book Collective. *The New Our Bodies, Ourselves.* New York: W. W. Norton, 1977.

Brenner, P. F. "The Menopausal Syndrome." *Obstetrics and Gynecology* 72 (November 1988):6S–11S.

Chapman, J. R., and M. Gates. *The Victimization of Women.* Beverly Hills, Calif.: Sage Publications, 1978.

Chervin, Ronda, and Mary Neill. *The Woman's Tale.* Boston: Beacon Press, 1976.

Chodorow, N. *The Reproduction of Mothering: Psychoanalysis and the Sociology of Gender.* Berkeley: University of California Press, 1978.

Clure, A. "The Relationship Between Psychopathology and the Menstrual Cycle." *Women and Health* 8 (1983):125–36.

Corea, G. *The Hidden Malpractice: How American Medicine Treats Women as Patients and Professionals.* New York: William Morrow, 1977.

Dalton, K. *The Premenstrual Syndrome and Progesterone Therapy.* Philadelphia: W. B. Saunders, 1977.

Donovan, Marilee Ivers, and Sandra Erdene Girton. *Cancer Care Nursing.* Norwalk, Conn.: Appleton-Century Crofts, 1984.

Dreifus, C., ed. *Seizing Our Bodies: The Politics of Women's Health.* New York: Vintage, 1978.

Eichenbaum, Luise. *Understanding Women.* New York: Basic Books, 1983.

Eskin, Bernard A., ed. *The Menopause.* New York: Masson, 1980.

Ferguson, K. J., et al. "Estrogen Replacement Therapy: A Survey of Women's Knowledge and Attitudes." *Archives of Internal Medicine* 149 (January 1989):133–36.

Fiore, Neil A. *The Road Back to Health: Coping with the Emotional Side of Cancer.* New York: Bantam Books, 1986.

Fogel, Catherine Ingram, and Nancy Fugate Woods, eds. *Health Care of Women.* St. Louis: C. V. Mosby, 1981.

Fried, Barbara. *The Middle-Age Crisis.* New York: Harper & Row, 1967.

Garcia, Celso-Ramon, et al., eds. *Current Therapy of Infertility, 1982–83.* Philadelphia: B. C. Decker, 1982.

Gates, C. C. "The 'Most Significant Other' in the Care of the Breast Cancer Patient." *Cancer: A Cancer Journal for Clinicians* 38 (May 1988):146–53.

Ghadirian, A. M., and L. S. Kamaraju. "Premenstrual Mood Changes in Affective Disorders." *Canadian Medical Association Journal* 136 (May 1987):1027–32.

Granstrom, S. L. "Spiritual Nursing Care for Oncology Patients." *Topics in Clinical Nursing* 7 (1985):1.

Grieze, I. H., and S. J. Ramsey. "Nonverbal Maintenance of Traditional Sex Roles." *Journal of Sociological Issues* 32 (1976):133–41.

Hammett, Jenny. *Woman's Transformations*. Lewiston, N.Y.: Edwin Mellen Press, 1982.

Harrison, M. *Self-Help for Premenstrual Syndrome*. Cambridge, Mass.: Matrix Press, 1982.

Hite, Shere. *The Hite Report*. New York: Dell, 1976.

Hongladarom, G., et al. *The Complete Book of Women's Health*. Englewood Cliffs, N.J.: Prentice-Hall, 1982.

Hunt, Swanee. "Pastoral Care and Miscarriage: A Ministry Long Neglected." *Pastoral Psychology* 32 (Summer 1984):265–78.

Jardine, Alice. *Gynesis: A Configuration of Woman and Modernity*. Ithaca, N.Y.: Cornell University Press, 1985.

Kaufert, Patricia. "Myth and the Menopause." *Sociology of Health and Illness* 4 (July 1982):141–66.

Kauffman, Donette G. *Surviving Cancer*. Washington: Acropolis Books, 1987.

Krant, M. J. "Psychosocial Impact of Gynecologic Cancer." *Cancer* 48 (July 1981):608–12.

Kuehn, Paul. *Breast Care Options*. South Windsor, Conn.: Newmark Publishing, 1986.

Leiblum, S. R., and L. C. Swartzman. "Women's Attitudes Toward the Menopause." *Maturitas* 8 (March 1986):47–56.

Leis, H. P. "The Diagnosis of Breast Cancer." *Cancer: A Cancer Journal for Clinicians* 27 (1977):209–32.

Leppert, P. C., and B. S. Pahlka. "Grieving Characteristics After Spontaneous Abortion." *Obstetrics and Gynecology* 64 (July 1984):119–22.

Littlefield, Vivian M., ed. *Health Education for Women: A Guide for Nurses and Other Health Professionals*. East Norwalk, Conn.: Appleton-Century Crofts, 1986.

MacNutt, F. *Healing*. Notre Dame, Ind.: Ava Maria Press, 1974.

Miller, Jean Baker. *Toward a New Psychology of Women*. Boston: Beacon Press, 1976.

Morgan, John H. "Caring for Parents Who Have Lost an Infant." *Journal of Religion and Health* 17 (October 1978):290–98.

Norris, R., and C. Sullivan. *Premenstrual Syndrome*. New York: Rawson, 1983.

Pariser, S. F., et al. "Premenstrual Syndrome: Concerns, Controversies, and Treatment." *American Journal of Obstetrics and Gynecology* 153 (November 1985):599–604.

"Psychological Response to Mastectomy: A Prospective Comparison Study." *Cancer* 59 (January 1987):189–96.

Quilligan, Edward J. *Current Therapy in Obstetrics and Gynecology*. Philadelphia: W. B. Saunders, 1980.

Reinharz, Schulamit. "What's Missing in Miscarriage?" *Journal of Community Psychiatry* 16 (January 1988):84–103.

Reitz, R. *Menopause: A Positive Approach*. New York: Penguin Books, 1977.

Rome, E. "Premenstrual Syndrome Examined Through a Feminist Lens." *Health Care for Women International* 7 (1986):145–51.

Sandelowski, M. *Women, Health and Choice*. Englewood Cliffs, N.J.: Prentice-Hall, 1981.

Schain, W. S. "The Sexual and Intimate Consequences of Breast Cancer Treatment." *Cancer: A Cancer Journal for Clinicians* 38 (May 1988):154–61.

Schindler, B. A. "The Psychiatric Disorders of Midlife." *Medical Clinics of North America* 71 (January 1987):71–85.

Schwartz, Harold P., ed. *Practical Points in Gynecology*. New Hyde Park, New York: Medical Publication Company, 1984.

Scully, D., and P. Bart. "A Funny Thing Happened on the Way to the Orifice: Women in Gynecology Textbooks." *American Journal of Sociology* 78 (1973):1045–50.

Seaman, B., and G. Seaman. *Women and the Crisis in Sex Hormones*. New York: Rawson, 1977.

Sheehy, G. *Passages: Predictable Crises of Adult Life*. New York: E. P. Dutton, 1974.

Solomon, B. H. *The Experience of the American Woman*. New York: Mentor, 1978.

Sorrentino, P., et al. "Mastectomized Woman's Acquired Knowledge About and Attitude Towards Breast Reconstruction: A Prospective Survey on 100 Cases." *Italian Journal of Surgical Sciences* 18 (1988):17–23.

Spots, S. "Love: Crisis and Consolation for the Middlescent Woman." *Advances in Nursing Science* 3 (1981):87–94.

Stoll, Ruth I. "Guidelines for Spiritual Assessment." *American Journal of Nursing* (1975):1574–77.

U.S. Department of Health and Human Services. National Institute of Health. *Taking Time: Support for People with Cancer and the People Who Care About Them*. Pub. No. 83-2059.

Vinokur, A. D., et al. "Physical and Psychosocial Functioning and Adjustment to Breast Cancer." *Cancer* 63 (January 1989):394–405.

Webb, C. "Feminist Methodology in Nursing Research." *Journal of Advanced Nursing* 9 (May 1984):249–56.

Williams, J. H. *Psychology of Women: Behavior in a Biosocial Context*. New York: W. W. Norton, 1977.

Zalon, Jean. *I Am Whole Again: The Case for Breast Reconstruction After Mastectomy*. New York: Random House, 1978.

NOTES

1. Vivian Littlefield, ed., *Health Education for Women: A Guide for Nurses and Other Health Professionals* (East Norwalk, Conn.: Appleton-Century Crofts, 1986), 10.

2. Paul Fink, "Psychological Myths of Menopause," in *The Menopause*, ed. Bernard Eskin (New York: Masson, 1980), 114.

3. Simone deBeauvoir, *The Second Sex* (New York: Alfred A. Knopf, 1961), 542.

4. Ibid., 541.

5. Ibid., 543.

6. Fink, "Psychological Myths," 127.

7. Jean Zalon, *I Am Whole Again: The Case for Breast Reconstruction After Mastectomy* (New York: Random House, 1978), 132.

8. Ibid., 120.

9. Ibid., 132.

CHAPTER 5

Sexual Abuse and Shame: The Travail of Recovery

NANCY J. RAMSAY

. . . .

To live with shame is to feel alienated and
defeated, never quite good enough to belong.
And secretly we feel we are to blame. The
deficiency lies within ourselves alone. Shame
is without parallel a sickness of the soul.[1]

Every pastor serves parishioners who know too well the consequences
of incest or sexual abuse. Perhaps one of them resembles Karen, an
attractive, intelligent, active new member. Karen is a single mother of
three who is now getting her college degree. In a recent home visit, she
disclosed her years of chemical and alcohol dependency and told of an
abusive former marriage. Waking up from a drug overdose, she said,
"I chose life." Without the addictions to numb her, however, memories
she had wanted to forget return to her. She remembers chronic sexual
abuse by her father and older brothers and has memories of her mother
allowing it to happen. She readily acknowledges many difficult days as
she works through the terror, betrayal, and rage that were too difficult
to acknowledge as a child. "But," she says, "I have my life."

Sometimes parishioners are more like Chris—friendly but shy. Chris
and her husband, John, have a three-year-old daughter, Claire. They
are active in the life of the congregation. Recently John asked the pastor
to come by, and Chris tearfully shared the fact that she had begun
having awful dreams of childhood experiences with an uncle; then
yesterday, when John took Claire up for her nap, Chris suddenly recalled
a time with her own father when that simple action filled her with
numbing fear. She said, "I don't want to believe those memories. I'm
so ashamed."

Occasionally the survivor of sexual abuse is herself a minister. Sarah is a supervising pastor in a local hospital who attends a congregation regularly. In her mid-forties, she is attractive but seriously overweight. She is competent, busy, even driven; the pastor likes her, but wonders if she is happy. One night after a committee meeting, Sarah hesitatingly visits the pastor's office to ask for support. Six months ago she entered therapy after beginning to remember fragments of childhood experiences. Her memories are still vague, "but I am sure that I was molested as a child. I have always been in control, but now instead of being numb to my own feelings, I am sometimes overwhelmed with sadness or anger. Tell me, where was God when this happened to me?"

Women like Karen, Chris, and Sarah are in every congregation. In this chapter, we will share further in their stories to understand the consequences of child sexual abuse and the process of recovery. We will give particular attention to the consequences of abuse for the survivor's spirituality and to theological issues posed by abuse. We will also focus on effective pastoral responses and on issues of religious leadership raised by the high incidence of incest and sexual abuse.

One in three girls and at least one in seven boys are sexually molested before the age of eighteen.[2] Between 75 and 90 percent of the time, the abuser is an adult the girl and those who would protect her know and trust, thus lowering the likelihood that she would reveal the identity of the perpetrator or that she would be believed if she did.[3] Estimates are that half of the incidents of sexual abuse occur in the immediate or extended family as incest. Sexual abuse in the family is likely to begin when the child is as young as three to six years of age and, if unreported, continues into adolescence.[4] In this country a girl is molested every ten minutes, and a daughter is molested by her father every thirty minutes.[5]

Molestation does not simply describe the explicit behaviors of oral, genital, or anal intercourse. It may include covert behavior such as sexualized touching or a parent's discussions of sexual needs or frustrations while thinly garbed in briefs. Both explicit fondling and implicit seduction are frightening and confusing to a child whose own emotional needs get put aside to meet an adult's.[6] Even the more covert seductions are abusive because the child's sense of safety, her need for protection, and her ability to say no are compromised.

Sexual abuse of children is not about sex or love. It is about the abuse of power, control, and authority.[7] Sexual abuse untreated is likely to cross generations with destructive consequences. In some treatment centers, 80 to 90 percent of the mothers who seek help to stop physically abusing their children report a history of incest in their childhood.[8]

The Family as Context

Ten to 25 percent of the time, sexual abuse is perpetrated by a stranger, does not become chronic, and is more likely to be reported. More often the child "knows" she would not be believed, obeys the injunctions of the family member or other trusted adult, and/or blames herself for remaining shamefully silent. Chris's father told her, "This is our special secret." Her family provided precious little affection, and she tolerated the awkward feelings. Later, when he became more demanding, he said, "If you tell your mother, it will hurt her very much." By definition, incest occurs in dysfunctional family systems determined to maintain patterns of denial, secrecy, and control, even at the expense of not "seeing" or responding to the child or children.

The current behavior and feelings of Karen, Chris, and Sarah help us to understand the consequences of the unspoken rules of their families.[9] The interpersonal and intrapsychic cornerstone of the dysfunctional family and of the victim is control—not control as authoritarianism but as the predictable management of affective experience. Chris certainly experienced such an environment through the manipulative behavior of her father and her sense that her needs were not as important as his or her mother's. Her family allowed no talk about difficult feelings. When her father's facade of control slipped, he blamed Chris, and she learned that response well, except that she could not tolerate the idea of his being at fault, so she blamed herself.

In Sarah's family, control yielded a similar facade of perfection. She treasured the attentions of her uncle, but the stigma of secrecy and the inability to say no took their toll. However, in her family, difficult feelings were not expressed. She learned to deny such feelings, including anger, because such problems could not be tolerated in a happy and successful family. In her family, intimacy, trust, and individual needs were subsumed by the family image.

In Karen's family, alcoholism and emotional abuse as well as sexual abuse taught her to expect vulnerability to inconsistent relationships. She knew not to "see" the addiction and so "joined" the family's commitment to keep its secrets at her own expense. Karen saw open but chronically unresolved conflict and learned how to listen carefully for the needs of others so as to avoid their anger if she could. Like Chris, she learned to blame herself for her abuse.

Affective and Behavioral Consequences

The behaviors these women developed to cope in their families of origin proved crippling to them as adults. Each was emotionally anemic. Each had an inordinate need for control, although they met that need differently. Each had very poor self-esteem and difficulty with trust and intimacy. Karen met her need for control by the compulsive use of drugs and alcohol. Having learned that love was sex, she became promiscuous. Having learned to be a victim, she entered several abusive relationships in which she acted out the worthlessness she felt. Alienated from her bodied self, sexuality was never a context for intimacy or trust.

Chris met her need for control by attending to the needs and expectations of others while repressing her intolerable feelings and memories. The isolation Chris felt in her childhood continues to plague her, fueled now by poor self-esteem. That among adults she carries herself as if she wishes she were invisible yet is grateful for every expression of friendliness is no accident. That Chris is a skillful and sensitive special education teacher is not surprising, for she is familiar with the needs of such children. Sexual intimacy and trust continue to be difficult for her in her marriage.

Sarah is also familiar with control. Rather than drugs, alcohol, or promiscuity, she has taken the perfectionism she learned well and become a workaholic in a helping profession that allows her to continue to deny her needs and feelings on behalf of others. Her poor self-esteem and alienation from her body contribute to her obesity. Instead of promiscuity, Sarah has denied her sexuality. Chronic depression—carefully masked—carries the anger she learned not to express.

The Intrapsychic Reality of Shame

Shame organizes the psychological reality of adults molested as children. Shame thrives in the control, denial, and secrecy of dysfunctional families. "Shame is an inner sense of being completely diminished or insufficient as a person. It is the self judging the self."[10] Shame is more primitive and punitive than guilt. In guilt, one's behavior, not one's identity, is questioned and repair seems possible. With shame the sense is not, "I have acted badly," but "I *am* bad." Karen did not attempt suicide because she thought she'd behaved badly but because she felt worthless. The wound of shame is not external but internal, and a woman cannot make it right by herself. The experience of incest or sexual abuse has profoundly destructive consequences for a child's emerging identity because of the intense feelings of shame internalized during development. Sarah has not shaken off her abuse; she has lived as if asexual for forty years.

Identity is that sense of individuality that has continuity over time. It is that "vital sense of who we are as individuals, embracing our worth, our adequacy, and our very dignity as human beings."[11] Ordinarily, identity emerges as a child's natural needs are met in mutually significant caring relationships. An inner sense of wholeness, belonging, and connection develops through a reciprocal process of identification and differentiation. Shame ensues when a devastating experience of rupture breaks that interpersonal bridge with trusted adults and brings a consequent sense of betrayal and the unexpected exposure of unmet internal need. Chris wanted and needed her father's affection; however, his manipulative, abusive behavior left her needs not only unmet but also exposed. When such experiences in relationships are not repaired or are chronic, they leave the individual's sense of herself diminished, painfully small or belittled, filled with self-doubt, and overwhelmed by self-consciousness.[12]

We all have some experiences of shame that allow us to learn to cope with the occasional failures, defeat, or rejection inherent in living. In the case of severe trauma and/or chronic trauma such as incest and sexual abuse, however, the interpersonal experience of shame is internalized. Once internalized, the distorting effects of shame may function apart from the original experience with the progressively destructive consequences we saw in the lives of Karen, Chris, and Sarah. Shame became a core dimension of their identity. Each woman internalized voices of contempt or blame and now can voice them herself, unprompted. Their experience of division within—self-hatred or worthlessness—was so painful that each sought to disown those hated parts of herself and set in motion the processes of repression and denial.[13]

Shame and Spirituality

The power of shame to undermine the victim's sense of self, her capacity to love and accept herself, and her capacity for genuinely giving and receiving love seriously erodes her capacity for religious belief and a healthy spirituality. Shame engenders deep estrangement within the self and between the self and others—and sometimes between the victim and God. Chris described herself as spiritually dead. Sarah put it another way: "How can you have a relationship with God without a self and without knowing what love is?"

Sexual abuse is particularly destructive for spirituality because the locus of violation and shame is the body itself. Alienation from one's bodied self is crippling for any experience of spirituality because spirituality is rooted in a sense of connectedness with those forces that give and sustain life. It involves a sense of meaning and the possibility for life that is larger than one's own efforts. In the lives of Karen, Chris, and Sarah, isolation and the absence of hope are striking themes. Karen anesthetized her body and exchanged intimacy for promiscuity. Sarah attempted a disembodied identity by insulating herself through obesity. She exchanged intimacy for an addiction to her work. In contrast, healthy spirituality involves feeling at home and at peace in one's body. Certainly an embodied spirituality is appropriate for Christian faith rooted in the phenomenon of incarnation.

A child's capacity for belief and her images of God emerge from her early interactions with parental figures.[14] Disturbances in those relationships distort not only the formation of her identity but also the possibilities for her experience of religious faith. As Erik Erikson's famous phrase suggests, "trust born of care" is central for the possibility of religious belief.[15] Caring that engenders the ability to trust in God's care involves how one's young bodied self was held and honored as well as verbal expressions of affection and experiences of trustworthiness and love. When such care is replaced by abuse of power, violation, and betrayal, then chronic fear, shame, and self-contempt replace trust and distort religious experience.

Somewhat like the rape of an adult, abuse is an experience of utter vulnerability compounded by the fact that it is done to a child, who is even less able to cope. Usually a child who is abused has no experience of a protector who seeks to defend the child. All too often, reported abuse is met with denial. The child experiences her family and world as not safe or trustworthy places.[16] Imagine how confused a child must feel upon simultaneously hearing that "Jesus loves you" and being a victim of molestation, or to have God portrayed as an all-powerful Father who loves the child and keeps her safe while she endures incest! Her logical conclusion is that somehow what is happening to her meets with God's approval and that God's love does not include her. Self-contempt, guilt, and shame emerge then to characterize a victim's religious experience. Karen self-destructively acted out her sense of worthlessness and self-contempt. Chris finally quit coming to church when the memories emerged and flooded her with shame. "I haven't been able to pray for months," she said. Sarah entered a church vocation and addictively sought to redeem herself and earn God's love. She said, "For a long time I've known there was no grace in my personal relationship with God. I was trying to deserve a love I couldn't even feel for myself." The poignant absence of hope and gracelessness are consequences of shame many survivors describe. Theirs is a faith shaped by obligation and alienation. Their pervasive shame begets a "sickness of the soul"—an inner, chronic hell.

Exploring the consequences of shame and sexual violence suggests a dynamic interaction of intrapersonal and relational issues with spirituality. Recovery involves addressing the woman survivor's spirituality alongside her intrapersonal and relational concerns. Rebuilding a healthy spirituality does not mean that religious faith is necessary for recovery. It does mean that to thrive people need a sense of connectedness with the human community that is life-giving and that gives a larger meaning and purpose to their lives beyond their own efforts.

Recovery as "Hearing into Speech"

The process of recovery for women molested as children is lifelong, but healing is possible and, although difficult, can be significant. A key element in this process is the experience of rebuilding the interpersonal bridge broken by the trauma and its shame. The levels of estrangement and alienation induced by shame gradually can be overcome as the survivor establishes a connection with a skilled therapist whose care she can trust. The supportive use of group therapy is also strongly encouraged for most.

The experience of recovery does not proceed in a linear progression but rather in a spiral process.[17] A woman explores issues, works on them, and then works them through repeatedly as she gains the strength to voice the reality of her story and disassemble the illusions by which she has lived. Although women survivors have predictable concerns, personal issues surface in no necessary sequence, and feelings about them vary in intensity. The issues most women encounter include breaking through denial and believing it happened, experiencing the anger and resentment that accompanies the recognition of abuse, grieving the many losses related to the trauma, remembering the abuse itself and the emotions felt at the time but suppressed or denied, and trusting themselves—their emotions and their own judgment.[18] Incest and abuse victims sometimes describe the recovery process in images of birth and delivery and describe therapy as midwifery. The passage from identity as victim to a new self-understanding as a survivor is not unlike the hard but rewarding work of labor, especially when the image of labor includes a support team.

Some women in recovery seek as a part of such a team pastors, especially pastors who are personally and professionally concerned about issues of sexual violence and are ready to respond. Although conversation about spirituality and God may well arise in more clinical therapeutic contexts, pastors may serve an important nurturing and interpretive function. Recovery begins when the secret is disclosed and the shackles of silence broken. A lifetime of silence has diminished the victim's sense of self and power to act.[19] Effective pastoral care may well be described by the feminist theologian Nelle Morton's phrase, "hearing into speech."[20] Beverly Harrison elaborates Morton's point by noting the importance of nurture as an expression of the constructive power of love "to-act-each-other-into-well-being."[21] Nelle Morton used hearing to mean more than listening. For her *hearing* was a direct, transitive verb.[22] Such hearing evokes life, new life, more authentic life. "Hearing into speech" is an act of nurture authenticating the life of the woman whose victimization robbed her of a sense of self. Karen, Chris, and Sarah each disclosed their secret to their pastor in hopes that they would be received with love and heard into new life. They did not expect their pastor to take away their pain but to validate them through listening to their story carefully and empathically. Such listening rebuilds the bridge of trust that was violently torn away earlier. Pastors hear not only as themselves but as representatives of Christ and thus convey God's love as well as their own. Quick or easy responses about love and forgiveness would only trivialize the depth of evil, pain, and shame that women such as Karen, Chris, and Sarah have experienced. Rather, pastors who listen patiently over time will find opportunities for theological interpretation that honor the woman's experience and may help to rebuild her sense of self in relation to God. The alienation from God described by Chris and Sarah certainly would present such opportunities in subsequent conversations. The pastor's role includes listening for and inviting reflection on the religious or theological significance of the woman's experience.

"Hearing into speech" requires courage, both for the survivor and for those who listen, for the story leads through the valley of the shadow of death. Often it includes the experience of the terror, pain, and anger of the victimized child and the anguish and rage of the adult who is now able to voice what she experienced and acknowledge the consequences for her life. Pastors who listen are called on to receive and validate those powerful feelings. Further, they need to be aware of and contain their own sometimes frightening and powerful responses if they are to remain available to the wounded victim.

The travail of recovery can include forging an authentic faith when women are able to face their experience of evil and find support in the struggle to discern meaning in their suffering.[23] For women molested as children, evil is not abstract or distant. They carry its cost in the shame and estrangement they embody. Recovery involves naming evil for what it is and raging against it. For many women the church is not exempt from evil, for the church failed to invite their stories, actively denied the truth, or responded to their situation with blame and guilt.

The process of recovery presents a host of theological issues for women seeking to reconstruct their lives and their faith and for pastors sharing in that journey. Such issues concern the nature of evil or sin, community, trust, embodiment, love and anger, theodicy, suffering, grief, and hope. Here we will pursue these issues briefly.

Returning internalized shame to its interpersonal origins and working through those relationships are important therapeutic tasks for recovery. In the process, the person is confronted with the destructive consequences of the sin of domination and betrayal, which are all the more powerful when perpetrated by a family member or trusted adult. Moreover, the child's notions of community and trust were further distorted by the fact that often her requests for help to mothers or other trusted adults were denied or the abuse was met with apparent indifference. That victims of sexual abuse often voice the sense that God betrayed them is not surprising. For some, recovery includes the recognition that in fact their abuse represents a betrayal of God. Pastors and congregations have the opportunity self-consciously to model community in which care is genuine, commitments are reliable, and each person's dignity and worth are affirmed. A woman like Chris, for example, will need special care and gentle encouragement as she begins the process of daring to believe she is a loved and valued member of the congregational family. Trusting will not come easily for her, but the experience of belonging offers healing and new hope for belief in a God whose love is reliable.

The evil of sexual abuse is particularly striking in the effect it has on the way victims feel about their bodies. The alienation and estrangement of sexual violence are all the more poignant because what is intended as the context for intimacy and care becomes the context of violation, domination, and betrayal. Theologians who have identified the connection between incarnation and embodiment are especially helpful in this regard because the church's embarrassed silence about sexuality only compounds the shame women such as Sarah, Chris, and Karen feel. The radical assertion that God came among us in human flesh (incarnation) contradicts cultural dualisms that divide spirit and body. As James Nelson suggests, "We either experience God's presence in our bodies or not at all."[24] This profound appreciation for the relationship between embodiment and spirituality may guide pastors for the relationship between embodiment and spirituality may guide pastors who talk with women like Sarah, who so fears her sexuality that she has attempted to deny it, or Karen, who escaped intimacy through promiscuity. Pastors may help such women work through the shame they feel about their bodies and recover the vitality and profound communion their sexuality may give them.

The good news is that those same bodies that felt the brunt of violence may be freed for the power to love. One of the most debilitating consequences of sexual abuse is the suppression of feelings. Understandably, victims cope by suppressing their terror, pain, and rage, but feelings cannot be suppressed selectively. Therefore, the power to love again comes at a dear price because the recovery of feeling also involves grief and anger. Ironically, pastors concerned that survivors of incest recover the capacity for love find themselves hearing such women into anger. For many caregivers as well as for those recovering from abuse, the experience and language of anger is at once more frightening and more intimate because it involves the loss of precious control.

Recognizing that anger and love are related is important. When anger is denied, the capacity for love atrophies.[25] Until women in recovery express anger, they are hostage to it, and healing will not happen. Anger signals the necessity for change and a sufficient sense of self to know that what they experienced was wrong. Despite popular understanding, Scripture does not describe anger as sin! It requires that we direct anger properly. The challenge for those recovering from child sexual abuse is to direct anger in nondestructive ways—not Karen's chemical dependency or Sarah's chronic depression and obesity. In directing anger outside themselves, survivors move from enrage to outrage.[26] Outrage here bespeaks courage. As Theresa Kane put it, "the heart of courage is just rage."[27]

A woman in recovery comes to terms with her deep resentment toward her mother for not protecting her from her father or another adult trusted by the family. This anger is understandable. Paradoxically, it is often more intense initially than the anger felt toward the perpetrator. Sometimes the child had little or no experience with her mother, as if her mother were absent or she assumed the mother knew of and was indifferent to her need.[28] As survivors work through this anger, they are better able to feel anger or rage toward those who actually abused them. Pastors must allow this anger to be expressed and validate it. They can also clarify that the scriptural injunction to honor parents includes the expectation of their responsible love and care for their children.[29]

Popular equations of sin and anger are especially problematic for the recovery of victims of abuse. All too frequently forgiveness is represented as an act that good Christians ought to do and could do if they wanted to. Many victims who are Christians use religion to sanction their fear of anger and disavow their understandable rage. Imagine the difficulty for a child or, for that matter, a mature adult who feels rage against her perpetrator—and is unable to consider forgiveness. Forgiveness is not something we can do but, as John Patton suggests, a discovery we make.[30] The capacity for forgiveness comes only by grace and transpires at some point deep into the process of recovery, if it comes at all. Most often the process of recovery simply yields a sufficient sense of resolution with the experience of abuse so that these women can put aside their identity as victim and claim the power and new life of a survivor.[31] The past is not forgotten, but it no longer claims the present and the future.

Anger and the experience of forgiveness with God are also painfully intertwined. God rarely escapes the survivor's anger or rage. Recovery for adults molested as children often requires a period of travail and of deep ambivalence and anger with God for leaving them unprotected. This anger is not unlike that directed to their mothers, the nonoffending but ineffectual parent.[32] Sarah, for example, feels this ambivalence deeply and angrily asks the pastor, "Where was this God of ours when I was as trusting and vulnerable as the children of this congregation?" Pastors must listen nondefensively to such expressions of anger and abandonment and acknowledge them as understandable. Anger with God has a valuable place in the recovery of faith. Scripture passages such as Psalm 22 demonstrate that anger and love are not opposites but rather different types of connectedness.[33]

For some survivors, God and the church are so complicit in their experience of abuse that their understandable rage reduces the usual approaches to God to irrelevance. Although such survivors may continue the search for a life-sustaining spirituality, the church and its theology may seem to be more a hindrance than an asset. When adults in recovery describe their awareness of God, they often speak of guilt and shame, such as the deadening feelings that distance Chris from God, or in terms of Sarah's explicit anger and charge of abandonment. Their reactions expose the vulnerability of traditional images of God. Tradition has long offered a monarchial image of an all-knowing God who rules with unlimited power (omnipotent) while remaining distant and unmoved by human experience.[34] These images leave victims such as Sarah angrily assuming God could have protected her but was indifferent to her pain. From the traditional perspective, God's power to save includes the power to keep safe.

In recent years, some theologians have searched Scripture for images of God's power that include God's compassion and vulnerability. Such an image would acknowledge the limitations on God's actions imposed by historical existence as created by God.[35] Their search has disclosed a rich legacy that is especially useful for victims of sexual abuse. This different perspective at once embraces God's primordial power as Creator and Redeemer, which acknowledges that God chooses to exercise such power as one intensely involved in historical existence. The consequence of that involvement is vulnerability to the pain and suffering of historical existence, for human freedom and the natural order present limitations on God's power. Although God's power to save is affirmed, it is not the power to keep safe.

When God's power is understood through the image of suffering love, pastoral responses can focus effectively on images of God's connectedness and presence in the midst of human pain, fear, and struggle. God's presence in the midst of human pain is especially apparent in the ministry of Jesus, who sought solidarity with the weak and vulnerable. God is present not as one who sends suffering but as one who shares in it, embodied it, and redeems it. The crucifixion does not justify or warrant involuntary suffering. It represents God's contradiction of death-dealing power with the power of love.[36] The meaning of Jesus' death is not found on the cross but in his behavior that led to it. Jesus was crucified "for refusing to abandon the radical activity of love—of expressing solidarity and reciprocity with the excluded ones in his community."[37] The resurrection witnesses to the power of the promise that nothing in all creation can separate us from such love.

The joining of God's power for redemptive transformation with God's suffering love offers a relational bridge of hope for those who long for an end to the alienation and gracelessness of lives lived apart from God's love. Chris, for example, is haunted by shame and guilt for her participation in her chronic abuse. Why did she not stop it? Chris cannot imagine God's forgiveness for her. Her experience of God's gracious forgiveness will come only as she faces the origins and consequences of shame and learns why the child in herself could not say no.

The experience of connection with God's gracious love is transforming and empowering. Most women who work through recovery move toward advocacy on behalf of victims. They embody the power of anger for the work of love through committed action and advocacy for those who are as yet vulnerable. Their anger, now assimilated and integrated, fuels action that nurtures life, relationships, and community.[38] Just as these women recovered the possibility for greater personal freedom through experiencing connection, they now are committed to building communities of care and justice.

Education and Advocacy

Just as recovery often results in the survivor's commitment to justice and advocacy, pastoral responses need to be broader than care for those immediately affected by sexual violence. Pastors and congregations can work effectively in a number of ways to enhance personal healing and take preventive and prophetic action.

As in the case of the victim, breaking the silence in congregations is the crucial first step for effective change. Although prevention of child sexual abuse may be an unlikely goal, more adequate and timely intervention is possible in the lives of victims, perpetrators, and families. Congregations and pastors can educate themselves and advocate systemic change in communities where better therapeutic and legal programs are needed. They can work to establish local chapters of such organizations as Parents United, where child victims, nonoffending parents, perpetrators, and adults molested as children are able to participate in an extended guided process of recovery through peer group experiences designed to augment personal therapy.

Pastors have many resources available to them in the work of breaking the silence about violence and abuse. As pastors begin to raise issues of sexuality, parishioners who have not felt free to speak through the deafening silence can begin to acknowledge the pain and struggle of their experience of rape, abuse, or incest and to describe problems associated with sexuality. Pastors must recognize the value of not avoiding biblical passages that deal with sexual violence, such as the incestuous rape of Tamar.[39] The theological as well as social and political themes in the story of Tamar are important for the congregation to hear. References to sexual abuse are also appropriate illustrations of such common biblical themes as betrayal, loss, and suffering.[40] In addition, the use of liturgy and ritual is an important asset in the care of individuals in recovery. *Sexual Assault and Abuse*[41] includes some liturgical resources useful with individuals and congregations who dare to include their sexuality among the life experiences that occasion praise, confession, and intercession.

Educationally, pastors and congregations have many opportunities with children, parents, and general classes to offer opportunities for correcting Christianity's complicity in sexual violence through its previous teaching, silence, or actual participation, especially with regard to women's sexuality.[42] In general, congregations have a potential role in helping persons value their sexuality and consider the responsibilities that accompany sexual expression. A better understanding of what being a family means and how to meet our commitments to one another is also a significant and related educational concern.

We have explored the consequences of sexual abuse, including incest in the lives of women molested as children. We have addressed the devastating impact of shame as a "sickness of the soul" and the consequences of shame for personality development, relationships, and spirituality. In particular, we have attended to some theological issues implicit in the process of recovery. Borrowing Nelle Morton's description of the constructive power of nurture, we have named pastoral care with victims in recovery as "hearing into speech." By this phrase we have emphasized the bondage of silence and the life-giving power that comes to those victims who dare to break that silence. Their courage in breaking familial and societal denial about child sexual abuse challenges pastors and congregations to break our silence that perpetuates that abuse.

BIBLIOGRAPHY

Bass, Ellen, and Laura Davis. *The Courage to Heal.* New York: Harper & Row, Perennial Library, 1988.

Belenky, Mary Field, et al. *Women's Ways of Knowing.* New York: Basic Books, 1986.

Cooper, Burton Z. *Why, God?* Atlanta: John Knox Press, 1988.

Erikson, Erik. *Childhood and Society,* 2d ed. rev. and enl. New York: W. W. Norton, 1963.

Fortune, Marie Marshall. *Sexual Violence.* New York: Pilgrim Press, 1983.

Fossum, Merle A., and Marilyn J. Mason. *Facing Shame.* New York: W. W. Norton, 1986.

Fretheim, Terence E. *The Suffering of God.* Philadelphia: Fortress Press, 1984.

Harrison, Beverly. "The Power of Anger in the Work of Love." In *Making the Connections,* ed. Carol S. Robb. Boston: Beacon Press, 1985.

Kaufman, Gershen. *Shame: The Power of Caring,* 2d ed. rev. Cambridge, Mass.: Schenkman, 1985.

Moltmann, Jurgen. *The Crucified God.* New York: Harper & Row, 1973.

Morton, Nelle. *The Journey Is Home.* Boston: Beacon Press, 1985.

Nelson, James B. *Between Two Gardens.* New York: Pilgrim Press, 1983.

Patton, John. *Is Human Forgiveness Possible?* Nashville: Abingdon Press, 1985.

Pellauer, Mary D. "A Theological Perspective on Sexual Assault." In *Sexual Assault and Abuse,* ed. Mary D. Pellauer, et al. San Francisco: Harper & Row, 1987.

Pellauer, Mary D. "Violence Against Women: The Theological Dimension." In *Sexual Assault and Abuse,* edited by Mary D. Pellauer, et al. San Francisco: Harper & Row, 1987.

Pellauer, Mary D., Barbara Chester, and Jane Boyajian, eds. *Sexual Assault and Abuse.* San Francisco: Harper & Row, 1987.

Pruyser, Paul W. *Between Belief and Unbelief*. New York: Harper & Row, 1974.

Rizzuto, Ana-Maria. *The Birth of the Living God: A Psychoanalytic Study*. Chicago: University of Chicago Press, 1979.

Robb, Carol S., ed. *Making the Connections*. Boston: Beacon Press, 1985.

Scott, Marshall S. "Honor Thy Father and Mother: Scriptural Resources for Victims of Incest and Parental Abuse." *Journal of Pastoral Care* 42 (Summer 1988):139–49.

Smith, Alexa. "Preaching the Tough Topics." Louisville, Ky.: Planned Parenthood of Louisville, 1988.

Suchocki, Marjorie Hewitt. *God, Christ, Church*. New York: Crossroad, 1982.

Summit, Roland. "Beyond Belief: The Reluctant Discovery of Incest." In *Sexual Assault and Abuse*, ed. Mary D. Pellauer, et al. San Francisco: Harper & Row, 1987.

Trible, Phyllis. *Texts of Terror*, Overtures to Biblical Theology. Philadelphia: Fortress Press, 1984.

NOTES

1. Gershen Kaufman, *Shame: The Power of Caring*, 2d ed. rev. (Cambridge, Mass.: Schenkman Books, 1985), 11.

2. Martha Kenney and Carolyn Lindsey, Pastoral Counseling and Consultation Center, Louisville, classroom presentations, 24 November and 1 December 1987.

3. Marie Marshall Fortune, *Sexual Violence* (New York: Pilgrim Press, 1983), 166; Roland Summit, "Beyond Belief: The Reluctant Discovery of Incest," in *Sexual Assault and Abuse*, ed. Mary D. Pellauer, Barbara Chester, and Jane Boyajian (San Francisco: Harper & Row, 1987), 176.

4. Fortune, *Sexual Violence*, 166.

5. Ntozake Shange, "With No Immediate Cause," n.p., cited by Mary D. Pellauer, "Violence Against Women: The Theological Dimension," in Pellauer, Chester, and Boyajian, *Sexual Assault and Abuse*, 50–52.

6. Merle A. Fossum and Marilyn J. Mason, *Facing Shame* (New York: W. W. Norton, 1986), 40–41.

7. Kenney and Lindsey, classroom presentations.

8. Summit, "Beyond Belief," 176.

9. Fossum and Mason, *Facing Shame*, 30–35.

10. Ibid., 5.

11. Kaufman, *Shame*, 7.

12. Ibid., 11, 29–30.

13. Ibid., 40.

14. Ana-Maria Rizzuto, *The Birth of the Living God: A Psychoanalytic Study* (Chicago: The University of Chicago Press, 1979); Paul W. Pruyser, *Between Belief and Unbelief* (New York: Harper & Row, 1974).

15. Erik Erikson, *Childhood and Society*, 2d ed. rev. and enl. (New York: W. W. Norton, 1963), 250.

16. Mary D. Pellauer, "A Theological Perspective on Sexual Assault," in Pellauer, Chester, and Boyajian, *Sexual Assault and Abuse*, 85.

17. Ellen Bass and Laura Davis, *The Courage to Heal* (New York: Harper & Row, Perennial Library, 1988), 58–59.

18. Ibid.

19. See Mary Field Belenky, et al., *Women's Ways of Knowing* (New York: Basic Books, 1986) for a further discussion of the debilitating developmental consequences of child sexual abuse.

20. Nelle Morton, *The Journey Is Home* (Boston: Beacon Press, 1985), 205.

21. Beverly Harrison, "The Power of Anger in the Work of Love," in *Marking the Connections*, ed. Carol S. Robb (Boston: Beacon Press, 1985), 13.

22. Morton, *The Journey Is Home*, 205.

23. Ibid., 15.

24. James B. Nelson, *Between Two Gardens* (New York: Pilgrim Press, 1983), 18.

25. Harrison, "Power of Anger," 14–15.

26. Conversation with Suzanne Holland, Louisville, Ky., 22 May 1989.

27. Theresa Kane, Women-Church Convergence Conference, Cincinnati, 1987.

28. Conversation with Martha Kenney, Louisville, Ky., 30 May 1989.

29. Marshall S. Scott, "Honor Thy Father and Mother: Scriptural Resources for Victims of Incest and Parental Abuse," *Journal of Pastoral Care* 42 (Summer 1988):139-49.

30. See John Patton, *Is Human Forgiveness Possible?* (Nashville: Abingdon Press, 1985) for an extended discussion of shame and forgiveness.

31. Kenney and Lindsey, classroom presentations.

32. Interview with Ann Letson, Chaplain, Norton Hospital, Louisville, Ky., and group facilitator with Louisville Chapter of Parents United, 8 March 1989.

33. Harrison, "Power of Anger," 14.

34. See Burton Z. Cooper, *Why, God?* (Atlanta, John Knox Press, 1988), 89 for a summary of this position.

35. See Jurgen Moltmann, *The Crucified God* (New York: Harper & Row, 1973); Marjorie Hewitt Suchocki, *God, Christ, Church* (New York: Crossroad, 1982); Terence E. Fretheim, *The Suffering of God* (Philadelphia: Fortress Press, 1984); and Cooper, *Why, God?*

36. Moltmann, *The Crucified God*.

37. Harrison, "Power of Anger," 18.

38. Ibid.

39. 2 Samuel 13:1-22 (RSV). For an incisive discussion of this passage, see Phyllis Trible, *Texts of Terror*, Overtures to Biblical Theology (Philadelphia: Fortress Press, 1984), 37–64.

40. Alexa Smith, "Preaching the Tough Topics" (Louisville: Planned Parenthood of Louisville, 1988).

41. Pellauer, Chester, and Boyajian, *Sexual Assault and Abuse.*
42. Fortune, *Sexual Violence,* 42–112.

CHAPTER 6

A Cry of Anguish:
The Battered Woman

JOANN M. GARMA

• • • • • • • • • • • •

Pastoral care providers must recognize the reality that the most violent group to which women and children belong is the family.[1] Pastors and church members view the family unit as a place where Christian values are taught and lived. They want to see the family as a haven for security, comfort, love, and joy. Such is the American dream. Nevertheless, the fact is that the family is a place where violence and tragedy can and do occur. The willingness and the ability to deal with the problem of violence in the family are a real challenge to the church, as is demonstrated by the following cases:

CASE 1: A middle-aged woman confided to her pastor that her husband had been beating her. She had been able to "live with" the beatings until recently, when she began to have health problems, and had become afraid that the beatings might exacerbate her illness. The church to which the couple belonged had a membership primarily of upper-middle-class families and was considered a moderate to liberal church within the major denomination. The couple were active members who gave a substantial pledge to the church. The initial reaction of the pastor to the woman's story was one of incredulity; then he felt compassion for the woman. As he continued to listen, he found himself becoming uneasy and then frustrated and angry because of her seeming sense of helplessness. He tried to sympathize with the woman, who came across to him as wimpy, and then he counseled her in terms of her passivity in allowing the beatings to take place.

Pastors view themselves as sensitive, compassionate, and competent people. A first reading of the above case might evoke the response, "I would not react like that pastor. I would be more sensitive and aware." Confronted with a battered woman's story, however, the pastor's skills are tested. Working with such women can make pastoral caregivers frustrated and then angry: How can you allow yourself to remain in such an abusive situation? Why not just leave? The decision to "just leave" is a difficult one for the battered woman. She often will not or cannot reach out until the possibility of her own death or the death of her child seems imminent to her. Even then, she may recant after the initial terror passes and become ambivalent. The outcome can be unnecessary tragedy. Like peace officers who are reluctant to become involved in domestic quarrels, the pastor usually finds such pastoral situations difficult and perhaps potentially dangerous.[2] The least demanding response for pastors is to deny and ignore that such situations exist. To the church community, the batterer may appear to be a responsible, gregarious person. To the pastor, this incongruity may validate taking a denial stance. The primary issue raised is this: Is domestic violence an issue in which the pastoral care provider needs to become involved and, if so, in what ways?

CASE 2: A young woman stood up in a workshop for women on marriage communication and stated that she was going to leave her husband because he beat her. The beatings had occurred throughout the four years of their marriage whenever he became upset over anything. Her attitude had recently changed because she felt that the safety of her baby daughter was threatened. She felt enormous conflict because she wanted to fulfill her Christian commitment and responsibilities as a wife, but she could not overcome or ignore her fear for her daughter's safety. Her statement was a cry for help, support, and direction, but a hushed silence fell over the workshop.[3] Two women stood up and broke the silence with the following:

> "You shouldn't leave your husband. . . . No matter what he does to you, God put him in charge of you. He's God's responsibility. If something he does to you displeases God, then it's up to God to stop him, not you." "That's right," the other woman added. "God made him your lord and master. Even if he tells you to jump out the window, you should do it. If God wants you or your baby to live, don't worry. He'll protect you somehow."[4]

Out of this experience, Holly Wagner Green wrote *Turning Fear to Hope: Help for Marriages Troubled by Abuse.* This book is directed at those churches that rely heavily on the literal translation of Scripture for guidelines about the conduct of marital relationships.[5]

This case illustrates the notion of male dominance and female submission that the church continues to maintain, sometimes overtly and sometimes subtly. The fact that male clergy fill most major church pulpits and female clergy have great difficulty in finding urban pastoral positions, even as associates, is evidence enough of the male-dominance value within the church. Even if a clergywoman does fill a pastoral position in a church, more than likely she does so at a lesser salary than her male counterpart. If a woman in an abusive marriage believes in the notion of female submission, it requires that she live in a physically and emotionally harmful and potentially life-threatening relationship. In this case, two women believe in and continue the notion of female submission. The larger question that must be answered is, Who supports and maintains such values? We might argue that the church hierarchy and its local clergymen do so.

CASE 3: A thirty-year-old woman was arrested for shooting her common-law husband of nine years. She had children by him and was the primary wage earner for the family. His family knew that he had been beating her because she had pleaded with them to talk to him. His family reasoned that he only did it when he was drunk and then he did not know what he was doing. They encouraged her to be more patient with him and to learn to avoid inciting him when he was drunk. Her pastor encouraged her to be "strong" and to pray for her husband that he might be "saved." He counseled that patience and strength in the face of suffering are Christian virtues. Over the years she had gone to the emergency room several times for the treatment of severe bruises and wounds. Acquiescing to her husband's pleadings, however, she had never pressed charges against him. He always gave contrite assurances that he would change. When her husband died of the gunshot wound, she was charged with first-degree murder. His family ostracized her and began proceedings to take custody of her children. Although her own pastor continued to maintain contact initially, he seemed to feel that he had somehow "failed" in his ministry to her and eventually stopped coming to see her in prison. As the case continued for many months in court, the woman became depressed. She confided to the prison chaplain that the outcome did not matter to her anymore. Even if she were to be released, she had no one and no place to go and she would have to live with the shame of having killed her common-law husband.

More than any other institution, the church has held firmly to the sanctity of marriage; from a healthy marriage, Christian morals and values can be passed from one generation to the next. Moreover, in the past, marriage was socioeconomically very important to women. Supporting herself or herself and her children was difficult for a woman to do outside the context of the family unit. Today, much is happening to challenge the traditional understanding of what marriage and family "should" be.

To hold the same values for the Christian married couple that were upheld fifty years ago is naive. Should a woman still be urged to remain in a marriage because "it's best for the children"? Are not men's and women's roles changing and being redefined? Are not women as working wives and single parents now in the work place in unprecedented numbers? If these and other questions were openly acknowledged and discussed in sermons and adult study classes, families in crisis could feel that their church is a sanctuary and a source of support as they work through what is best for them. To remain in an abusive marriage "at all costs" can become a tragic dictum.

Myths and Realities

The National Coalition Against Domestic Violence lists four major myths about battered women: Abuse of women is not common, abuse is limited to a particular socioeconomic and racial group, battered women provoke violence, and battering stems from an individual pathology rather than the patriarchal structures and practices of society.[6] Most pastoral care providers know little about battered women and may not realize that each of these commonly held opinions is wrong.

To begin with, violence against women occurs across ethnic, socioeconomic, and religious lines. Some devoutly committed Christian women find that their acquired religious and community values keep them trapped in dangerously abusive marital relationships. Spiritual issues rooted in religious beliefs can be as punitive as the beatings. Although the church itself is changing, albeit slowly, the church's "language" (its Scripture, ritual, hymns, and theology) remains predominantly patriarchal. This orientation is mirrored and supported by a society in which women are less "powerful"; that is, they earn less and hold fewer leadership positions. Given that the church has such an orientation, the question of the place and status of women in the church must be addressed.

Domestic violence against women is shockingly common. According to the National Crime Survey, 2.1 million women (married, divorced, or separated) were victims of physical abuse (aggravated assault, simple assault, rape, and robbery) by their partners at least once in a twelve-month period. Of these 2.1 million victimized women, 32 percent (672,000) were physically abused at least a second time. This study's estimate is that physical battering is perpetrated on some woman every fifteen seconds.[7] The FBI Uniform Crime Report states that 30 percent of all female homicide victims are killed by their husbands or boyfriends.[8] The U.S. Surgeon General's Report states that physical battering is the single largest cause of injury to women in the United States; it surpasses muggings, rapes, and automobile accidents combined.[9]

According to the National Center on Women and Family Law, in 72 percent of the states (thirty-six states), a husband can legally rape his wife.[10] As of 1982, more than a million women each year seek medical help for injuries derived from physical battering, and 20 percent of these visits are to emergency medical services.[11]

These data demand the concern and involvement of pastoral care providers. Everyone within the church has a vested interest in helping the battered woman and in stopping the domestic violence in our society that touches the lives of millions of families each year, crossing all lines of culture, ethnicity, race, social class, denomination, and economic status. They might start this work by learning that battered women do not somehow bring the violence on themselves.

Identifying the Battered Woman

When listening to the battered woman's story, the pastoral care provider may feel overwhelmed by the woman's inability to act on behalf of herself or her children. The woman's passivity may seem exaggerated, unreal, or even repulsive. The questions often raised are, How can any able-bodied person allow herself to remain in such a dangerous situation? Why not just leave? The decision to "just leave" is a difficult and complex one.

Lenore Walker, who has conducted research on the battered woman, proposed that the theory of learned helplessness describes why women remain in abusive relationships.[12] Her theory is that the battered woman's response to her abuse comes out of a sense of helplessness or a sense that she has no control over the abuse, even though in reality she may have control. Her belief or her expectation that she has no control is the crucial factor in the learned helplessness response to abuse. According to Walker, "Once we believe we cannot control what happens to us, it is difficult to believe we can ever influence it, even if later we experience a favorable outcome."[13] A sense of helplessness is learned when the woman comes to believe that no matter what she does to try to avoid the batterings or to control the batterer's anger, the batterings still occur. The woman may attempt to initiate problem-solving techniques to assuage the batterer's anger, but to no avail. With each failure, subtle changes occur in the woman's psyche until all motivation to avoid the batterings seems to disappear, and the woman becomes more passive in her response to the batterer's anger. The battered woman's experience does include moments of tenderness and affection from the batterer, especially after the beatings. These interludes maintain some motivation and perhaps a glimmer of hope because the woman looks on these moments as being achievable for the relationship as a whole. That she experience such respites, however, is crucial to the three-stage cycle of woman battering.[14]

The first stage is the tension-building stage.[15] The woman denies her own needs and feelings (such as anger) in an attempt to assuage the batterer's anger. At one extreme, she may attempt to stay out of his way, or on the other she may try to meet his every need. When the batterer does become angry during this stage, the woman rationalizes that somehow she may have done something to make him angry, that his anger could have been worse than it was, or that he was out of sorts on that day. What the woman is doing during this stage is accepting responsibility for the batterer's abusive behavior and simultaneously communicating to him that she accepts his abusive behavior toward her.[16] As Walker states, "It is not that she believes that she should be abused; rather, she believes that what she does will prevent his anger from escalating."[17]

What happens, however, is that the batterer's anger does escalate into stage two, the acute battering incident, an uncontrollable discharge of the tensions that were built up during the first stage.[18] The process from stage one to stage two moves from minor battering incidents into a major destructive incident characterized by a complete lack of control on the part of the batterer.[19]

> His rage is so great that it blinds his control over his behavior. He starts out wanting to teach the woman a lesson, not intending to inflict any particular injury on her, and stops when he feels she has learned her lesson. By this time, however, she has generally been very severely beaten.[20]

This stage is usually short-lived, from two to twenty-four hours, but has been known to go on for a week. The batterer is in complete control of this stage and is the only one who can end it. Exactly when the stage will begin and the amount of violence that will be inflicted are totally unpredictable. If the woman has experienced the battering cycle several times, she knows that the second stage is short-lived. She may then prefer to "push" the inevitable because she also knows that the third stage will bring about a period of calm.[21]

The third stage is the kindness and contrite loving behavior stage, which is characterized by overwhelming calm and good will.[22] The batterer knows that he has gone too far, becomes extremely loving and tender toward the battered woman, and asks for her forgiveness. His behavior is quite contrite. He truly believes that she has learned her lesson and that he will never again beat her. Each time he manages to convince himself and everyone concerned that he has battered his wife for the last time. He may even change some behavior (for example, drinking) to prove that he will change. The batterer also seems to be able to mobilize and utilize the influence of any or all family members to convince the battered woman to "take him back." His pleadings work on the battered woman's guilt. How can she deny the children their father's presence? Does she not know that the batterer needs her help if he is to change?[23]

> Since most battered women adhere to traditional values about the permanency of love and marriage, they are easy prey for the guilt attendant on breaking up a home, even if it is not a very happy one. They have been taught that marriage is forever, and they believe it.[24]

The batterer's reasonableness finally convinces the woman that he will change. The woman wants to believe that the behavior of the batterer in stage three truly represents who the man is without considering that he is also the person who brutally hit her. In her own mind, she convinces herself that with her support and with proper help, the batterer can change. As long as the battering couple remains together, however, the batterer will not seek the help to change. The exact length of stage three is not clear. It is longer than stage two but shorter than stage one.[25]

The battered woman has low self-esteem.[26] She does not believe in her own abilities, especially her ability to make competent decisions concerning her life. Her sense of her own value comes from outside herself. If she is told that she is a "good" mother, wife, housekeeper, cook, lover, or provider, then she is a "good" person. Because of her low self-esteem, she relies heavily on feedback from others (especially her husband) and is easily influenced by what others say. In addition, she firmly believes in the old values about marriage and family in which the ultimate and full responsibility for the success or failure of the home lies with the woman alone. She is the one who must maintain the peace and tranquillity of her family at all costs. Walker notes, however, that the battered woman does possess sufficient strength to manipulate her situation enough to avoid being killed. Her sense of personal value, perceived as coming from outside and not from within herself, makes her an easy prey to the cycle of learned helplessness; she feels she has little or no control of her life, and she believes that she "ought" to have more control. As she fails with each effort to maintain peace in her family, she perceives herself as even more of a failure, which, in turn, lowers her self-esteem. She continues to work at finding a solution, but to no avail.[27] As Walker states, "Most of the women interviewed eventually got around to saying that they were still not completely sure that there was not something they could have done differently that might have made the batterer cease his abusive behavior."[28]

Walker further suggests that the way a woman perceives causation in general influences her perception of her control of events in her own life. For example, those Walker labels "externalizers" believe they have less control over events that happen to them than those who are "internalizers," those who believe that they have a great deal of influence over what happens in their lives.[29] Walker states, "Some people believe that most of the events that occur in their life are caused by factors outside themselves. . . . Deeply religious people fall into this category, as do people who believe in strictly following rigid rules and regulations."[30] Although Walker notes that research remains to be done in discovering whether battered women can be classified as externalizers, she does raise the issue of the role of religious beliefs and values in the life of the battered woman.

The church has a long history of projecting external dictums on the woman, especially the battered woman. The worldview taught by the church subjugates the woman to the authority and control of the man through the patriarchal language of its Scripture, ritual, hymns, and theology. The woman's God is *Father,* her Redeemer is *Son,* and her priest or pastor, who theologizes, teaches, and preaches about her God and Redeemer is usually a man. The woman is taught to believe that the patriarchal ideologies come from God and are therefore true. The dominant language and symbols of the church give the woman little with which to identify; if she is a battered woman committed to the male ideology of the Christian faith, she has even less with which to build her self-esteem.[31]

With each battering, the woman's self-esteem as well as her body is beaten. To question or to show initiative is interpreted as prideful and willful on the woman's part. The woman is metaphorically beaten into a dark abyss from which she sees no escape. The woman experiences shame in the way that Nancy Ramsay describes shame in the chapter on sexual abuse. Whatever "love" she receives is earned and is usually withheld when her husband perceives her as not being "good." She is never quite "good enough." Her spirituality is experienced in terms of sin, judgment, and the call to "perfection" that is never attainable. The woman, therefore, remains bound by feelings of self-blame and guilt. Because the battered woman's values are defined by male symbols, male dominance, and the patriarchal hierarchy, she is kept in her abusive bondage. Like her husband, her God seems to be punitive and distant.[32]

Her suffering then is perceived as a means to attain penance and "perfection." As Christ suffered for the sins of others, so should the battered woman suffer for her own sins and those of her abuser. She must believe that her suffering in some way will lead her batterer to change; therefore, his redemption becomes her task as a Christian. She must remain faithful and humble if her man is to find salvation.[33]

The battered woman experiences forgiveness as something outside herself. She learns to live in a state of personal guilt for all the "wrongs" she has done. Yet, she is quick to forgive her batterer, often with the encouragement of her pastor, family, and friends. Because of her shame and low self-esteem, the battered woman believes that forgiveness for herself is beyond her reach. Forgiveness comes to people whose homes are peaceful, whose lives are orderly, and whose husbands and children are happy.[34] Over the years, however, the woman's own stifled feelings of anger build. Sometimes these pent-up emotions explode in a reciprocal violent reaction to the abuse that may result in the abuser's death. The battered woman then finds herself in the crux of a dilemma because she cannot forgive her batterer now that he is dead. Moreover, how can she ever be forgiven or forgive herself? Here again, Nancy Ramsay's discussion of anger and the process toward healing (forgiveness) in the case of sexual abuse is helpful in understanding the spiritual dilemma of the battered woman.

Identifying the battered woman helps the pastoral care provider come to some understanding of why she cannot "just leave" her abusive relationship. She is a woman who adheres strongly to her learned Christian beliefs and to societal values about marriage and family. She believes in her place in the family and the societal structure. She finds herself caught in a web of manipulation, coercion, and violent abuse. Such a woman neither belongs to "other" churches, nor lives in someone else's neighborhood. She is your neighbor who sits in your church each Sunday searching for help and for the answers to her plight. Her cry of anguish may be a silent one. If not heard and answered, it can rend the very fiber of the church's call to renewal.

The Battered Woman's Needs

The battered woman needs the pastoral care provider to face the fallacy of family bliss and to put it to rest. Husbands do beat their wives and children, both physically and emotionally. The "loved one" is most likely to commit assault, rape, and murder. The media emphasize the dangers that lurk in the streets, but the fact is that most cruel abuse happens at home. The church and society at large are reluctant to view the home as a place where brutality and coercion take place.[35] In *Violence Against Wives: A Case Against Patriarchy,* Dobash and Dobash state:

> Despite overwhelming evidence to challenge it, the myth of family bliss and security survives almost totally intact. The official statistics, which have long been available, clearly show the high incidence of violence among family members; yet these figures have usually been ignored or given scant notice of treatment (especially when compared with the concern about violence in other settings). It is almost as though we have averted our eyes from violence in the family because we do not want it to happen and believe that it should not happen. When forced to acknowledge its existence, we attempt to deny that it is widespread or severe or that it happens between "normal" people.[36]

Recognizing the existence of violence in the family is crucial if ministry is to be provided to those within the church community who live in quiet desperation. Pivotal questions must be raised: What is at stake that the reality of family violence must be denied so persistently? Why hold on to values that are no longer helpful to families in a constantly changing world? What value and place does the woman have in today's church? The struggle to come to some resolution around these questions not only can bring consolation and support for the battered woman and her plight but also can be a catalyst for renewal within the church as it faces liberation, feminist, and womanist issues.

The battered woman needs the pastoral care provider to understand and believe her.[37] To do so, the pastoral care provider must be informed. The National Coalition Against Domestic Violence (P.O. Box 15127, Washington, D.C. 20003-0127) can be helpful in gathering resource materials and information. After becoming informed, the pastoral care provider can then apply and include what he or she has learned about the issue of battered women in sermons, group discussions, adult church school classes, and workshops. As interest and a sense of commitment to the issue develop, a decision must be made concerning how and to what extent the pastoral care providers will become involved. A process of pastoral contact, support, and referral should be developed. What helpful services, other than a listening ear, does the pastoral care provider have to offer the battered woman who musters enough courage to make contact? Can the pastoral care provider offer legal aid or a safe place to stay? Although a local church may not have the facilities to house a battered woman and her children, it can work with local shelters to make such assistance available. Because shelters typically have difficulty in maintaining funding, an appropriate outreach program may be to assist local shelters in their fund-raising efforts.

In working with battered women, the pastoral care provider must be aware of tendencies to minimize the severity of the batterings. The usual reaction is to deny that it is "that bad," especially if the batterer claims that the woman is exaggerating. The pastoral care provider must also be aware of the battered woman's ambivalence about identifying her husband as a batterer and about labeling herself as a battered woman. She may be inclined to rescind her decision to leave her husband if he comes to her in a "penitent" manner. Take the woman seriously, however, and begin the process of pastoral support and referral. The battered woman's basic need is empowerment, both personally and within the church. Rita-Lou Clarke speaks of the basic issues of the battered woman and the pastoral care that can be offered in *Pastoral Care of Battered Women*. She brings together the ideas of many feminists, biblicists, and theologians and utilizes their interpretations to reframe traditional beliefs and values that can empower women in general and battered women most particularly. Providing the battered woman with Marie Fortune's *Keeping the Faith: Questions and Answers for the Abused Woman* can be helpful and supportive to her. Carol Bingham's *Doorway to Response: The Role of Clergy in Ministry with Battered Women* can be utilized as an orientation resource.

The National Coalition Against Domestic Violence has a crisis line (1-800-333-7233) that provides support as well as referral services to local community shelters that are available to the battered woman. The local church can make the crisis line available to its church membership by publishing it periodically in the church news bulletin. The crisis line can also direct the pastoral care provider to resource people within the local community who would be available for consultation. The primary purpose of the crisis line is to assist the battered woman toward help and empowerment.

To empower a woman is to offer her an identity within the church by utilizing inclusive language and symbols. It is to see her as a person with gifts and personal worth of equal and complementary value to those of a man. It is to value and encourage her claim to her place within the church that has been thus far overlooked and denied. To empower a battered woman is to assist and enable her to free herself from the bondage of an abusive relationship. It is to help her see herself as a person of value and worth. It is to denounce the abusive acts that are perpetrated against her and her children. It is to demand that legal action and community aid be provided to her.

Christian women being brutally beaten by their husbands or boyfriends is a reality. Domestic violence must be seen as a problem that occurs daily within the families of the church. Brutal violence against women and children is not something that takes place in "other" families of "other" churches that are located in "other" neighborhoods. Women who are members of your church are victims of violent physical and emotional assaults. The statistics can no longer be denied or ignored. "Keeping a woman in her place" is a potentially lethal stance.

Understanding the personality of the battered woman can be frustrating, and developing an appreciation for the dynamic of learned helplessness is most helpful. She lives in a three-stage cycle of battering that enhances the learned helplessness response to her battering. Her low self-esteem makes her susceptible to participating in a relationship in which she will be battered. Her self-worth comes from outside rather than from within herself. Her emotional and spiritual life is filled with guilt, judgment, fear, and, at the core of herself, shame. She receives no relief or support from a patriarchal church that teaches that the man is dominant in his value as a person and in his place within the church.

The church is being called to face what is taking place among the most "devout" of couples. Judgment and condemnation from the church are not needed. Understanding, sincere compassion, patience, tenacity, and the inclusion of women within the total structure of the church are required to help the battered woman help herself and to break the cycle of violence.

BIBLIOGRAPHY

BOOKS

Ackerman, Robert J., and Susan E. Pickering. *Abused No More: Recovery for Women from Abusive Co-Dependent Alcoholic Relationships*. Blue Ridge Summit, Pa.: Human Services Institute/TAB Books, 1989.

Alsdurf, James, and Phyllis Alsdurf. *Battered into Submission: The Tragedy of Wife Abuse in the Christian Home*. Downers Grove, Ill.: InterVarsity Press, 1989.

Bailey, Abigail Abbott. *Memoirs of Mrs. Abigail Bailey*. Ed. by Ethan Smith. New York: Arno Press, 1980.

————. *Religion and Domestic Violence in Early New England: The Memoirs of Abigail Bailey*. Annotated and introduced by Ann Taves. Bloomington: Indiana University Press, 1989.

Bauschard, Louise, and Mary Kimbrough. *Voices Set Free: Battered Women Speak from Prison*. St. Louis: Women's Self Help Center, 1986.

Beaudry, Micheline. *Battered Women*. Translated by Lorne Huston and Margaret Heap. Buffalo: Black Rose Books, 1985.

Bingham, Carol F., ed. *Doorway to Response: The Role of Clergy in Ministry with Battered Women*. Springfield, Ill.: Interfaith Committee Against Domestic Violence, 1986.

Blixseth, Edra D., and Cheryl Hodgson, eds. *Uncharged Battery*. Portland, Ore.: Portland Entertainment Publications, 1988.

Bochnak, Elizabeth, ed. *Women's Self-Defense Cases: Theory and Practice*. Charlottesville, Va.: Michie Company, 1981.

Borkowski, Margaret, Mervyn Murch, and Val Walker. *Marital Violence: The Community Response*. New York: Tavistock Publications, 1983.

Bowker, Lee H. *Beating Wife-Beating*. Lexington, Mass.: Lexington Books, 1983.

Browne, Angela. *When Battered Women Kill*. New York: Free Press, 1987.

Carr, Brian F., and Joseph Mathews. *Woman Abuse Bibliography*. Monticello, Ill.: Vance Bibliographies. 1979.

Clarke, Rita-Lou. *Pastoral Care of Battered Women*. Philadelphia: Westminster Press, 1986.

Costa, Joseph. *Abuse of Women: Legislation, Reporting, and Prevention*. Lexington, Mass.: Lexington Books, 1983.

Dellacorte, Betty. *Shelter from the Storm: A Personal Story*. Glendale, Ariz.: Villa Press, 1985.

Dickstein, Leah J., and Carol C. Nadelson, eds. *Family Violence: Emerging Issues of a National Crisis*. Washington, D.C.: American Psychiatric Press, 1989.

Dobash, R. Emerson, and Russell Dobash. *Violence Against Women: A Case Against Patriarchy*. New York: Macmillan Co., 1979.

Dutton, Donald G. *The Domestic Assault of Women: Psychological and Criminal Justice Perspectives*. Boston: Allyn & Bacon, 1988.

Ellwood, Garcia F. *Batter My Heart*. Wallingford, Pa.: Pendel Hill Publications, 1988.

Englund, Steven. *Man Slaughter*. Garden City, N.Y.: Doubleday & Co., 1983.

Ewing, Charles P. *Battered Women Who Kill: Psychological Self-Defense as Legal Justification*. Lexington, Mass.: Lexington Books, 1987.

Fedders, Charlotte, and Laura Elliott. *Shattered Dreams: The Story of Charlotte Fedders*. New York: Harper & Row, 1987.

Finkelhor, David, et al., eds. *The Dark Side of Families: Current Family Violence Research*. Beverly Hills, Calif.: Sage Publications, 1983.

Fortune, Marie M. *Keeping the Faith: Questions and Answers For the Abused Woman*. San Francisco: Harper & Row, 1987.

Frank, Jan. *A Door of Hope*. San Bernardino, Calif.: Here's Life Publishers, 1987.

Gelles, Richard J., and Claire P. Cornell. *Intimate Violence in Families*. Beverly Hills, Calif.: Sage Publications, 1985.

Gillespie, Cynthia K. *Justifiable Homicide: Battered Women, Self-Defense, and the Law*. Columbus: Ohio State University Press, 1989.

Gondolf, Edward W. *Man Against Woman: What Every Woman Should Know about Violent Men*. Bradenton, Fla.: Human Services Institute, 1989.

Gondolf, Edward W. with Ellen R. Fisher. *Battered Women As Survivors: An Alternative to Treating Learned Helplessness*. Lexington, Mass.: Lexington Books, 1988.

Green, Holly W. *Turning Fear to Hope: Help for Marriages Troubled by Abuse*. Nashville: T. Nelson Publishers, 1984.

——. *Turning Fear to Hope: Women Who Have Been Hurt for Love*. Grand Rapids: Pyranee Books, 1989.

Gintz, Joy. *Victim/Survivor of Domestic Violence*. Tiffin, Oh.: Sagger Print, 1985.

Grudko, Susan J., and Ellen Boylan. *Domestic Violence: A Guide to the Legal Rights of Battered Women in New Jersey*. New Brunswick: Legal Services of New Jersey, 1986.

Hartik, Lorraine M. *Identification of Personality Characteristics and Self-Concept Factors of Battered Wives*. Palo Alto, Calif.: R & E Research Associates, 1982.

Hintz, Joy. *Victim/Survivor of Domestic Violence*. Tiffin: Sayger Print, 1985.

Hofeller, Kathleen H. *Battered Women, Shattered Lives*. Palo Alto, Calif.: R & E Research Associates, 1983.

Horton, Anne L., and Judith A. Williamson, eds. *Abuse and Religion: When Praying Isn't Enough*. Lexington, Mass.: Lexington Books, 1988.

Johann, Sara L., and Frank Osanka, eds. *Representing Battered Women Who Kill*. Springfield, Ill.: Charles C. Thomas, 1989.

Johnson, Norman, ed. *Marital Violence*. Boston: Routledge & Kegan Paul, 1985.

Jonathon, Janet. *He Hits! Hope for Battered Women*. Wilson, N.C.: Star Books, 1989.

Jones, Ann. *Everyday Death: The Case of Bernadette Powell*. New York: Holt, Rinehart & Winston, 1985.

Jordon, Merna. *Physical Violence Against Women in Barbados, 1977–1985*. Barbados: Bureau of Women's Affairs, 1986.

Kennedy, Jan. *Touch of Silence: A Healing from the Heart*. San Diego: Cosmoenergetics Publications, 1989.

Kilgore, Nancy. *Every Eighteen Seconds: A Personal Injury into Domestic Violence*. Eugene, Ore.: L.I.F.T. Press, 1983.

Leehan, James. *Pastoral Care for Survivors of Family Abuse*. Louisville: Westminster/John Knox Press, 1989.

Loving, Nancy. *Spouse Abuse: A Curriculum Guide for Police Trainers*. Washington, D.C.: Police Executive Research Forum, 1981.

McNulty, Faith. *The Burning Bed*. New York: Harcourt Brace Jovanovich, 1980.

Maguire, Patricia. *Doing Participatory Research: A Feminist Approach*. Amherst: Center for International Education, University of Massachusetts, 1987.

Mains, Karen B. *Abuse in the Family*. Elgin, Ill.: David C. Cook Publishing Co., 1987.

Martin, Del. *Battered Wives*. San Francisco: Volcano Press, 1981.

Monfalcone, Wesley R. *Coping with Abuse in the Family*. Philadelphia: Westminster Press, 1980.

Neidig, Peter H., and Dale H. Friedman. *Spouse Abuse: A Treatment Program for Couples*. Champaign, Ill.: Research Press Company, 1984.

NiCarthy, Ginny. *Getting Free: A Handbook for Women in Abusive Relationships*. Seattle: Seal Press, 1986.

————. *The Ones Who Got Away: Women Who Left Abusive Partners.* Seattle: Seal Press, 1987.

————, and Sue Davidson. *You Can Be Free: An Easy-to-Read Handbook for Abused Women.* Seattle: Seal Press, 1989.

————, Karen Merriam, and Sandra Coffman. *Talking It Out: A Guide to Groups for Abused Women.* Seattle: Seal Press, 1984.

Olson, Esther Lee, with Kenneth Perterson. *No Place to Hide, Wife Abuse: Anatomy of a Private Crime.* Wheaton, Ill.: Tyndale Press, 1983.

Pagelow, Mildred D. *Woman-Battering: Victims and Their Experiences.* Beverly Hills, Calif.: Sage Publications, 1981.

Pahl, Jan M. *A Refuge for Battered Women: A Study of the Role of a Women's Centre.* London: Her Majesty's Stationery Office, 1978.

————, ed. *Private Violence and Public Policy: The Needs of Battered Women and the Response of Public Services.* Boston: Routledge & Kegan Paul, 1985.

Pascoe, Peggy. *Woman's Work for Woman: The Search for Female Moral Authority in the American West, 1874–1939.* New York: Oxford University Press, 1989.

Pellauer, Mary D., Barbara Chester, and Jane A. Boyajian, eds. *Sexual Assault and Abuse: A Handbook for Clergy and Religious Professionals.* San Francisco: Harper & Row, 1987.

Porterfield, Kay M. *Violent Voices: Twelve Steps to Freedom from Emotional Abuse.* Deerfield Beach, Fla.: Health Communications, 1989.

Pressman, Barbara M., Gary Cameron, and M. A. Rothery, eds. *Intervening with Assaulted Women: Current Theory, Research, and Practice.* Hillsdale, N.J.: Erlbaum, 1989.

Reidman, Larry. *Battered Women and the New Hampshire Justice System: A Consultation.* Washington, D.C.: U.S. Commission on Civil Rights, 1980.

Roberts, Albert R., ed. *Battered Women and Their Families: Intervention Strategies and Treatment Programs.* New York: Springer Publishing, 1984.

Roberts, Albert R., with Beverly J. Roberts. *Sheltering Battered Women: A National Study and Service Guide.* New York: Springer Publishing, 1981.

Rouse, Linda P. *You Are Not Alone: A Guide for Battered Women.* Holmes Beach, Fla.: Learning Publications, 1986.

Roy, Maria. *Children in the Crossfire: Violence in the Home—How Does It Affect Our Children?* Deerfield Beach, Fla.: Health Communications, 1988.

Roy, Marcia, ed. *Battered Women: A Psychological Study of Domestic Violence.* New York: Van Nostrand Reinhold, 1977.

Savina, Lydia. *Help for the Battered Woman.* South Plainfield, N.J.: Bridge Publishing, 1987.

Scarf, Mimi. *Battered Jewish Wives: Case Studies in the Response to Rage.* Lewiston, N.Y.: Edwin Mellen Press, 1988.

Schechter, Susan. *Women and Male Violence: The Visions and Struggles of the Battered Women's Movement.* Boston: South End Press, 1982.

Schulman, Mark A. *A Survey of Spousal Violence Against Women in Kentucky: Conducted for the Kentucky Commission on Women.* New York: Garland Publications, 1981.

Scott, Catherine L. *Lovestruck*. Denver: Accent Books, 1988.

Silverman, Phylis R. *Helping Women Cope with Grief*. Beverly Hills, Calif.: Sage Publications, 1981.

Sinclair, Deborah. *Understanding Wife Assault: A Training Manual for Counselors and Advocates*. Toronto: Ontario Government Bookstore, 1985.

Sonkin, Daniel J. *Domestic Violence on Trial: Psychological and Legal Dimensions of Family Violence*. New York: Springer Publishing, 1987.

Stark, Evan. *Wife Abuse in the Medical Setting: An Introduction for Health Personnel*. Rockville, Md.: Clearinghouse on Domestic Violence, Yale Trauma Program, Yale University, 1981.

Strom, Marshall. *In the Name of Submission: A Painful Look at Wife Battering*. Portland, Ore.: Multonamah Press, 1986.

Suttor, Cathy A., and Howard Green. *A Christian Response to Domestic Violence: A Reconciliation Model for Social Workers*. St. Davids, Pa.: North American Association of Christians in Social Work, 1985.

Switzer, M'Liss, and Katherine Hale. *Called to Account: The Story of One Family's Struggle to Say No to Abuse*. Seattle: Seal Press, 1987.

Talbert, Marc. *The Paper Knife*. New York: Dial Books for Young Readers, 1988.

Teske, Raymond H. C., and Mary L. Parker. *Spouse Abuse in Texas: A Study of Women's Attitudes and Experiences*. Huntsville, Tex.: Survey Research Program, Criminal Justice Center, Sam Houston University, 1983.

Turner, Janine. *A Crying Game: The Diary of a Battered Wife*. Edinburgh, Scotland: Mainstream Publications, 1984.

Walker, Lenore E. *The Battered Woman*. New York: Harper & Row, 1979.

———. *The Battered Woman Syndrome*. New York: Springer Publishing, 1984.

———. *Terrifying Love: Why Battered Women Kill and How Society Responds*. New York: Harper & Row, 1989.

Warner, G. Richard Braen, and Carmen Germaine Warner, eds. *Management of the Physically and Emotionally Abused: Emergency Assessment, Intervention, and Counseling*. Norwalk, Conn.: Appleton-Century-Crofts, 1982.

Wohl, Agnes, and Bobbie Kaufman. *Silent Screams and Hidden Cries: An Interpretation of Artwork by Children from Violent Homes*. New York: Brunner/ Mazel (Coalition for Abused Women), 1985.

Zambrano, Myrna M. *Mejor Sola Que Mal Acompanada: Para La Mujer Golpeada (For the Latina in an Abusive Relationship)*. Seattle: Seal Press, 1985.

JOURNALS

Anderson, G. "Battered Women (letter)." *American Family Physician* 37 (April 1988):55.

Bassuk, E. L., and L. Rosenburg. "Why Does Family Homelessness Occur? A Case-Control Study." *American Journal of Public Health* 78 (July 1988):783–89.

Benton, D. A. "Battered Women: Why Do They Stay?" *Health Care for Women International* 7 (1986):403–11.

Bergman, B. K., "Battered Women: Their Susceptibility to Treatment." *Scandinavian Journal of Social Medicine* 16 (1989):155–60.

———. "Psychiatric Morbidity and Personality Characteristics of Battered Women." *ACTA Psychiatric Scandinavica* 76 (December 1987):678–93.

———, et al. "Aetiological and Precipitating Factors in Wife Battering: A Psychological Study of Battered Wives." *ACTA Psychiatric Scandinavica* 77 (March 1988):338–45.

Bowker, L. H., and L. Maurer. "The Medical Treatment of Battered Wives." *Women and Health* 12 (1987):25–45.

Bradley, D. "Battered Women: An Important Nursing Issue." *Imprint* 33 (Sept.–Oct. 1986):24–25.

Brismar, B., et al. "A Battered Woman: A Diagnostic and Therapeutic Dilemma." *ACTA Chirurgia Scandinavica: Supplementum* 153 (January 1987): 1–5.

Bullock, L., et al. "The Prevalence and Characteristics of Battered Women in a Primary Care Setting." *Nurse Practitioner* 14 (June 1989):47, 50, 53–56.

Campbell, J. C. "Nursing Assessment for Risk of Homicide with Battered Women." *ANS Advances in Nursing Science* 8 (July 1986):36–51.

———. "A Survivor Group for Battered Women." *ANS Advances in Nursing Science* 8 (January 1986):13–20.

———. "A Test of Two Explanatory Models of Women's Responses to Battering." *Nursing Research* 38 (Jan.–Feb. 1989):18–24.

Christiano, M. R., et al. "Battered Women: A Concern for the Medical Profession." *Connecticut Medicine* 50 (February 1986):99–103.

Epstein, S. R., G. Russell, and L. Silvern. "Structure and Ideology of Shelters for Battered Women." *American Journal of Community Psychology* 16 (June 1988):345–67.

Frazer, M. "Domestic Violence: A Medicolegal Review." *Journal of Forensic Sciences* 31 (October 1986):1409–19.

Gianakos, I. and E. E. Wagner. "Relations Between Hand Test Variables and the Psychological Characteristics and Behaviors of Battered Women." *Journal of Personality Assessment* 51 (Summer 1987):220–27.

Gross, T. P., and M. L. Rosenberg. "Shelters for Battered Women and Their Children: An Under-Recognized Source of Communicable Disease Transmission." *American Journal of Public Health* 77 (September 1987):1198–1201.

Grusznski, R. J., J. C. Brink, and J. L. Edleson. "Support and Education Groups for Children of Battered Women." *Child Welfare* 67 (Sept.–Oct. 1989):431–44.

Hartman, D. "Battered Women: The Fight You Can Help Them Win." *Nursing Life* 7 (Sept.–Oct. 1987):36–39.

Helton, A. S., M. McFarlane, and E. T. Anderson. "Battered and Pregnant: A Prevalence Study." *American Journal of Public Health* 77 (October 1987):1337–39.

Hughes, H. M. "Psychological and Behavioral Correlates of Family Violence in Child Witnesses and Victims." *American Journal of Orthopsychiatry* 58 (January 1988):77–90.

Jaffee, P., et al. "Emotional and Physical Health Problems of Battered Women." *Canadian Journal of Psychiatry* 31 (October 1986):625–29.

McCleer, S. V. "The Role of the Emergency Physician in the Prevention of Domestic Violence." *Annals of Emergency Medicine* 16 (October 1987): 1155–61.

McCleer, S. V., and R. A. Anwar. "A Study of Battered Women Presenting in an Emergency Department." *American Journal of Public Health* 79 (January 1989):65–66.

McCleer, S. V., et al. "Education Is Not Enough: A Systems Failure in Protecting Battered Women." *Annals of Emergency Medicine* 18 (June 1989):651–53.

Mehta, P. and L. A. Dandrea. "The Battered Woman." *American Family Physician* 18 (June 1989):651–53.

Moehling, K. S. "Battered Women and Abusive Partners: Treatment Issues and Strategies." *Journal of Psychosocial Nursing and Mental Health Services* 26 (September 1983):8–11, 15–17.

Ryback, R. F., and E. L. Bassuk. "Homeless Battered Women and Their Shelter Network." *New Directions of Mental Health Series* 30 (June 1986):55–61.

Stark, E., and A. H. Flitcraft. "Women and Children at Risk: A Feminist Perspective on Child Abuse." *International Journal of Health Services* 18 (1988):97–118.

Stern, P. M. "Students Aid Battered Women." *Journals of American Women's Association* 43 (March–April 1988):44, 58.

Smith, L. S. "Battered Women: The Nurse's Role." *Nurse* 2 (Sept.–Oct. 1987):21–24.

Tilden, V. P. "Increasing the Rate of Identification of Battered Women in an Emergency Department: Use of Nursing Protocol." *Research In Nursing and Health* 10 (August 1987):209–15.

Tilden, V. P., and P. Shepherd. "Battered Women: The Shadow Side of Families." *Holistic Nursing Practice* 1 (February 1987):25–32.

Walker, L. E. "Psychology and Violence Against Women." *American Psychologist* 44 (April 1989):695–702.

Wolfe, D. A., et al. "Child Witnesses to Violence Between Parents: Critical Issues in Behavioral and Social Adjustment." *Journal of Abnormal Child Psychology* 14 (March 1986):95–104.

NOTES

1. R. Emerson Dobash and Russell Dobash, *Violence Against Wives: A Case Against Patriarchy* (New York: Free Press, 1979), 7. The "Pastoral Care Provider" denotes clergy and church members or parishioners.

2. According to Joel Garner and Elizabeth Clemmer, "Danger to Police and Domestic Disturbance: A New Look," in *Research in Brief* (Washington, D.C.: U.S. Department of Justice, 1986), recent research has found that domestic violence is not the primary source of bodily harm or death to police officers.

3. Holly Wagner Green, *Turning Fear to Hope: Help for Marriages Troubled by Abuse* (Nashville: T. Nelson Publishers, 1984), xi.

4. Ibid.

5. Ibid.

6. The purpose of the National Coalition Against Domestic Violence (NCADV) is threefold: (1) NCADV is the key lobbyist in the U.S. Congress that focuses on the issue of violence against women; (2) it is the national organization that networks with local shelters for battered women; and (3) its purpose is to empower women in general and battered women in particular.

7. Patrick A. Langan and Christopher A. Innes, *Bureau of Justice Statistics Special Report*, "Preventing Domestic Violence Against Women," U.S. Dept. of Justice, August 1986.

8. *Uniform Crime Reports for the United States, 1987* (Washington, D.C.: Federal Bureau of Investigation, 1988), 11.

9. United States Surgeon General, 1984.

10. *Marital Rape Exemption* (New York: National Center on Women and Family Law, 1987).

11. Stark, Evan, and Anne Flitcraft, "Medical Therapy as Repression: The Case of the Battered Woman." *Health and Medicine* (Summer/Fall 1982).

12. Lenore E. Walker, *The Battered Woman* (New York: Harper & Row, 1979), 45–51.

13. Ibid., 47.

14. Ibid.

15. Ibid., 56–59.

16. Ibid.

17. Ibid., 56.

18. Ibid., 59–65.

19. Ibid.

20. Ibid., 60.

21. Ibid.

22. Ibid., 65–70.

23. Ibid., 65–66.

24. Ibid., 67.

25. Ibid., 68–69.

26. Ibid., 32–33.

27. Ibid., 33–34.

28. Ibid., 33.

29. Ibid., 48.

30. Ibid.

31. Rita-Lou Clarke, *Pastoral Care of Battered Women* (Philadelphia: Westminster Press, 1986), 62.

32. Ibid., 77–78.

33. Ibid., 74–77.

34. Ibid.

35. Dobash and Dobash, *Violence Against Wives*, 7.

36. Ibid., 7–8.

37. In a telephone interview on 25 August 1989, Barbara Davidson, educational resource person with the Louisiana Coalition Against Domestic Violence (P.O. Box 2133, Baton Rouge, LA, (504) 389-3001) noted that through an informal survey with a group of battered women in Baton Rouge, she found that battered women were often reluctant to confide in their male pastors because of their feelings of guilt and shame, and because they assumed that the clergymen would identify with their husbands. She also noted that the women indicated that their husbands often forced them to stop attending church and thus isolated them from outside help.

CHAPTER 7

Women's Depression: Lives at Risk

CHRISTIE COZAD NEUGER

. . . .

Becky came to pastoral counseling wondering why she kept ending up in dead-end jobs. She had no energy for herself, her friends, or her work. She was having trouble sleeping but could not seem to get up in the mornings. She often seemed to be lost deep inside herself. She could not eat. She could not concentrate. She did not know how she could go on feeling this way.

Mary had always wanted to be a clergywoman. Unfortunately, she had run into roadblock after roadblock in her conservative denomination. The latest had been a referral to pastoral counseling so that "she might find and come to terms with her true vocation." Mary no longer knew what "true" was, and she felt abandoned by the very God who had called her into service. She felt that she had no direction for her life.

Carol was both angry and hopeless when she walked into the pastor's office. She'd had another argument with her husband, and it had again ended with him beating her. She was bruised in spirit and body. She wondered why God was letting this happen to her. She went to church. She was faithful to her husband, even though when he was home he was angry and when he was out he was drinking. She had kept hoping that her life would turn around or that she would find out how to make things better. However, her hope had run out, and she was desperate.

An Epidemic

All of these women are depressed. Yet each has different life circumstances and different kinds of feelings, thoughts, and behaviors, and each of them sought help from a pastor. They all knew that their depression affected their lives at the deepest psychological, social, and spiritual levels. Pastors must be prepared to hear the stories of depressed women at these complex and profound depths because depression, in its various forms and contexts, is one of the most common problems brought to pastoral counseling.

Depression is a very broad term for experiences that range from a passing bad mood to a chronic withdrawal from reality. What really constitutes depression has generated considerable debate and no firm agreement on what causes it or how best to care for those suffering with it. What is clear is that various forms of depression are very common in the general population, that women suffer from depression in particularly high numbers, and that depression is a seriously debilitating psychospiritual condition that takes a great toll on the lives of those who suffer with it.

Depression exists in a startlingly high percentage of the population. In the 1978 Midtown Manhattan Study, 23.6 percent of the surveyed group had symptoms of depression.[1] According to Robert Hirschfeld of the National Institute of Mental Health, approximately one in five Americans have at least moderate depressive symptoms.[2] When *depression* is defined in more clinical terms, counting only those people who seek treatment because of their depression, the numbers are still as high as one depressed person out of every ten Americans.[3]

These numbers suggest that depression is at epidemic proportions in our culture. The occurrence of depression in women is even more disturbing. Figures differ depending on the studies and surveys, but at a minimum twice as many women are depressed as men, and the numbers range as high as six times as many women. The lower figure means we are talking about as many as 26 million women who struggle with feelings of depression at some point in their lives; more than one out of four women experience at least mild depression. Myrna Weissman of the Yale University Hospital Depression Unit suggests that the numbers of depressed women have been steadily rising in the past decade.[4] If you ask any psychotherapist or counselor who they see most often in counseling, the answer will more than likely be "depressed women."

Approaches To Depression

Why are more women than men depressed, and why is women's depression at an epidemic level? The statistics themselves have been questioned along the line of reasoning that statistical bias occurs in reporting and gathering data and that depression labels are used more frequently for women than for men. Although both statistical problems exist, the consensus is that many more women than men are depressed. Consequently, other theories try to explain this high level of depression in women. Some theories emphasize potential chemical imbalances and hormonal variations in women. In other theories the focus is on sex roles that leave women with few options for building self-esteem and a sense of competency. Yet other theories accent sociocultural differences for women and men, such as the fact that women are taught to have higher dependency needs and are more vulnerable to depression when they lose important relationships. Finally, some theories of women's depression are built around the idea that living in patriarchy is more stressful and damaging to women than to men.

Representative theories.   Traditional psychological approaches have seen depression in a variety of ways. Psychoanalytic theory has understood depression primarily in terms of intrapsychic loss, suggesting that the young child experiences significant loss when she realizes that the parent is not the perfect need-meeting person. This loss creates rage in the child that must be suppressed in order to avoid risking total rejection by the parent. Consequently, the child turns the anger against herself, and this sets the stage for depression. Later losses trigger this depressive rage, and depression is the result. Loss of self-esteem and rage turned inward are the major ingredients of depression. Interestingly, Freud noted that it was "the good, capable, conscientious woman who is more likely to become depressed."[5] Freud, however, did not go on to make the connection between society's pressured definition of the "good" woman and her vulnerability to depression. This missing link is key.

Psychoanalytic theory is still influential today in thinking about depression, and it has been expanded by ego psychology, object-relations thought, and feminist theory. The difficulty with psychoanalytic interpretations of depression (along with the consequent therapeutic approach) is that the link between a culture that is oppressive to women and women's vulnerability to depression is often missing. In addition, environmental stressors are often not adequately considered. Without these connections, depression becomes something that exists in women's psyches alone. The depressogenic nature of the culture for women is not fully appreciated.[6] The male-defined norms of health and pathology are not critiqued. Moreover, environmental realities are often not addressed. Therefore, a traditional psychoanalytic treatment for depression is generally inadequate by itself.

Another major approach to depression is that of the cognitive-behavioral theorists. This theory suggests that depression is a learned response to a frustrating or negative environment. Depressed people generally have a set of "negative cognitions," which one writer calls "self-critical tapes."[7] Cognitive theory suggests that depression occurs, in large measure, because people have learned to interpret situations through a negative lens and consequently have bad feelings about themselves. Living in a culture that sends many negative messages to them, women tend to internalize these negative messages and interpret life situations through them. Counselors who use cognitive-behavioral theory to understand depression attempt to help women acknowledge the self-interpretive process by teaching them to pay attention to their negative thoughts. Women are then taught to stop those negative thoughts and use a more neutral set of thoughts to interpret events. This process strengthens self-esteem and lessens the depression.

Recent research has shown cognitive therapy to be useful with depressed women. Training in assertiveness, negative thought stopping, and feeling assessment in light of distorted thinking are all part of the therapeutic process. Research has demonstrated that depressed people tend to think pessimistically, to have low self-esteem, to expect the worst in any situation, and to blame themselves for trouble. Because self-image and self-interpretation are generally distorted in women through their life development within a sexist culture, learning to challenge that distorted thinking can help. The limits here again include the fact that changing one's thinking does not change an environment that continues to send negative messages to women. Also, the depressogenic realities in women's lives cannot be changed by revising their thinking patterns.

A third influential theory is the biochemical approach to depression. This theory suggests that depression is the result of chemical changes within the body that create depressed feelings and behaviors. These biochemical difficulties often are the result of a genetic predisposition. The treatment of depression in this model is chemical in nature, generally the prescription of antidepressant medication. Treatment might also include other biological approaches such as electroconvulsive therapy or psychosurgery. Some types of depression do seem to be biochemical in origin and can be greatly helped through medication, although in some cases knowing which came first—the chemical imbalance or the environmentally caused depression—can be difficult. However, most depression does not seem to be biochemical or helped by biological treatment. Theorists who work from a women's perspective are, on the whole, very cautious about biological approaches as the history of mental health reveals a tendency to overmedicate women as a response to their "illnesses" or distresses.

Another theoretical approach to depression is through the lens of family systems theory. The emphasis in systems theory is on the role depression plays in the overall family system. In other words, how does this depression in one family member fit the rules and roles of the overall family system? This way of looking at the depression in a larger context can be valuable, and it may open up some issues that help to rebalance the family and reduce the kinds of stress that keep the depression in place. Nevertheless, one significant difficulty with family systems theory in relation to depression in women is that systems therapists tend to see the family roles as equal in power and to ignore the fact that women have significantly less power in terms of cultural value, economic independence, vulnerability to physical abuse, and so on. Rachel Hare-Mustin, in addressing this tendency to ignore the reality of power differences among family members, suggests that "by ignoring gender differences, the therapist supports them."[8]

The human potential school of thought emphasizes growth and self-actualization. This humanistic model lends itself to a nonsexist approach because it advocates the power within every individual to grow and change and the right of every person to a full and valuable life. Humanistic counselors have worked to empower women and men to determine their own lives and not to give their power away to oppressive situations. This concept is central for women. The human potential perspective has its limits, however, as it puts the responsibility for transcending depression within the women herself and does not make the link between a society that has the power to oppress women and women's own self-empowerment. Because this model has been an important influence in the pastoral counseling movement, pastoral caregivers must not overlook this flaw in humanistic counseling. It perpetuates the myth that depression is a problem of individual pathology.

Each of these theoretical approaches to the problem of depression in women has value. However, without a thorough critique from the standpoint of women's lives in a patriarchal culture, that value is distorted and lost. Pastors must be able to integrate a feminist critique, with its theological, psychological, and sociological implications, into their counseling perspectives.[9]

Developing nonsexist and feminist approaches.   A pastor who takes these critiques of the standard approaches to depression in women (and men) seriously must then find ways to use these therapeutic perspectives to provide as much healing as possible and, at the very least, to do no harm. A nonsexist or feminist approach is essential in counseling with depressed women.

A nonsexist approach to counseling recognizes the injustice of sexism. Counselors work to help women and men develop themselves in self-actualizing ways, regardless of sex role stereotypes. The focus is on the individual in that each woman or man is seen as having the right to her or his own personal fulfillment and the right to become whomever God is calling her or him to be.

A feminist approach concentrates more on the need for women to understand their own lives in the context of cultural sexism, with the recognition that health and wholeness can happen only when women and men work to change the injustices of patriarchy. Power dynamics in relationships, in families, and in institutions are taken as seriously as various psychological symptoms.

In 1975 an American Psychological Association survey identified five areas in which counselors operated with sexist implications and consequences. Cecelia Foxley identifies these as: (1) fostering traditional sex roles with women, (2) having lower expectations for women clients, (3) using psychoanalytic concepts in sexist ways, (4) viewing women as sex objects, and (5) sexually exploiting or harassing female clients.[10] According to recent studies, therapists have begun to take these cautions more seriously, especially in terms of breaking down sex role stereotypes. However, these five areas of sexist practice are still operating in many counseling offices.

The theoretical overview and critique just offered may be helpful to pastoral caregivers as they develop their own approaches to counseling depressed women. In order to operate as nonsexist counselors, we must avoid theory that does not take seriously women's experience or that in any way denies women's full worth. As most psychologies of women have been developed out of a male experience and often with male norms and subjects, we have to bring a thorough critique to every psychological theory we explore. All counseling must be done with a sense of suspicion as to our own collusion with the culture's pervasive sexism.

Many people concerned with depression in women feel that nonsexist counseling does not go far enough toward helping women move beyond depression. Feminist approaches see depression primarily as an attempted adaptive reaction to a destructive culture. Miriam Greenspan, a feminist psychologist, writes about the prevalence of depression in the lives of women and surveys the various approaches that have been used to counsel with women who are depressed. She concludes that survey with a suggestion that "one reason why none of these methods works very well is that they all fail to get at the underlying cause of most women's chronic depression: an abiding, unconscious rage at our own oppression which has found no legitimate outlet."[11] Her statement represents a widespread feeling among feminist therapists who work with depressed women. Women and men live in a culture that is powerfully depressogenic for women, and any counseling that is to be effective must pay attention to this cultural reality. The counseling must help the woman identify, claim, and value her own story while it also helps her find ways to live in and change the culture that has set the context for her depression.

Causes of Depression

Because much of the research on women's depression hinges on the importance of the larger environment, we ought to look at some of the cultural causes that women theorists name as being responsible for depression. Miriam Greenspan, after listing typical symptoms, writes, "The obvious reality is that in a woman-hating culture it is normal for women to hate themselves. Depression is, for one thing, a survival strategy adopted by women in a society that devalues women while demanding and idolizing femininity."[12] These words are powerful. She and others who focus on the effects of patriarchy realize that the culture has been and continues to be damaging to women.

Abuse.   As the last chapter indicated, attacks by husbands on wives result in more injuries requiring medical treatment than rapes, muggings, and automobile accidents combined. One third of all women slain are killed by their husbands or boyfriends.[13] Approximately 50 percent of all women experience violence in their marriages. Current statistics suggest that somewhere between 2 and 6 million women in the United States are battered annually. Studies show that between 15 and 30 percent of all American women are victims of incest. Approximately 750,000 women are raped yearly in the United States. Statistics about women and violence validate those who call the culture "woman-hating" and depressogenic.

Economics.   According to the 1983 World Health Organization Report, two thirds of the world's work is done by women, but they receive only a tenth of the world's income. The report also says that two thirds of the world's poor adults are women.[14] A 1980 article in the *Boston Globe* reported that women are increasingly segregated into lower-paying jobs; 78 percent of women who work do the lowest-paying work.[15] In 1987 women earned sixty-nine cents for every male dollar earned.

Education.   Children's books often still feature men who achieve and women who are passive and get rescued. In various studies, boy-focused stories outnumbered girl-focused stories five to two. Male biographies outnumber female biographies six to one. The androcentric bias is pervasive; language and imagery still tend to be male focused; women are still often excluded from history. The bias is even more extreme for women of color.[16] This trend has been changing significantly over the past five to ten years, especially in the secular literature. In addition, important work, especially by feminist theorists and theologians, has begun to rename women's experiences and reclaim women's roles in history. These changes are crucial in combating the stereotypical images of women and men.

Self-esteem.   Strong links have been made between self-esteem and depression. The statistics discussed here just give a beginning feel to the systematic attack on women's self-esteem from the time of infancy through adulthood. Mary Ellen Donovan and Linda Tschirhart Sanford's extensive study on women and self-esteem concludes that

1. Low self-esteem is primarily the result of being female in a male-dominated culture.
2. Low self-esteem is at the root of many of the psychological problems that women experience, and attempts to cure these problems without addressing the causes of low self-esteem lead to other problems.
3. Low self-esteem and the resultant psychological problems continue the problem because women are easier to "keep in their place" when they are depressed and feeling powerless.
4. Women must develop self-esteem as individuals and as a group in order to be able to challenge the oppressive status quo.[17]

Spirituality and Depression

Low self-esteem is at the heart of most depression, and the cultural messages of patriarchy are damaging to self-esteem in women. What happens to women's spiritual health? Depression is a psychospiritual problem. Are our faith lives a resource or a curse in terms of women's vulnerability to depression?

Religion.   As pastors we must look at our theological resources with as much clarity and honesty as we look at our psychological and sociological resources. Like the culture in general, religion has also tended to perpetuate low (spiritual) self-esteem in women. Through religion, we raise and explore the fundamental questions about our lives. We try to understand the purposes of our lives, our relationship with God and with creation, the meaning of our vocations, and who we are at our deepest levels. As religious people, our spiritual inquiries are at the heart of our search for meaning.

Theology.   Women have not fared well for the most part in traditional theology. They have been seen as the cause of all evil in the world through the story of Eve's role in creation. Throughout much of the church's writings, women were held accountable for sin and evil. During the Middle Ages, somewhere between 30,000 and 9 million people were executed as witches (embodiments of evil), and most of them were women. Despite the fact that we do not currently base much of our theology on these aspects of our history, the themes persist and run deeply in our traditions. The sense of being to blame and bearing the shame of that blame is a strong, recurrent theme in depressed women, and much of theology reinforces this theme. (See Nancy J. Ramsay's article for a further discussion of shame.)

Most church doctrine is also strongly embedded in patriarchy. The fatherhood of God as a fixed and determining image for God has kept women from finding validation for themselves in being created in God's image. Not only is the richness of God reduced by limiting God to maleness and fatherhood but also the injustice of a patriarchal culture is theologically reinforced. Men are granted a more "divine" status if God is male and sexism receives religious approval. When God is defined by male values and experience, is named as male, and gives males the right to name, then the "natural order" is defined and established as male. Women in this system are clearly the other, and their experience is not received as being of the divine. Women have consistently been seen as less holy than men in their attempts to live their lives and carry out their spiritual vocations.

In addition, certain beliefs have contributed to women's vulnerability to depression. The doctrine of original sin, which holds women to blame from the moment of birth, and the belief in the godliness of suffering are two beliefs that have been particularly destructive for women. Many women have stayed in an abusive situation out of a sense that it is their "punishment" in life and that somehow their undeserved suffering "saves" them in God's eyes. Moreover, the belief in the pervasive sexual seductiveness of women has been used to hold women as the guilty ones for their own rapes and experiences of incest.

We, as ministers, have to claim our own accountability in these issues and work to bring an appropriate critique of the damaging sexist assumptions in our theological positions. We need to reaffirm God's creative and redeeming presence along with the theme of God's love for all people. God's people have always been called to recognize those who have been oppressed, even in the name of religion, and to empower and bring liberation to them. We need to listen to those who have been hurt by the sexism in our traditions and to renew our theological resources accordingly. In addition, we must help women learn to name their experiences of God and to claim those experiences as holy. Helping women learn to tell their spiritual stories is important. The theological tradition is virtually devoid of images born of women's experience, and as women reach out to name God and the reality of creation, they are also beginning to name themselves. As Mary Daly has said, "In hearing and naming ourselves out of the depths, women are naming toward God which is what theology always should have been about."[18]

Spiritual aliveness is an important component of creative, nondepressed living. The questions that can be answered only in dialogue with God's power and presence still lie at the heart of every life. The reality of the living God, not the idolatrous God of our own patriarchal past (a fiction), must be the presence we mediate in our pastoral counseling with depressed women. With the power of God's spirit, we can find ways to know God, ourselves, and one another through stories and images that enhance, rather than damage, spiritual self-esteem. The church, despite its embeddedness in patriarchy, has often been a place of healing, refuge, and empowerment for women. It has served as a place of leadership and community. The power of God's spirit to empower, even in the midst of oppression, is a clear beacon of hope. The church and its representatives must work to dismantle patriarchy and to bring justice and wholeness to the women and men in its midst.

The Counselor's Assessment

The pastoral caregiver has to understand the psychological, social, and theological dynamics of patriarchy in working with women who are depressed. Putting the depression in the context of these sociocultural realities changes the counseling agenda. However, we must also understand how depression develops, its symptoms, and the possible avenues of care.

Defining *depression* is a difficult task. It can be seen as a chemical imbalance, distorted negative thinking, the loss of a love object and the consequent internalized rage, a response to the needs of a family system, or an attempt to live within and adjust to an oppressive environment. As long as all of these understandings are tested by the reality of women's lives in this culture, they can be helpful perspectives through which to explore a woman's experience of depression.

Depression has been likened to a gray fog, to numbness, to waves of sadness, to a hopeless and helpless vision of the future, to a black hole, and so on. The primary characteristics of depression combine to create these powerful images. Those common depressive symptoms include a sense of being slowed down; fatigue; sad feelings or sometimes a numbness of feeling; inability to concentrate; sleep disturbances; a sense of tiredness and weakness; digestive difficulties; a lack of enjoyment in things that once brought pleasure; a loss of interest in sexual activity; a sense of loss, guilt, self-blame, pessimism, and hopelessness; a tendency toward indecision; negative thinking; and a sense of helplessness about feeling differently. These symptoms may be mild or intense or somewhere between. The more intense the symptoms, the more likely are striking physical symptoms like a complete loss of appetite (anorexia), insomnia (or sometimes a need for constant sleep), general retardation of motor functions, loss of ability to think clearly, and a change in the rhythm of the depression, with the worst time being the morning and a gradual improvement throughout the day. With more intense symptoms, a biological problem is more likely, and medication may be needed. More serious characteristics generally indicate the need for referral to a psychiatrist who is trained in women's psychology and depression.

Three types of depression.   Depression can be categorized in many ways. The psychiatric manuals of diagnosis tend to see three distinct types of depression that are not unrelated to each other.

One type is dysthymia or depressive neurosis. It is the most common type of depression and the one that the pastor will encounter most often. It responds best to counseling and does not generally respond well to medication. It is the kind of depression that we have been talking about throughout most of the chapter.

A second type is major depression. It includes unipolar (or recurrent) depression and tends to be more serious, with the more intense symptoms or characteristics. What is most obvious about major depression is the significant slowing down of motor activities—of talking, of physical processes, and of thinking. This type of depression also needs the kind of empowerment counseling that we have been talking about, but the woman may also be a high suicide risk and may need medication to help address the debilitating physical symptoms. She should be referred for consultation with a psychiatrist. Anyone who comes to counseling with depression symptoms ought to have a physical examination. Some illnesses mimic symptoms of depression.

A third type of depression is characterized by swings in mood. The mild kind of bipolar disorder is called *cyclothymia* and often does not need medication. A person who comes for counseling when she is in the depressed phase may greatly benefit from it. In the manic phase, the woman is at risk for poor impulse control and may come for help with that problem. The more severe form is called *bipolar disorder* and involves swings from serious depressive symptoms to a manic phase characterized by everything being speeded up. In the manic phase, the woman tends to talk fast, make impulsive decisions, spend too much money, and take physical risks. This bipolar disorder seems to be primarily a chemically based, genetically linked problem, and it can often be helped with the drug lithium. However, the diagnosis has to be carefully made before chemical treatment is chosen.

Assessing suicide risk.   Along with assessing the kind of depression a woman has, the pastoral caregiver must assess suicide risk. Most depressed people have had thoughts of suicide. A person who is able to identify stronger reasons not to live than to live is in danger. If she has thought about how she would commit suicide and can tell you her plan, and if she has the means to carry out that plan, you need to consider whether she needs to be in a safe environment. Asking people directly if they are thinking of hurting themselves or if they are thinking about suicide is useful. Often people are relieved to have their feelings spoken out loud. If suicide is a likely option, the person should be referred to a psychiatrist who can facilitate medical supervision or to a psychotherapist trained in working with suicidal situations. Of course, the pastor should make sure that the suicidal person has followed through with the referral. If a psychiatrist or psychotherapist is not available, then the pastoral caregiver ought to go with the depressed person to a hospital emergency room and help her to be admitted and kept safe until she can work through the suicidal danger.

Other signs that would indicate the need for consultation with a specialist in counseling and mental health would be severe withdrawal, depression that continues to get worse, bizarre thoughts or speech, and the kinds of depressive symptoms that cause organic problems like insomnia, anorexia, and retarded thinking. The ethics of caregiving mandate that a counselor seek to avoid harm, maintain confidentiality, maintain the trust of the care receiver, and not work beyond his or her competency. These guidelines are helpful in considering the need to refer.

The Counselor's Action

Most of the depressed people the pastor sees in the counseling office are of the milder type. We may refer to it as a mild depression, but it can create tremendous pain in individual lives. These depressed women need the kind of care that gives them the ability to discover the truth about themselves as valuable people in God's creation. Women need to hear their own stories, and they need to hear other women's stories. The cultural and theological messages of worthlessness and weakness need to be dispelled by the gathering together and telling the truth—of naming the reality of women's lives.

Mary Ballou and Nancy Gabalac propose a process for this kind of counseling—"corrective action."[19] Its purpose is to help undo the damage done by what they call "harmful adaptation" or what we have suggested to be a depressive adjustment to a destructive culture. The purpose of corrective action is to replace the sense of shame and low self-esteem with a more positive sense of self and with accurate information about being a woman in patriarchy. The point is empowerment so that self-esteem is rebuilt and depression is replaced with a sense of power, competency, and support.

Corrective action.   Corrective action consists of five steps, not necessarily in this sequence:

1. A movement toward *separation* of the woman from the pervasive negative messages encourages her to tell her own story to the counselor and to other women. As she tells her own story and hears others' stories, a greater sense of the reality of the world around grows, as does her confidence in her ability to know what is real.
2. In the story-telling process, the counselor works for *validation* of the woman's experience and helps her affirm her strengths, which may have been defined as weaknesses all of her life.
3. *Association* with other women is a crucial part of counseling. Women's groups should be available for women's affiliation and empowerment.
4. *Authorization* is learning to be strong and accountable for oneself. It does not mean falsely independent but rather knowing oneself well enough to have boundaries and still to recognize interdependence.
5. The *negotiation* phase is the testing out, with the ongoing support of counselor and group, of these new behaviors and thoughts in the woman's day-to-day environment.

This model of corrective action offers a helpful vision of the kind of counseling that takes into consideration women's individual depression as well as the impact of the culture in creating the vulnerability to that depression. It is a loose and flowing process that varies from person to person and that names the essential aspects of empowerment for depressed women.

Other feminist counselors suggest similar processes. Miriam Greenspan, for example, feels that both facilitating the story of the counselee and creating support groups of other women are essential ingredients of effective counseling. Joan Laird talks about the centrality of women's story telling because their stories have been denied to them in so many ways. She also talks about the process of co-interpreting stories so that together women find new meanings as the stories are told.

The counseling relationship is the central therapeutic tool for the pastoral caregiver. The caregiver must be willing to nurture and support the counselee as she works to integrate a new understanding of herself and her world and yet to engage in the counseling process with a sense of mutuality and respect.

The pastoral caregiver must help depressed women look at the various dimensions in their lives that contribute to their depression. This help might include family, personal history, work life, economic situation, coping skills in regard to a sense of powerlessness, and spiritual hopes and fears. Despite the fact that the story will include these areas, the caregiver should not "push the process" or try to determine the speed and the structure through which the story will unfold. The counselor's role is, as Nelle Morton so beautifully phrased it, "to hear the woman into speech."[20] The co-interpretation of the story is a secondary process of the telling of it. Moreover, the spiritual life and journey of the woman must be a part of the story telling. At this time, the woman must be encouraged to see her life experiences, including her experiences of God, as being worthy of naming. Despite her lifelong training that her experience is not valuable or even normative, naming and claiming her story in the presence of one who represents God helps to open up a woman to the powerful presence of the Spirit. Spiritual renewal and movement out of the depression may very well be the result of this kind of care. Listening skills and authentic respect for the counselee are the most important gifts that a counselor can give.

In telling the story, many feelings emerge for the counselee, and very frequently the expression of those feelings has been forbidden. The counselor cannot be afraid of the expression of anger and rage, which are essential feelings to uncover in the healing of depression. Catharsis, or expression of the feelings, is not enough in and of itself, but it is a fundamental part of the process.

Finally, the use of imagination is a very useful resource in pastoral counseling with depression. Often women have no vision for how their stories can have new chapters or how new endings can be rewritten. The use of imagination, whether in formal, guided imagery or in the use of images and metaphors that offer powerful new possibilities for creative life, are invaluable in moving beyond depression into hope. Women imaging together create a new future for themselves and new hope for all women. Through the use of imagination, women can reconnect in community with themselves, with one another, and with the Holy Spirit as they seek to be true to God's call to become all that they can be and to be coauthors of God's ongoing creation.

BIBLIOGRAPHY

Anderson, Carol M., and Diane P. Holder. "Women and Serious Mental Disorders." In *Women and Families: A Framework for Family Therapy*, ed. Monica McGoldrick, Carol Anderson, and Froma Walsh. New York: W. W. Norton, 1989.

Ballou, Mary, and Nancy Gabalac. *A Feminist Position on Mental Health*. Springfield, Ill.: Charles C. Thomas, 1985.

Greenspan, Miriam. *A New Approach to Women and Therapy*. New York: McGraw-Hill, 1983.

Guttentag, Susan Salasin, and Deborah Belle, eds. *The Mental Health of Women*. New York: Academic Press, 1980.

Hare-Mustin, Rachel. "The Problem of Gender in Family Therapy Theory." In McGoldrick, Anderson, and Walsh, eds., *Women in Families*.

Holder, Diane, and Carol Anderson. "Women, Work and the Family." In McGoldrick, Anderson, and Walsh, eds., *Women in Families*.

Laird, Joan. "Women and Stories: Restorying Women's Self-Constructions." In McGoldrick, Anderson, and Walsh, eds., *Women in Families*.

Morton, Nelle. *The Journey Is Home*. Boston: Beacon Press, 1985.

Sanford, Linda Tschirhart, and Mary Ellen Donovan. *Women and Self-Esteem*. Baltimore: Penguin Books, 1984.

Scarf, Maggie. "The More Sorrowful Sex." *Psychology Today* 12 (April 1979): 45–52.

Wetzel, Janice Wood. *The Clinical Handbook of Depression*. New York: Gardner Press, 1984.

NOTES

1. Daniel W. Badal, *Treatment of Depression and Related Moods: A Manual for Psychotherapists* (Northvale, N.J.: Jason Aronson, 1988), 23.

2. Maggie Scarf, "The More Sorrowful Sex." *Psychology Today* 12, no. 11 (April 1979):45–52.

3. Badal, *Manual*, 25.

4. Scarf, "The More Sorrowful Sex," 51.

5. Janice Wood Wetzel, *The Clinical Handbook of Depression* (New York: Gardner Press, 1984), 34.

6. The word *depressogenic* refers to circumstances that either set the stage for or actually foster a state of depression.

7. Linda Tschirhart Sanford and Mary Ellen Donovan, *Women and Self-Esteem* (New York: Penguin, 1984), 294.

8. Rachel Hare-Mustin, "The Problem of Gender in Family Therapy Theory," in *Women in Families: A Framework for Family Therapy*, ed. Monica McGoldrick, Carol Anderson, and Froma Walsh (New York: W. W. Norton, 1989), 69.

9. As Mary Ballou and Nancy Gabalac suggest (*A Feminist Position on Mental Health* [Springfield, Ill.: Charles C. Thomas, 1985], 73):

Conventional criteria for mental health . . . are not appropriate. The medical model holds mental health to be the absence of pathology. . . . Defining through absence is not helpful. Significant questions must be raised about the criteria used for pathology. The behavioral orientation of reality therapy and related theories use basic notions of effective behavior and responsible actions as criteria. However, they offer inadequate analysis of the determinants of effective behavior or responsible action, leaving one to again assume conformity to the dominant social norms. Hence, adjustment to dominant social norms is the implicit or explicit notion of mental health within these orientations. Since dominant social norms are in large part determined by power systems, uncritical adjustment to them colludes with the power system and has little to do with mental health.

10. Cecelia Foxley, *Nonsexist Counseling: Helping Women and Men Redefine Their Roles* (Dubuque, Iowa: Kendall/Hunt, 1979), 30.

11. Miriam Greenspan, *A New Approach to Women and Therapy* (New York: McGraw-Hill, 1983), 300.

12. Ibid., 191.

13. Hare-Mustin, "The Problem of Gender," 64.

14. Ballou and Gabalac, *A Feminist Position*, 69.

15. Diane Holder and Carol Anderson, "Women, Work and the Family," in McGoldrick, Anderson, and Walsh, eds., *Women in Families*, 360.

16. Sanford and Donovan, *Women and Self-Esteem*, 180.

17. Ibid., xiv.

18. Mary Daly, "Why Speak About God?" in *WomanSpirit Rising: A Feminist Reader in Religion*, ed. Carol Christ and Judith Plaskow (San Francisco: Harper & Row, 1979), 213.

19. Ballou and Gabalac, *A Feminist Position*, chap. 4.

20. Nelle Morton, *The Journey Is Home* (Boston: Beacon Press, 1985), 24.

CHAPTER 8

Life-styles:
A Culture
in Transition

PRISCILLA L. DENHAM

. . . .

In 1970 the letters *r* and *is* caused a furor by their absence. The letters were the missing parts of the titles *Mrs.* and *Miss.* Instead of these titles, some women began using an alternate title—*Ms.* A culture that loves fast foods and easy solutions to gaps of knowledge should have welcomed the change. It did not. Instead, *Ms.* stirred up anger, dissension, and derision in homes and boardrooms. *Ms.* gave women the option of a title that did not designate marital status. In a culture that had developed a punctuational code to clearly designate a woman's legal relationship to a man (that is, Miss Jane Smith is unmarried; Mrs. Henry Jones is married; and Mrs. Jane Jones is divorced), for a woman to call herself "Ms. Jane Jones" was unsettling. Equally unsettling was a woman using a hyphenated last name, and most unnerving of all was a married woman calling herself "Ms. Jane Smith," just as she had before marriage. *Ms.* was both the vehicle and the symbol for women naming themselves (literally and dynamically) rather than being named by marital status. The idea was really not so radical; it is the same linguistic construct used for men. However, many religious leaders loudly and publicly decried the "new" grammatical construct as an "attack on the American family."

The conflict over women's titles corresponded to other issues of women's presence in the church. Men and women alike began to notice that women could bake communion bread at home but could not stand in the sanctuary to distribute it. Women could teach Sunday school, but these same women could not read Scripture or offer prayer during worship. Women who ran the complex organizations of their homes or businesses were not eligible to be elected deacons or elders. Countless women in the 1970s and 1980s began to feel that to be the women they were becoming, defined and functioning as themselves, was not possible within the church.

We will look briefly at the history of women's role in the church with particular emphasis on U.S. churches. Broad comparisons will be drawn to help us understand the differences between women approaching churches in the 1950s and in the 1980s. Because of changes in the social context, our society now has unprecedented numbers of divorced, never married, widowed, and lesbian women, any of whom may also be single parents. To help us understand what ministry issues may be involved with women who function without male partners, we will focus on five stories that embody dynamics we need to see and discuss salient commonalities. We will examine the practical concern for pastoral care to and with these nontraditional churchwomen and conclude with a reflection on the theological implications of a more inclusive church.

Women in the Church's History

Beginning with the ministry of Jesus Christ, the early church (until the third century) made a startling statement regarding women to the surrounding cultures. In the Gospel accounts, we are sometimes told of a woman's relationship to a man (husband, brother, son, or father) but only when it has significance to the story or is used for identification. Rather, women were defined, not by a man's name or status, but by relationship to Jesus Christ and faithfulness to the church. In Paul's letters to the fledgling churches, he was clear in applauding the work of numerous women (for example, Rom. 16:1-15). Even when he was chastising, Paul addressed the women directly in egalitarian communication. From his assertion of equal desires and rights for husband and wife (1 Cor. 7:2-5) to his prophetic vision that "There is neither male nor female; for you are all one in Christ Jesus" (Gal. 3:28), Paul expressed a recognition and respect for women amazing in its context.[1] Given the social patterns and the Jewish laws that informed the early church, the respect, affirmation, and acknowledgment of women as individuals—significant in their own right as members and leaders—was a powerful message.

During the Middle Ages, being a nun was accepted as a valid "career option" for women who did not choose marriage. Women's religious orders gave women a place and a way to function as independent adults unique for many centuries. The historian Lawrence Stone, however, notes that the growth of Protestantism effected a parallel growth in patriarchy, and women's position (in and out of the church) went into a "Dark Age" all its own. Not only did the Protestant churches have nothing of comparable status and function to a nun but also the domestic religious functions married women had performed under Catholicism were diminished. "In 1528 Luther himself boasted of bringing order, discipline and obedience to his family as well as to society as a whole."[2]

By the time the English colonies were developing, parallel liberalizing social movements were afoot in the American churches. Despite the acceleration of patriarchy in the sixteenth and seventeenth centuries through Protestantism, women again became visible agents in the church. Indeed, churches became a primary arena for women to function outside the home. "Almost from the beginning of settlement in the English colonies, religion and the churches were a special sphere of activity for women."[3] Depending on the denomination, women's acceptance as church teachers and evangelists varied. "Among certain Protestant sects, especially Quakers and Baptists, there were some opportunities for women to be leaders and preachers. The Quakers in particular made few role distinctions between the sexes."[4] Regardless of their official leadership role, the church made a notable impact on women's autonomy because "for many married women religious activities opened up new horizons without calling into question their domestic duties or outlook."[5] The other side of women's autonomy within the church is that the American church has—in reciprocal measure—depended on married women to do much of the lay work of the church without having to question its outlook about them.

Through work in the church and in the social reform movements that were born out of religious concern in this country (for example, the antislavery movement, temperance movement, child labor laws, and the women's rights movement), women were training for participation in the public sphere and developing a respect for themselves and their gender that was not dependent on their marital status or their economic power. In this country, women have been associated with the guardianship of the home and (as an extension of that) responsibility for public morality. The church, as the institution associated with the keeping of morality, has utilized and benefited because women shouldered this responsibility.[6]

Whether by necessity, choice, or divine inspiration, the Christian church has, from its inception, valued women. The American church has depended on the participation of women as an important resource for the ongoing life and social justice concerns of the church. However, many of the major transitions in American life over the last twenty-five years have pivoted on changes in women's lives. The impact of these changes has been felt as surely in the life of congregations as in the hearts of individual women.

The Last Twenty Years

The churches in the 1950s grew apace in suburbanizing America. Then the 1960s, with the sexual revolution, changing divorce laws, integration and civil rights, the Vietnam war, and the emerging women's rights movement, changed the needs, pastoral expectations, and available energy of women. I suggest that part of the decline of church membership over the last two decades is because the church has lost touch with the personal and social revolutions of women. Despite the church's historical dependence on women as a major resource, the church has been slow to recognize and/or respond to the pastoral needs of single parents, Vietnam widows, and families who struggle with divorce and/or blending. Those family units who do not conform to the image of the "traditional family" look for spiritual resources and seldom find them in mainline churches. Women and men who recapitulate the values of the 1950s have found support for their understanding of life in fundamentalist denominations and TV ministries. However, women whose life processes have moved them—either by chance or choice—into nontraditional family patterns[7] encounter difficulty in finding churches that acknowledge, accept, and understand their life-styles.

In the last twenty years, the role of women in our culture has changed profoundly. Many factors have influenced this change. Perhaps the single most dramatic factor is the tremendous rise in the rate of divorce. Another social change has been the increased visibility of people who openly live their homosexuality. With women's growing ability to control economic life through their own careers, women who have never married are choosing to bear or adopt children without a male partner.

At the same time that women became visible and valued in the business and professional world, church leaders have been discussing what role a woman should have within the church.[8] As we enter the 1990s, women are often still encouraged to fulfill the roles women filled in the 1950s (for example, working with youth and children, preparing social events or food for the congregation). The problem is that even those women who are in traditional positions as wives with children are different from the same women who populated the church two decades ago. Over half the married women in this country hold a job outside the home. For more than ten years, the divorce rate has been half the marriage rate. Consciousness-raising and patterns of independent competence develop in a woman during and after a divorce. These insights do not go away, even though she might remarry and become an "invisible divorcee." The Vietnam war, nuclear arms, and ecological concerns also have affected the way women think, function, and utilize their time.

As the church approaches the twenty-first century, it faces a profound challenge. For almost two millennia, the church has relied on women for support of church activities and the work of the clergy. Now women expend tremendous energy outside the home. Many receive both a paycheck and appropriate authority for tasks done in the marketplace. More single women are in our culture and in our churches today. Divorced women grapple daily with being the economic and emotional head of household. As always, widows come in all ages; loneliness and the need for appropriate sexual expression is not confined to young women. Many lesbians have not rejected their Christian upbringing and are looking for a church home where they can be open regarding sexual identity. The single parent is no longer a rarity. However, the church does not seem to have caught up with a vision of ministry equal to the parishioners it faces.

Only the exceptional church or clergyperson has addressed—pastorally, structurally, or theologically—the needs and life-style dynamics of the women who incarnate the transitions of our culture. The task is not a small one. It involves struggling with new questions regarding sexuality. It means taking a fresh look at structures that have been in place for many years and often discovering that new wine will not fit into old wineskins. It means education for both ministers and laity. At the same time the nontraditional issues are addressed, the clergyperson must also take seriously the anxiety, discomfort, or fear of the more traditional church members regarding "the new." How do these various groups relate to each other? The challenge for the church of the twenty-first century is gaining the courage to recall its roots; the first-century church incorporated widely dissimilar people into one group on the basis of one unifying principle—the belief in Jesus Christ as Lord in their lives.

Life-styles That Challenge

No single story can say everything about being divorced or being widowed, but a story can exemplify representative characteristics, dynamics, and pastoral issues. The biblical stories alternate with stories shared by women I have known professionally. As stated earlier, the Bible seldom mentions a woman's male partner, so we cannot be sure of a woman's marital status. The biblical vignettes are chosen because they clearly show pastoral issues for each of the categories. I have used stories that allow the women, their actions, and the situation to speak for themselves.

The never married—untouched, afraid, risking (Luke 8:43-48).
Apparently a significant story to the early Christian community, recorded in all three Synoptic Gospels, this woman's story is one of only
two instances in which a woman is cited as initiating a healing encounter
with Jesus. Two thousand years ago, the rules prohibited a woman
from speaking with a man publicly. Rabbinic law decreed a woman
with any flow of blood should not be touched, lest that touch render
the other unclean. Against all common sense, this bleeding woman
risked contact with a noted religious leader. Jesus was on his way to
the important task of healing the daughter of a powerful man in the
community. This woman must have been compelled by a desperate
desire for healing that would allow her back into her community of
faith and into the normalcy of life that her malady had denied her. She
seemed utterly alone. No one claimed kinship with her or stood by her.
Because of the nature of her illness, she probably would have been
unable to bear children, making her not valuable in the marriage marketplace of her time. She was an insignificant, alienated woman, invisible
to everyone except Jesus. Luke tells us that "when she saw that she
was not hidden, she came forward trembling." Jesus' response to her
must have shocked all who heard it. He did not embarrass, condemn,
or shame her for her action, which would have been considered inappropriate on so many levels. Instead, he called this woman "daughter."
The only time recorded in the Gospels where he calls anyone his son
or daughter, here Jesus himself claims a kinship with this woman who
was so alone. Then, in the presence of the people who knew her malady
and knew that she had been unclean for twelve years because of it, he
made a statement affirming her faith and its power.

This story contains many characteristics of the modern-day experience of women who have never married. Most dominant is the dynamic
that they stand alone in their life activities. Contact with others—
emotional or physical—must be chosen. It can never be taken for granted
and may be somehow suspect. Fear is another dynamic. Many women
say they must train themselves and learn how not to be afraid of being
alone. Many women who have chosen not to marry are still faced with
labels of "old maid" and the cultural "given" that married is better.
The unmarried woman has no one to speak her concerns for her; she
must speak on her own, often without support or encouragement.
"Kinship" with others develops only with time, work, and some risk.
A single woman may carry no weight in a congregation oriented to
family ministry. Sometimes other women may be anxious or distant,
assuming the single woman is eager to catch any man, even a married
one. Simply by her presence, she challenges the life-style choice of most

other church members. Her "difference" may be interpreted as "sickness."

Maria: a faith journey through divorce.   Maria was in her early thirties, happily married, and had a child she adored. She was attractive, intelligent, and proud of her work in the church, which utilized her musical training and abilities. One piece, however, prevented the positive parts of her life to come together into an integrated whole. Maria had married young to a man who felt free to abuse her physically and emotionally. She had stayed in the marriage for eight years, trying "to make it work" and struggling with her Catholic upbringing, which did not permit divorce. Eventually she began working with a psychiatrist "who probably didn't have any religious belief." This man, over three years' time, was able to help her realize her marriage was destroying her. She finally filed for a divorce. After some time she dated and married John, a man with a quiet spiritual life of his own tradition. They become involved in a church of his denomination that was enriching and satisfying. However, after five years of marital happiness and after three years in this theologically compatible Protestant church, Maria still could not resolve her religious conflict regarding her divorce and remarriage. She faced no external questions or criticisms, as her divorce was an invisible part of her history. Her new church home never mentioned divorce, however, and Maria took the silence to mean it was shameful, not to be discussed in church. If the Catholic church was so overtly against what she did and her Protestant church was so silent, surely it must be wrong. How could God accept it or her? As she understood herself, she had been able to decide for a divorce only because she had "borrowed" her psychiatrist's secularism. Now that she was once again within a church and trying to be in relationship with God, the guilt and confusion resurfaced. She sought out a pastoral therapist to help her integrate her existential reality with her faith. She did not feel she could get that help from her church or her pastor.

Maria's story includes many elements typical of "good church people" who divorce. The first thing to note is that in her first marriage Maria was married in the church of her upbringing—her religious "family"—to a man of that same faith group. For her, as for many others, the question of divorce was not only a question of separating from an individual but also a serious breach with the larger family. Her divorce was not only painful in and of itself but also was felt to be "disobedient" or sinful. She was unable to find permission to do what she intellectually knew she needed to do within her church structure. A second key element was the transference of her belief that if the church was critical of her action then God must be also. It is a sad theme I have heard many women express. I do not know if churches are really so negative about divorced women, but many women feel that their individual pain is not as significant to their church as is a dogma regarding divorce. Contrary to the statement that "people get divorced so easily these days," the women I know have lived through this decision only with much soul-searching and doubt, despite the wisdom of such a decision to an outsider. (A therapist I know spoke of a woman client, an active church member, who had gone through two divorces and spent months trying to work through her guilt and shame. He commented, "She spent so much time trying to figure out why her marriages had failed. I couldn't see how she made them last as long as she did.") Another truth contained in Maria's story is the abiding power of unresolved spiritual questions. Women who have internalized so much condemnation regarding divorce may not have the courage to ask whether a church will accept them, but their silence does not mean they feel religiously content or secure. Many women assume that silence on the part of the church about a difficult issue probably implies condemnation. The woman caught in the act of adultery and taken to Jesus was not freed simply because she was not stoned. She had to hear an overt pastoral voice say, "Neither do I condemn you. Go in peace and sin no more," before she could really go on with her life (John 7:53—8:11).

The widow—abandoned, condemned, resourceful (Genesis 38).   The story of Tamar is a complex one, and the intervening centuries between her time and ours make a simple transposition of situations difficult. Nonetheless, it has some lessons to be learned. Tamar was widowed before she became pregnant by her husband. Following the ancient custom of levirate marriage, her brother-in-law, Onan, was sent to "perform of the duty of a brother-in-law to her." Although willing to have sex with her, Onan was not willing to impregnate her, "So . . . he spilled the semen on the ground, lest he should give offspring," and he died, too. Then Judah, her father-in-law, sent Tamar home to her father until the youngest brother-in-law should come of age. Apparently, Judah had no intention of filling his parental obligation to her for fear of losing his youngest son also, so Tamar was abandoned in her father's house. Judah's wife died, and after a time of grieving, while visiting a friend, Judah had sex with a woman he takes to be a temple prostitute. She is Tamar in disguise. Three months later, when Judah learned that Tamar is pregnant, Judah was quick to condemn, saying that she should be brought out and burned. At this point, Tamar revealed that her "sexual infidelity" had been with Judah himself. Acknowledging her resourcefulness in tricking him to keep his obligation to her, Judah finally acknowledged that "she is more righteous than I."

Tamar is a reminder that widows are not always women who have most of their lives behind them. Widows of any age may be lonely and wish for appropriate sexual expression. Although this story is almost three thousand years old, the religious, righteous indignation of the father-in-law who invokes levitical law (Lev. 21:9) to have Tamar killed for her sexual behavior has a contemporary tinge. He clearly sees her behavior as much worse than his own sexual behavior after the death of his spouse. Today, too, a double sexual standard continues. Widowhood itself is not criticized by the church as it is not something a woman has chosen. The church does, however, often act as though a woman's sexuality died with her spouse—compounding the feelings of abandonment that come with death—with the message that the woman's own vitality must be sacrificed at the same time. Three widows of different ages in different towns have expressed to me the frustration that after their husbands' deaths the church began to focus its relating around "the grief issue" alone so that each felt her identity became that of "the dead man's wife." Each of these women felt her life issues were more difficult for the church to respond to than her identity as a "wife," even though her husband was no longer living.

Susan: a choice for love.   The most striking feature about Susan was her warmth and gentleness. She was loving and respectful when approaching my one-year-old son and equally caring when approaching the bedside of a patient. She had gone through college and seminary without emotional or financial support from her family. Susan had, in fact, fled from her home and had been "in hiding" for the last four years. She had been beaten routinely by her mother and father for eighteen years and had been sexually abused by both until she was physically large enough to defend herself. Some of the beatings she had endured were the result of a conscious choice on her part for her attempts to defend her younger siblings from abuse. Somehow, despite the horror that had been her upbringing, Susan had not become an embittered or violent person herself. Instead, drawing on the few supports she had— friends and her church—Susan had gathered the courage to be in positive relationship with others. She found, however, that the only way she could relate to men was through the safety of a structured relationship (such as student and teacher or chaplain and patient). To relate to a man as a close friend or a potential partner was terrifying for her. Women were less frightening, but even then feeling comfortable with much closeness was difficult for Susan. In seminary, she had a sexual experience that did not immobilize her when she was able to be loved by another woman. Coming from a conservative denomination where homosexuality was a foregone sin, she needed to reconcile her history, her faith, and her sense of call with her sexual self. Although Susan was not driven by strong sexual desires, she was starved for human closeness that did not hurt and affection that was not self-serving. She could not simply stay away from relationships. She had already been deprived of intimacy and tenderness from others for years. She wanted a church home where she could work with children (the one part of humanity of whom she was not automatically afraid), and she longed to have a loving partner to whom she could come and replenish herself emotionally after giving so fully of herself at work.

Susan's story is more dramatic than many. For some women, lesbianism is something they have simply discovered after years of marriage and of being unable to find sexual pleasure with their husband. Others have known from early adolescence that their sexual attraction was to females rather than to males. Many lesbians have found words of peace and comfort from the biblical account of Jesus' ministry. They have sought that same acceptance and respect in a church and have had great difficulty in finding it. What many lesbians have done is to "stay in the closet" within their Christian community. The problem for these women often comes when they feel a lack of integrity in separating out who they know themselves to be from the person they are known as in their church. If they have children, the secretiveness becomes an even more difficult issue. Many lesbians must ask the question every day, With whom is it safe to share this piece of information about myself? Christian lesbians struggle with the confusion between their experience of love and acceptance from God and/or Jesus Christ and the supreme difficulty of finding a church that embodies that same message. Some Christian lesbians, like Susan, are caught in the dilemma of feeling the "Christian" part of them condemning the homosexual part of them. For Susan, beginning to experience the same pastoral compassion for herself that she gave so regularly to her patients was a long and painful process. I felt blessed to be with Susan as her faith allowed her to transform self-condemnation into genuine understanding that perhaps a miracle had occurred that God had enabled her to be able to love anyone. Given the trauma of her history, for Susan to be able to risk intimacy without total immobilizing terror was the grace of God, the creator of our sexuality.

The single parent—foreign, determined, caretaking (Matt. 15:21-28).
To the Gospel writers the most significant thing about this mother was that she was a foreigner, a non-Jew coming to ask help from a Jewish

rabbi. Second, she was a woman approaching a man in public.[9] I use the story to illustrate single parenting because, within the context of this exchange, a mother does come alone to plead for her child, risking the trespassing of not one but two different cultural barriers. She is determined to get help for her daughter. Jesus does not make her task any easier. Her first request is ignored. His disciples beg him to dismiss her; his apparent agreement occurs through his response that he is focused on the needs of Jews, not Gentiles. She comes and kneels before him to request again. Again he refuses, this time insultingly alluding to the Canaanites as dogs. Still she persists, using the metaphorical insult to press her point once more. Finally Jesus responds, praising her faith and granting her daughter health.

The dynamic most parallel to today's single mothers is in the woman's persistent efforts to take care of her child. This woman is willing to endure insults, break the cultural rules, approach a foreigner—anything that might help. Obviously this woman does not fall back on an alternate recourse. No one else will plead for her child. Perhaps like most single mothers, she has become accustomed to doing alone whatever she needs to do to take care of the child she loves. This story is the only instance in the Gospels (other than the woman with a flow of blood) in which a woman initiates contact with Jesus to request healing. Note that Jesus was denigrating of her nationality but showed no disrespect for her gender.

The only information more startling about the American family than the tremendous increase of divorces in the last twenty years is the statistic regarding single-parent families.[10] Single parents, who are mostly women, now head more than one out of every four families with children. They are single parents as a result of divorce, separation, widowhood, and never having married.

Despite their large numbers, single mothers do not feel a part of a group that supports or enriches. Instead, what single mothers share most often is the feeling of being alone, alone in the all-encompassing and sometimes overwhelming experience of responsibility for their children.[11] Most mothers do not have support from the other parent of the child. Single mothers say that often, if the father is involved with the child, he is likely to use his power (for example, threatening to cut off child support, refusing to see the child at all) against the mother rather than for the child. Along with the mother's heavy responsibility is the reality that women have less power (economic and cultural, for example) than their male counterparts.[12] Being a single parent also raises questions in others' minds regarding the mother's past. Were the mother and father married? Why a divorce? The visible child begs the question of the mother's invisible history.

Single parenting is a physically exhausting job. All of the labor of a household must be carried out by one adult. *Labor* includes work outside the home, childcare, house maintenance, the character building of the child, chauffeuring, recreational activities, maintaining family ties, and more. As one mother put it, "I not only bring home the bacon, I have to cook it, make the kids eat it, and clean up afterwards." Single mothers need to hear a word of compassion that they do not and cannot do it all. Whenever I speak to displaced homemaker groups or to individual single mothers, I share, "To the child of a working mother, a pizza with mushrooms is a hot meal with vegetables." The response is always the laughter of recognition and relief.

The single parent who is lesbian faces many complications. Because she is living a life-style that is criticized by many heterosexuals, the lesbian single parent has a reduced number of options for support if she is open regarding her sexuality. If she is trying to stay "in the closet," her children increase the difficulty of secrecy.[13] The gay community is not focused around the needs of children, so few supports come from that direction either. Sadly, the church of Jesus Christ, which preaches that nothing can separate us from the love of God (Romans 8:31-39), is not a beacon of compassion. The church has sometimes implied a gradation of sin—with homosexuality being "one of the worst"—despite a gospel that preaches "all have sinned and come short of the glory of God." The lesbian single parent is not likely to have much support from secular sources, straight or gay. The church needs to check its self-righteousness and propensity to evaluate others' sins. It can ask instead how it might be both prophetic and pastoral without simply conforming to the secular values of the world.

Many in our society—including single mothers—believe that single parent families are "sick," "a problem," or bad for the children. The church should not participate in fueling this fallacy. Many mothers have become single parents to protect their child(ren) from emotional, physical, or sexual abuse. A single-parent home may be less conflicted, rigid, or enmeshed than another home that looks "normal" to an outsider. A family's "problem-ness" should not be decided on the criterion of the number of parents in the home. A single parent who is divorced from the father of the child(ren) must affirm the child(ren) while continuing her own life task of emotionally ending the marriage. This task of separating from a spouse while loving the child who is the embodiment of that union is always difficult. It is not made easier if the single mother must also battle poor self-esteem or guilt that she is inadequate simply by virtue of being a single parent.

Life-styles of Grace, Creativity, and Resourcefulness

Women in traditional family units can be nonconforming in their thinking. The women discussed in this chapter constitute nontraditional family units regardless of personal conventions. As women they may value their role in defining a new reality regarding families, or they may not. However, like left-handed people in a right-handed world, these women approach typical situations from an atypical perspective and must be flexible enough to adapt when necessary. Women who do not live out the "and they lived happily ever after" myth know that other cultural myths as well will not offer sufficient foundation for them in the face of crisis. Because the informal rules of our culture do not work so neatly in their own lives, these women may have a much needed perspective on the existential reality of living by grace instead of by religious rules. Ministry with these women may be a challenge because the platitudes of religious dogma will not stand in the face of their reality. Like the Canaanite woman who challenged Jesus' Jewish boundaries, these women offer a prophetic voice. They ask us, also, to stretch our narrow outlook and call us to a more comprehensive ministry.

A second feature common to women living through personal and cultural transitions is their creativity. This creativity may be born out of their different vantage point on the church and community, or it may develop from the necessity to evaluate the limitations of the community in responding to their needs. Whatever the reasons, these women, who have had to travel the road of their adulthood along unmarked paths, have often devised innovative methods to accomplish life tasks. This creativity can be a powerful leavening agent if the church will risk using it. The answers and the questions these women bring to their communities may be an everyday gift of God to keep the church from falling into a spiritual rut.

A third reality the women in cultural transition often experience is the practical restriction of their resources. Not only do they not have the financial resources of a two-paycheck family but also they often have less income than a single male of their same age and educational background. Single mothers may not have the free backup for childcare that a married woman has. Moreover, any woman who works outside her home and then comes home to cook, clean, shop, check homework, and so on is not likely to have excess energy for church projects during the week. However, these women who have had to be creative in apportioning their limited time, money, and energy at home may be equally adept at rethinking a church budget or restructuring church assignments. Most of them have learned how to compromise gracefully and make do with less. Many churches would do well to have members who understand stewardship and conservation of resources so thoroughly.

The church claims to value discernment as a spiritual gift. Women who live without the sanctions of traditional cultural values may be particularly gifted in the discernment of anger both in themselves and in others. The grief and abandonment such women experience through death or divorce allow them a unique awareness of this difficult interpersonal dynamic. Perhaps more than most, these women can provide guidance on the interpretation of Paul's injunction to "Be angry, but do not sin" (Ephes. 4:26). They may still fear their anger or that of others, but they are not naive as to its reality and presence in all people. They may be able to help others understand how often anger masks fear or hopelessness. I hope the church can become a place where women are not told to stifle their anger at any cost, a message that society often gives indirectly as women are either nudged toward prescription drugs that will "calm them down" or encouraged to prefer "ladylike" depression to clean, outward expression of anger. The church might be a place where women could experience a transformation of cultural expectations rather than pressure to conform to the secular expectation that anger should be muted.

Although awkward for the church to discuss, sexuality is a reality. The church takes comfort in the belief that a married woman's sexuality is kept under the bedclothes of the marital bed. If a woman does not have a male partner, the question of how she handles her sexuality raises anxiety. In the midst of a culture that focuses heavily on sexual relating, few ministers have the incredible self-confidence that Jesus seems to have in his dialogue with the Samaritan woman, or even the bumbling courage of Paul to address directly the sexual questions of a congregation. A wise pastor knows that the anxiety he or she feels comes from the sexual questions that are unanswered in each of us. The minister would do well to remember that God, the Creator, made each of us a sexual being. Our sexuality is the embodiment of our divine need for relationship. Women who are not married have needs for adult companionship that may be served well through their relationship with the church. In turn, the church can benefit from this resource of relationship energy as a catalyst for new programs or support for existing committees and activities.

Criticism and Response

We have looked at pain when relationships die, at conflict when relationships are not socially acceptable, and at the incredible responsibility in the relationship between a single mother and her children, but the ultimate question for us is, What will be the relationship of the church to nontraditional family units, women who are not defined by a male partner? Given the continuing reality of a large divorce rate, the numbers of single parents, and the increasing openness of homosexuality, the question is not if the church will relate to these women but what kind of relationship the church will pose as an ideal toward which it struggles.

The track record of the church in regard to women who live outside a traditional life-style has not been good. It is, however, difficult to chronicle because the church has been guilty of more sins of omission regarding women than sins of commission.[14] By that I mean what the church has not done—by the silence that has been kept—rather than overt attack. The most visible sign of our failure may be the declining membership in churches because these women have felt ignored. Failure may also be demonstrated in the lack of creative response to the needs of women that are particular to those who do not have a male partner.

> The promotion of family and devoted parenting and the touting of motherhood somehow dissolved quickly on divorce, as if such conceptions are only valuable when a man is a part of the family unit. The church's ministry seems to focus on traditional nuclear family only. This unwittingly excludes the majority of families today.[15]

The perspective of those who live in alternative family units is that the church has not been pastoral in response to them.

One single mother tells of going to church on Mother's Day wanting to hear a word of grace and understanding regarding the job she had been doing for twenty-four hours a day, seven days a week, for the past two years. What she heard instead was a sermon based on Proverbs 31 that focused on the virtuous wife who is the pride of her husband. Instead of a sermon on mothering, which applied to her either in relation to her son or her own mother, she instead heard a sermon about the job of a "wife" with which she felt no connection except failure. She felt angry, frustrated, and, most significantly, not ministered to that day. When she wrote a note to her pastor to share her concern that perhaps others in the congregation (married and unmarried alike) would not have felt cared for by a Mother's Day sermon that focused on wifely duty, she got no response from him and she left the church. She left, she said, not because of the sermon alone. As she thought back, she realized sadly she had heard that text and basically the same sermon preached on Mother's Day in other congregations. The compelling reason for her leaving was that having her note ignored made her feel like a leper, one whose life circumstance was not to be touched! Singles programs in the church leave many women (whether never married, divorced, or lesbian) feeling that the only response the church wishes to make to them is to put them in a singles' ghetto, a place where hopefully they will meet other singles and get married, thus placed in the traditional family mold as quickly as possible. The criticism, then, is that the church *a*bandons at the point of crisis, *e*vades responsibility, *i*gnores the issues, *o*versimplifies the problem, and *u*ndermines the self-respect of those who must deal with painful life situations—the vowels of bad ministry.

What suggestions, then, can we make to address the ministry needs of these women without alienating others in the church? Two basic ideas that have been suggested repeatedly are that the church (1) should affirm the feminine element within the church and (2) not create structure according to marital status. Neither suggestion denigrates any other person in the church nor precludes the traditional marital and family patterns that are a part of every congregation. What it could mean is that a pastor might preach on women in the Bible or biblical feminine images of God. Women might be utilized as lay readers or guest preachers. Sermon illustrations and Sunday school lessons using examples of women as respected role models (such as women missionaries, women artists, the saints, or the usually invisible women workers in that particular congregation) are statements of the worth and dignity of all women. Allusions to American church history can note that Quakers, Christian Scientists, and the Salvation Army are religious groups that were founded primarily by women. Painful issues such as rape or incest (crimes usually committed against women) need to be addressed directly within the church. Thoughtful Christians, both male and female, need to be in dialogue about these topics as pastoral issues. Scriptural texts are available for these discussions and for discussion of women's unique biological crises, whether the usually happy crisis of childbirth or the more difficult crises of menopause, miscarriage, or infertility. (The inability to create a child has different meanings for men and women. Both need to be recognized as real pastoral concerns.)

Structuring units and/or activities along nonmarital definitions may occur merely by renaming certain groups or it may mean creating new curriculum options within a church. Not only does a deacons' wives' auxiliary create a problem if the deacon's "wife" is a man but also the name itself implies that deacons should not be women or single. A Sunday school class for the parents of teenagers could include single parents as well as both members of a couple. Activities based on interest rather than marital status, gender, or age allow for a cross-section of people within the church to meet each other based on common interests rather than organizing around data that separate them from others.[16] Evening activities give working women the option to attend. Choir practice may still not be a true option for single parents if no childcare is available through the church. The cost of a babysitter may limit a single parent's ability to become involved and productive in a church except on Sunday mornings. Adult Sunday school curriculum that focuses on Bible studies, ethical issues, or even the church's concern about life-style issues can involve all interested adults in an inclusive way. The vowels of good ministry with nontraditional women are the same ones for any ministry—to accept and acknowledge people as they are, to enable, engage, and empower the congregation, to include all people, to open opportunities for involvement, and to utilize the unique gifts of every person.

Wholeness through Faith

Look at the theological implications of what we have been discussing. Several of the healing pericopes of Jesus' ministry end with his words "Go in peace, your faith has made you whole." One image of healing is of something like a broken bone being mended. Some think of ministry as "mending" people or "fixing" the problems they have. This idea of health as repair work is shallow compared to Jesus' idea of healing as wholeness. The words of Jesus are a challenge for us—the challenge to see other people, even nontraditional women, as whole in their own right. The challenge is also whether the church itself can become whole, inclusive of people who do not fit traditional formulations. This challenge is impossible to meet except through faith. Only through faith can a Christian look at herself or himself and accept the brokenness that is there. Only through faith can we look at others who are broken in different ways and accept that they, too, are the beloved children of God. Faith allows access to our incompleteness without condemnation, and faith liberates us to experience wholeness, both as individuals and as congregations.

Studying the Exodus story, I am convinced that a faith journey is neither simple nor implies a foregone conclusion. If we fully enfranchise nontraditional women into our congregations, we cannot know what the church will become. I can only imagine how frightening it must have been for first-century Christians to grapple with the "shaking of the foundations" of their culture as they experienced slave and master as equals in the church. How strange for a Jew to incorporate the reality of the Savior's love of the Gentile. Just as the early church had to struggle to incorporate an uncomfortable vision of equality and integrate on a personal level all the people who came together in the name of Christ, so we, almost two thousand years later, must struggle to incorporate and integrate those who do not fit into our expectations of what the church should be. We sometimes have difficulty living out the belief that God, author of all creation, is still involved in the creating process—and that we are still being created into new beings. The challenge of faith is also the promise of faith: that we can become whole as individuals and as congregations by incorporating nontraditional people into church. We can be certain that pastoral issues with no easy answers will be likely to surface. Just as certain will be new opportunities for ministry. If the women I have described become a part of the congregation, they will surely bring their gifts of creativity, organizational skills, and relationship energy to deal with new questions as surely as they will bring new questions.

Jesus Christ allowed himself to be challenged by a nontraditional woman from Canaan. He allowed himself to be touched by a woman who was considered unclean. He regularly risked ridicule by speaking with women in public. He kept himself available to those culturally uncomfortable ones who needed his presence and allowed the vision of his ministry to be shaped by them. The effect on him and his early followers was so profound that the role of women in the Christian religion stood out as significantly different from other women in that part of the world. What a miracle we would witness if today's church could present an equally fresh vision of compassion and respect to today's world. Let us hear again the word of Jesus—despite the fear of breaking cultural boundaries, the discomfort of being honest about our inadequacies, and the very real, practical problems of incorporating a new social order into the church. The ultimate word of Jesus Christ is that of grace; we may go in peace, and faith can make us whole.

BIBLIOGRAPHY

Biblical Perspectives on Women and Women's Issues

Engelsman, Joan Chamberlin. *The Feminine Dimension of the Divine.* Philadelphia: Westminster Press, 1979.

Mollenkott, Virginia Ramey. *The Divine Feminine: The Biblical Imagery of God as Female.* New York: Crossroad, 1983.

————. *Women, Men and the Bible.* Nashville: Abingdon Press, 1977.

Russell, Letty M., ed. *Feminist Interpretation of the Bible.* Philadelphia: Westminster Press, 1985.

Stagg, Evelyn, and Frank Stagg. *Women in the World of Jesus.* Philadelphia: Westminster Press, 1978.

Swidler, Leonard S. *Biblical Affirmation of Women.* Philadelphia: Westminster Press, 1979.

Trible, Phyllis. *God and the Rhetoric of Sexuality.* Philadelphia: Fortress Press, 1978.

Ethical and Theological Issues from a Feminist Perspective

Rothman, Sheila M. *Women's Proper Place.* New York: Harper Colophon Books, 1978.

Ruether, Rosemary Radford. *Sexism and God-Talk: Toward a Feminist Theology.* Boston: Beacon Press, 1983.

Russell, Letty M. *The Future of Partnership.* Philadelphia: Westminster Press, 1979.

Schecter, Susan. *Women and Male Violence.* Boston: South End Press, 1982.

Harrison, Beverly Wildung. *Our Right to Choose: Toward a New Ethic of Abortion.* Boston: Beacon Press, 1983.

Worship Resources

Inclusive Language Resources. 1977. Available from Church Leadership Resources, Box 179, St. Louis, MO 63166 ($1.00).

Spinning a Sacred Yarn: Women Speak from the Pulpit. New York: Pilgrim Press, 1982.

Stanton, Elizabeth Cady. *The Woman's Bible.* 1895. Order from Coalition on Women and Religion, 4759 15th Avenue, N.E., Seattle, WA 98105 ($6.95 plus 50 cents postage).

Watchword, Women and the Church. Available from National Ministries, ABC/USA, P.O. Box 851, Valley Forge, Pa. 19482-0851.

Watkins, Keith. *Faithful and Fair: Transcending Sexist Language in Worship.* Nashville: Abingdon Press, 1981.

Women Doing Theology. Available from Church Women United, Room 812, 475 Riverside Drive, New York, NY 10115 ($1.50).

Relationship Issues

Belenky, Mary Field, et al. *Women's Ways of Knowing.* New York: Basic Books, 1986.

Bianchi, Eugene C. and Rosemary R. Ruether. *From Machismo to Mutuality: Essays on Sexism and Woman-Man Liberation.* Paramus, N.J.: Paulist Press, 1976.

Collins, Emily. *The Whole Single Person's Catalog*. New York: Peebles Press, 1979.

Gilligan, Carol. *In a Different Voice: Psychological Theory and Women's Development*. Cambridge: Harvard University Press, 1982.

Pogrebin, Letty Cotlin. *Growing Up Free*. New York: Bantam Books, 1980.

Rich, Adrienne. *Of Woman Born, Motherhood as Experience and Institution*. New York: W. W. Norton, 1986.

Washbourn, Penelope. *Becoming Woman: The Quest for Wholeness in Female Experience*. San Francisco: Harper & Row, 1977.

NOTES

1. Henry Chadwick (*The Early Church* [Baltimore: Penguin Books, 1967], 58–59) notes, "Christianity seems to have been especially successful among women. . . . Christians believed in the equality of men and women before God, and found in the New Testament commands that husbands should treat their wives with such consideration and love as Christ manifested for his church. The Christian sex ethics differed from the conventional standards of pagan society in that it regarded unchastity in a husband as no less serious a breach of loyalty and trust than unfaithfulness in a wife. . . . Christianity cut across ordinary social patterns more deeply than any other religion."

2. As Lawrence Stone (*The Family, Sex and Marriage* [New York: Harper & Row, 1979], 111) makes clear, "the triumphant emphasis on patriarchy as one of the benefits of the Lutheran Reformation is here unmistakable. All the magisterial reformed churches stressed the subordination of wives to husbands . . . nor was this all. The shift to Protestantism meant the loss by the wife of control over the domestic rituals of religious fasting and feasting on the appropriate days. Lastly, the doctrine of the priesthood of believers meant in practice that the husband and father became the spiritual as well as the secular head of the household."

3. Carl Degler (*At Odds* [New York: Oxford University Press, 1980], 298) discusses women's role in the American church: "This did not mean that women were ministers or even officers of the church . . . [though] most women did not lead in the churches, they were conspicuous from the outset as members. As early as the 1650s, for example, women outnumbered men in the churches of New England . . . one observer wrote in 1823 that women outnumbered men two to one among the denominations in the district. In the evangelical churches in the southern states at the end of the eighteenth century, white women outnumbered men almost two to one even though men actually outnumbered women in the population."

4. Ibid., 302.

5. Ibid.

6. For one discussion of this idea, see Robert N. Bellah, et al., *Habits of the Heart* (New York: Harper & Row, 1985), 85–86.

7. The traditional pattern of wage-earning father, stay-at-home mother, and two children actually represent fewer than 15 percent of all American families. For a current picture, see Diane Hales, *The Family* (Edgemont, Pa.: Chelsea House, 1988).

8. Most major denominations have had highly visible controversy regarding the ordination of women as clergy or as deacons and/or elders. Most denominations, however, have apparently not realized the radical restructuring of the family and its impact on women. *The American Baptist* (Sept.–Oct. 1989) has a brief, perceptive article, "Beyond Dad, Mom and the Kids," which describes how some churches have begun to focus on this new reality.

9. In *Women in the World of Jesus* (Philadelphia: Westminster Press, 1978), Frank and Evelyn Stagg make clear that "A man in the Jewish world did not normally talk with a woman in public, even with his own wife" (p. 116).

10. In a 1986 Associated Press article, Randolph Schmidt quotes the Census Bureau that "single parents accounted for 26 percent of all family groups with children under 18 years old in 1985, a proportion twice as large as in 1970."

11. In a front-page article for *Family Therapy News*, the newspaper of the American Association for Marriage and Family Therapy, in January 1989, William J. Doherty states that "Non-custodial fathers tend to have unreal relationships with their children. National data indicate that fifty percent of children have not seen their non-custodial father in the past year, and only sixteen percent see him once a week or more."

12. Despite the law, single mothers across the United States report they have a hard time getting a house or car loan, renting certain apartments, and sometimes getting a job. Women make less money than men. Some apartments do not allow children. Some employers feel a woman will just "take off work" if a child is sick. The rationale of twenty years ago was that "men should get paid more because they have to support a family," but it is not being argued in the case of single-parent mothers today.

13. Betty Sagle (*Family Therapy News,* Jan. 1989, 19) notes it is sometimes dangerous to be gay, and children increase one's visibility and vulnerability. "Fear is often translated into anger and hostility or even violence against such families." She mentions ministers (among others) as a group whose values might need to be selectively rejected.

14. Letha Dawson Scanzoni (*Daughters of Sarah,* Jan. 1989, 15) says, "A wife who is left at mid-life . . . is likely to feel terribly betrayed—not only by her husband but by the church and society whose rules she followed so carefully and faithfully. Instead of being rewarded, she is deserted."

15. Fay Blix (*Daughters of Sarah,* Jan. 1989, 23) says that the church has added to the lack of dignity and self-respect of divorced women (and/or single parents) by "adopting priest-levite attitudes and passing gingerly by on the other side, looking away."

16. A good example of what a church can do occurred in a group called the "Yo Yo's" (You're Only Young Once). This group met monthly for a social activity open to anyone in the church who was college age or older. Married

couples would have a monthly "date." Singles were welcome by themselves or with a friend. Childcare was provided so single parents could afford to come. Activities ranged from swimming parties to a sock hop to a Christmas carol fest. It was a structure that did not "ghettoize" any adult in the church.

PART THREE

Transition

CHAPTER 9

Travail as Transition

MAXINE GLAZ AND
JEANNE STEVENSON MOESSNER

Experience shapes our perception of reality. Perception determines the theological questions we ask and at least some part of the answers we formulate in response. Feminine experience, we believe, bears a significant relationship to the pastoral questions we ask. It also informs how we think theologically about those questions. Yet some aspects of women's experience have not been obvious to clergy who, either through gender or schooling, are immersed in a male-normed environment.

Parts One and Two introduced an alternative point of view—a deeper look at the feminine perspective. Part One outlined historic contributions to the psychology of women that have been offered within this century. It also offered a theory of women's psychology constructed from current psychoanalytic thought. This theory further informs approaches to the pastoral care of women and to the pastoral care movement as a whole. Part Two suggested several of the identifiable pastoral questions that occur more often among women. These chapters inform theological reflection and approaches to caring for the specific pastoral concerns of women.

Two important tasks were begun in the previous sections. First, we have developed a new awareness of pastoral care and pastoral theology in transition toward inclusivity. Second, the contributors' divergent approaches to an understanding of women's experience and distinctive ways of addressing the pastoral and theological concerns, although not initially designed as such, serve as a casebook of methodology in pastoral care and theology.

Pastoral Care in Transition Toward Gender Inclusivity

The evolving lives of women in a social era permeated by change suggest a shift in consciousness both for women about themselves and for those ministers who respond to women pastorally. Not all women are pleased with these redefinitions and with the openness in gender expectations that has accompanied the women's movement. At the same time, most women's lives are affected by the new interpretations of women's experience. What is needed if these shifts in consciousness are to culminate in compassionate pastoral care? What are we to do, how are we to respond, when we hear the cry "as of a woman in travail"?

This volume has addressed the issue of a new pastoral care for women in a variety of ways. As our collaboration progressed, four patterns emerged.

1. *Modes and methods of pastoral care are contingent on the recognition of pastoral need.* The recognition of pastoral need is inevitably made as a social and theological judgment that is contingent on a contextual understanding of who warrants care and what issues invoke concern.[1] The pastor who disregards the reality of battering, to say nothing of the needs of the batterer, or the possibility of incest in a middle-class congregation, will inevitably miss an opportunity to provide care. The pastor who cannot recognize and accept a Christian family consisting of a divorced or lesbian mother and her children will not be able to respond with sound pastoral concern for such families, even though she or he might relate very well to a more traditional family in a crisis. When we paint a picture of family bliss as the norm of Christian life or confuse faith with material advantage or class standing, we limit our opportunity to see our church members and clients as they are in fact. As a result, we miss occasions when we might offer real help or prevent greater harm.

Struggles described in this book—such as the conflict between work and love, the greater incidence of depression, and the recovery from sexual abuse—are typically recognized as women's problems. However, we have not described many additional issues common to women, such as the tensions created by the responsibility of caring for aging parents and the higher levels of poverty and social isolation among elderly women. Our lack of attention to these special needs makes telling us their difficulties harder for these individuals and deepens their feelings of shame. We cannot think theologically or offer pastoral concern when we do not recognize the issues that perplex our church members.[2]

As specialists in pastoral care, we are accustomed to thinking of social issues such as sexism and racism as important occasions for the attention of those in ministry. We know that the pastoral concern of the church is related to social and cultural norms. We were reminded, as Part 2 of this book evolved, that the need for ministry is evidenced in a social context, even when an individual is involved or when an individual minister is the pastoral caregiver. We realize, in a new way, that pastoral care takes place or does not take place at the vector of social context and personal need. Although ministers are understandably apathetic to pain that is not recognized, pastoral care should not be reserved for those whose wounds have our approval. We need to be reminded that we are not just shepherds managing and dividing herds of sheep and goats; we are called to be, as proposed in Chapter 10, the neighbor.

2. *Moments of failed ministry with women occur when a pastor simply does not understand what to say or do for a parishioner. Good intentions are not sufficient for helpful presence.* Theologically speaking, pastoral care efforts fail when we attempt to fix the problem rather than evince God's presence. We suspect that women are especially sensitive to a minister's thoughtless response. Because women are ordinarily socialized to be caregivers, they readily recognize the absence of an empathetic reaction.

Sometimes a minister could be helpful to a woman but is not. At other times a minister can actually be harmful, even while intending to offer help. We do not presume that such failures are dependent on the minister's gender or that one's sex determines adequacy as a minister! Both men and women pastors have made the errors chronicled in this book. These errors may be overstated numerically—we believe that many of the positive contributions of ministers are not remembered and that the horror stories are not easily forgotten—but are nonetheless endemic to the profession.

How do we account for these failures? What we are about to say is not new to the pastoral care literature, but it bears repeating. Clergy giving pastoral care are often not able experientially to distinguish projection from overidentification, nor are they able to distinguish either of these from empathy. By *projection* is meant the counselee's attribution to other people of her or his own feelings and difficulties. By *overidentification* is meant the counselee's attribution to her or himself the feelings and characteristics of the other so that the counselee confuses the other's affect with his or her own. By *empathy* is meant the capacity to participate appropriately in the ideas, feelings, and experiences of another.

In our introductory story, the pastor was unable to empathize with June's fright over childbirth and death. Pastoral empathy was so impaired that neither words of personal concern nor theological reassurance accurately responded to her turbulence. Clergy cannot minister (we are not concerned here with psychological knowledge but with human compassion) when they do not recognize the inner dilemma of their parishioners because they are caught up in their own difficulties.

In fact, the minister's response to June connotes a projection (June should feel gratitude) suggestive of the minister's unrecognized fear of her potential aggression toward the infant or of an overidentification with the newborn. The mistaken response does not occur simply because the pastor is out of touch with feelings; June's pastor was nearly overwhelmed by affect. However, this minister was unaware that the primary feelings being attended to were his, not June's.

Poor pastoral care occurs when pastoral anxiety becomes heightened in critical moments so that inner tension and confusion interfere with empathy. On the one hand, we may wait, speechless, because we are afraid to test our intuitive sense of the experienced world of the parishioner. On the other hand, projection supplants empathy when the minister presumes to know how the parishioner feels. We disown our own feelings and ascribe them to another instead, responding to the experience as we assume it is or should be! Empathy is thus inhibited by the interference of our own affective needs.[3] Overidentification occurs when the feelings of any party in the pastoral interchange cause so much resonance that we become, as it were, emotionally fused and cannot distinguish or separate our own intense affective response from that of the parishioner. In such instances, empathy exists but is out of control. Affective congruence is present but impaired by overinvolvement; we may be too closely identified to be pastorally helpful. Both projection and overidentification are more likely to occur when anxiety about adequacy, performance, or the need to find solutions supersedes or interrupts the capacity for empathic presence.

What is also impressive about the damaging and cavalier responses that ministers sometimes offer to women is that clergy can be oblivious to their own professional impact. If you do not think what you say matters very much to anybody, you end up saying things that matter all too much! We came to the conclusion that too many clergy suffer from what might be called "professional narcissism." Authority flounders on the defensive belief that ministry is of utter importance (grandiosity) as when clergy overidentify with divine power. Authority also flounders on the equally defensive belief that ministry is of no value (devaluation, also grandiosity) as clergy disavows their potential impact on others. Such pastors suffer from a debasement of their own confidence. They lack an authentic sense of the significance of their work in ministry and pastoral care. As a result, they may place great import on what they expound, but their proclamation suffers because they do not understand what they convey. These pastors appear to others to be either unnatural or without integrity. They may or may not know their tradition well enough to interpret it. If the religious tradition is mediated by individuals who do not embody its values and do not live with a sense of grace, pastoral care inevitably suffers. Managing one's inner life and anxiety—the continual transformation of self—is an essential component of pastoral presence.

Another possibility, a more social-psychological understanding of the problem, still exists. We can wonder if the real issue is that clergy, whether male or female, see women as relatively unimportant and are blindsided by culturally reinforced sexism. Whereas perhaps all people are at least somewhat sexist, we would argue that people who are especially unhelpful to women are those who suffer most from their own problems with personal—and therefore professional—self-esteem. Being merciful requires that we have experienced mercy.

We have intended the accounts of clergy and women in this book, and their implied criticism, as illustrative without believing that ministers are universally guilty of these offenses or that they are misogynists or women-haters. Although this book is at times provocative, our purpose has been to inspire. We wrote and edited with the conviction that, as women's issues are understood, ministers will do a better job of pastoral care with women.

3. *Women's experience, behavior, and psychology are related to biology, neurology, and culture.* All contributors to this volume have been deeply affected by the second wave of the women's movement, and we share a skepticism about theories of anatomic determinism. We are also convinced that cultural views of women's inferiority are too common and cannot be supported scientifically. Since Freud, in particular, we have witnessed a revolution in attitudes about women. The revolution is neither universal nor complete, but women's views of self and cultural views of women have greatly improved as compared with attitudes toward women that pervaded Western consciousness prior to 1600.[4] We are, in fact, free to think about sexual differences and wonder about biologic reality without compromise to feminine self-esteem.

Thus, the reality of woman's experience, as organized but not limited by biology, is developed within this book in two striking ways. First, the issue of rhythmicity, as underscored in Chapter 1 and developed in Chapter 4, struck us as essentially correct. We were moved by the acknowledgment of our own natural biologic functioning and threatened by the reality that on occasion (even while this book was being written) our lives are made more complicated by it. The feminist desire for a theology more easily related to nature has an understandable appeal.

Without some connection of revelation to nature, an important component of feminine experience is disenfranchised.

Second, we wonder to what extent phylogenetic aims direct the organization of women's life experiences toward a moral stance of immediate rather than delayed responsiveness in caregiving. Concerns for family and children often deter women from other work so that they sometimes have difficulty discerning when they falter on the side of neglect of people or of tasks. We believe that part of the feminine contribution to culture is that women experience these dilemmas. As the new literature on fathering achieves popularity, we hope that more men will recognize the importance of their contribution as parents and caregivers.[5] At least, women would find great comfort in being able to draw on a pastoral theology that identifies and responds to our dilemma. We wish that more men shared our concern about their greater involvement in the public domain than in the family and the personal realm! If pastors could talk knowledgeably and sympathetically about the ethical dilemmas inherent to sorting out personal and community demands, then women would be encouraged and relieved. Bonnie Miller-McLemore is correct in describing the dilemma of work and love. Her chapter begins a task that should not be left in the hands of theorists outside the church, nor should it be the sole deliberation of women within the church.

4. *Finally, both male and female clergy need to respect those with whom we minister, particularly when they are different from us.* Whether as men offering pastoral care to women or as women offering pastoral care to men, we need to avoid thinking that whoever is unlike us needs to be controlled, domesticated, or educated or—as dangerous a thought—that the person is so much an "other" that she or he is a nonperson to be ignored. Pastors who harbor a Pygmalion-like view of women will not be helpful to them. Pastoral care is not something that we do (or do not do) to others; empathic care takes its lead from the needs of others as they identify those needs.

We have argued that women's development must be taken more seriously in order to understand the experience of being female in our culture. We have described many special concerns of women. We invite you to use this new knowledge to view women with greater compassion and therefore to offer them more sustained and empathic pastoral care. A developmental perspective can inform pastoral care when ministry is dialogical and mutual. Even a developmental viewpoint might be harmful to women, however, if it persuades you that you can now assume a more knowing stance toward women rather than learning together as you work. Respect for others means that your pastoral care will never be a monologue. It involves the pastor in an effort to demonstrate regard for the feelings, experience, and circumstance of the people to whom you hope to offer care.

Women's Experience and Methodology in Pastoral Theology

This book assumes that the minister's care of women could be enhanced by knowledge of women's experience. Each contributor formulated an approach to pastoral problems through the lens of her experience as a woman to focus theological reflection. Yet, the ways we have each envisioned experience as a component of the pastoral dilemma, along with the varied approaches to theological reflection that are offered, suggest many methodological options within pastoral theology.

Methodological approaches.   Mary Dean and Mary Louise Cullen (chap. 4) describe the experience of women through their interviews of women in health care crises. Their conception of an appropriate pastoral response is also drawn directly from their interviews of the women themselves. The methodological assumption is that pastoral intervention follows existential need and is best matched by existential presence on the part of pastors.

Nancy Ramsay draws on her work with incest survivors and on the literature about incest for an analysis of the pastoral problem (chap. 5). She creates an image of the survivor and indicates how the church and its pastor may respond to the challenge of managing the powerful effects of incestuous overstimulation. She uses this psychological portrait to suggest that an abused individual will be in theological crisis. Questions about injustice and about God's beneficence and omnipotence are corollary concerns for the woman who has endured incest. The methodological approach is a carefully drawn description of how the pastoral situation focuses theological reflection. The problem of abuse is then addressed by the church in assisting the survivor as she faces her own anguish, the unknown future, and her questions about God and community.

Christie Cozad Neuger (chap. 7) establishes the social context of women's depression and critiques psychological approaches that implicate an individual woman's psyche as the source of her own malaise. She takes the view that women's experience is substantially derived from a sexist cultural background. Her understanding of women's experience is organized by a sociopolitical view, and her understanding of the minister's pastoral response is organized by an understanding of church as community. The central theological thrust is that we are to be advocates for equity, both in our work with individuals and within the body of Christ. Concerns for justice are at the core of the pastoral response.

JoAnn Garma (chap. 6) describes the interactive relationship of the abuse of women to social assumptions about the family that are embedded in religious belief. The pastoral caregiver needs to become more critical of cultural assumptions posing as theological requirements. We are asked to empathize with the victim, provide for her protection from family abuse by physical and spiritual means, and endorse interventions to deal with the perpetrator. Methodological focus is placed on the critique of certain forms of theological statement and on their correction. The critique is organized by her understanding of women's experience of family violence.

Bonnie Miller-McLemore (chap. 3) describes women's experience of conflict over work and love as an important question for practical theology. She reviews the writings of several women who address women's everyday life and everyday events through the politics of male and female relationships. Through this material she builds a critique of their underlying beliefs about human nature in order to press for theological discernment. She describes how, at the level of metaphor, these writings may be in conflict with basic assumptions of the Christian tradition. Pastoral thought holds psychological and political theory in tension with Christian understandings of experience and is concerned with individual church members, the life of the congregation, and societal and institutional structures.

Jeanne Stevenson Moessner (chap. 2) presents historical silhouettes of the thinking of three representative women who have made important contributions to psychological thought. From these vignettes she derives insights about women that inform our pastoral understanding of them. Later (chap. 10) Jeanne develops an exegetical understanding of the Good Samaritan passage to elaborate a new paradigm for ministry to women. She engages Scripture and experience in a dialogical, if not dialectical, relationship. Thus, experience does not reign supreme, unintentionally establishing another hierarchical pattern.

Maxine Glaz (chaps. 1 and 2) presents a constructive critique of developmental themes in women's experience. The psychological bases for these themes are evaluated for their congruence with the Christian tradition. The themes are then used to reinterpret theological images and motifs that might shift our understanding of pastoral theology. Through these themes she introduces the pastoral theologian to new areas of reflection on practice.

Priscilla Denham (chap. 8) writes about those women whose lives are in transition. Through exegetical work and historical reflection, she argues that our pastoral concern for these women and for their inclusion within the community of faith has precedents.

Although obviously we write about pastoral theology from different vantage points, we share a concern with women's experience. Still, does only gender hold this book together?

Epistemology and pastoral practice. At the outset many of the contributors knew each other slightly. All of us are women, but most of us had male mentors. Each of us felt our theological and pastoral education had had a missing component, the procedural and subjective knowledge that is accrued by living as women within our culture.[6] We reside in different parts of the country and are variously educated to be deliverers of pastoral care. Reflection on the methodology of pastoral theology, with several exceptions, has not been central to our education. In the United States before the 1970s, such discussion was relatively rare. We suppose, because the explicit discussion of methodology is relatively new among pastoral theologians,[7] that the experience of most men in the field parallels our experience in this discussion.

However, we also understand that male procedural knowledge, whether or not it is acknowledged, informs the present understanding of pastoral care and theology and assumes declarative power among pastoral theologians. Our conviction is that in order to develop a gender-free understanding of human experience, we first need to develop the *voice* woman-centered formulations that have escaped conscious articulation. We are equally convinced that as a result pastoral theology and practice will become more discerning in understanding situations and in appreciating the way God is revealed and involved in the life of the world.

Thus, our primary aim has been to identify in a preliminary way aspects of women's experience that might further inform our work. We seek to identify the knowledge that is embedded in feminine experience and suggest how this experience becomes a formative part of the declarative knowledge within the field.[8] Within this book is a persistent methodological shift in that all contributors take seriously women's experiences, feelings, and formulations. This shift involves, but is not reduced to, an epistemological stance that has most often been unacknowledged because it is based on procedural and subjective knowledge that is inaccessible, except through experience. Morris Taggart writes:

> Women's realization that *they* are the ones to define their nature and place in human affairs points to a radical break with past definitions of both theory and knowledge.

....

In both the epistemology and the society constructed by men, the real and material relationships between human beings, as well as those between humans and the natural world, are obscured. Committed as they are to severing culture from nature, knowledge from politics, biology from history, and self from body, and family therapy from a fully human way of life, men avoid material (corporeal, sensuous, practical, relational) reality and structure their social relations (and their understanding of social relations) in abstract and idealized terms. Though women have the potential to experience their lives differently, men's conceptual schemes are the ruling ones. Women are thus alienated from their own experience, and this is the essence of their oppression.[9]

A New Paradigm for Ministry

The final chapter of this book suggests a new model for pastoral ministry that many women will find to be more congruent with their life experience as women. Men, especially those who have given up an authoritarian posture, will also discern the helpfulness of a paradigm change. The parable of the neighbor, which demonstrates greater affinity to the nonhierarchical preferences of women and suggests their desire for community, is offered to modify ministry.

On the face of it, this paradigm shift may not seem like a substantial change in point of view. Yet, governed by our concern for women, who have long been kept in deferential positions and have had so little voice in the development of an understanding of pastoral ministry, the familiar story of a Samaritan takes on new meaning. This parable better describes for women what receiving ministry means, and it better describes for women what ministering means. Pastoral care is not simply the domain of the leaders of the flock. Its basis is found in the sustaining internalizations of love within the self, in the continuing power of community, and in divine hope beyond ourselves, that is, in God.

NOTES

1. We are indebted to Jim Poling, Colgate-Rochester Divinity School, who shared this insight with Maxine Glaz in the context of a meeting of the steering committee of the Society for Pastoral Theology, August 1988.

2. For example, a woman who used a wheelchair once told a group of pastors that attending worship in their buildings was impossible without access ramps in place. One pastor responded: "We have no parishioners in wheelchairs." The woman replied: "Build the ramps, and you will have parishioners in wheelchairs."

3. Ralph R. Greenson, *The Technique and Practice of Psychoanalysis* (New York: International University Press, 1967).

4. Eli Sagan, "Tyranny and Equality," in *Freud, Women, and Morality: The Psychology of Good and Evil* (New York: Basic Books, 1988), 27–49.

5. See, for example, Joseph D. Lichtenberg, "The Attachment-Affiliation Motivation System: Part Two," in *Psychoanalysis and Motivation* (Hillsdale, N.J.: Analytic Press, 1989), 95–124.

6. *Women's Ways of Knowing: The Development of Self, Voice, and Mind*, ed. Mary Field Belenky et al. (New York: Basic Books, 1986).

7. The Society for Pastoral Theology first met at the Brown Palace, Denver, Colorado, in June 1985. A primary motivation for the society's creation was to further the methodological ferment in pastoral theology that was begun in the writings of Wolfhart Pannenberg and Edward Farley.

8. Declarative knowledge has more to do with how one organizes or what one says about experience. We assume that pastoral theology as practiced by women will be different from pastoral theology as practiced by men. The writing of pastoral theology by women, based on knowledge of women's experience, will inevitably present new paradigms for pastoral care and theology.

9. Morris Taggart, "Epistemological Equality as the Fulfillment of Family Therapy," in *Women in Families: A Framework for Family Therapy*, ed. McGoldrick, Aranson, and Walsh (New York: Norton, 1989), 100, 108.

CHAPTER 10

A New Pastoral Paradigm and Practice

JEANNE STEVENSON MOESSNER

· · · · · · · · · · · ·

Ann was a patient on an addictive disease unit in a psychiatric facility; she entered group therapy after leaving the detoxification unit. As was customary at the beginning of each group session, the patients and counselors introduced themselves. When Ann's turn came, she had difficulty with the counselor's request: Tell us about yourself.

> ANN: I take care of people; I'm a nurse. I'm a mother; I take care of my daughter. I'm a daughter; I take care of my mother who has Alzheimer's. She lives with us.
>
> COUNSELOR: Tell us something about yourself.
>
> ANN: I can't. I don't know who I am.

PASTORAL PARADIGM: IN SEARCH OF THE ELUSIVE SELF

Ann's comment illustrates the difficulty many women have in establishing a sense of identity. This phenomenon has been encountered by several researchers. Lillian B. Rubin, for example, studied 160 women who had difficulty answering the question, Who am I? This difficulty was attributed to the mystery about women's nature, *the elusive self.*[1] Rubin's "elusive self" is not far removed from the work of pastoral theologian Orlo Strunk, who speaks in terms of the "Secret Self,"[2] the central region of the person, a private centerpoint in each of us that is good, and the internal essence of who we authentically are that resists external demands of compliance and conformity. Lacking adequate knowledge of who they are, women often exhibit low self-esteem.

We see this problem particularly among women who have identified themselves in conformity with our culture's traditional feminine stereotypes. Women in this situation commonly describe themselves as wives, mothers, and kind, caring, and unselfish people.[3]

They have followed society's ideal of the good woman, yet society has not reciprocated by rewarding their ideal qualities. In her exemplary care of the "other," something is amiss in the woman's care of herself. Professional and paid caregivers must confront the paradoxical question, What is a useful ministry with women who have so often excelled as caregivers themselves?

Much of women's caregiving, unfortunately, is intricately involved in their pleasing others. To be "pleasing," subordinate, subservient, and dependent is a *cultural archetype* of what being "feminine" means.[4] One theologian has named the characteristics that accompany such an archetype as sins; these feminine "sins" include diffuseness, dependence on others for self-definition, lack of an organizing center, and distractibility.[5] These characteristics and the tendency to be pleasing and passive have contributed to the exploitation, battering, sexual abuse, psychological abuse, and role conflict that are discussed in Part 2 of this book.

Because women have traditionally been primary caregivers, they actually wield great power over infants and children. "Mother's power" over life nurturance and death avoidance is remembered, revered, feared, and envied. The all-powerful mother can be a terrifying and capricious image, causing some women to avoid powerful authority lest they be regarded as a modern Medea.[6] Those who envy a woman's innate power can respond with reprisals. As women's power has become more obvious and organized, men have become more insecure and misogynist.[7] Pastoral caregivers may ask themselves, When ministering to women, how can we better monitor our own vulnerability to women or our own insecure and misogynist reactions to previous experiences of a woman's authority as mother?

These considerations bring us to the question, What is a healthy paradigm for pastoral care of women? This chapter offers a substitute for the prominent shepherding paradigm extracted from John 10 and presents theological foundations for the pastoral care of women.

The paradigm developed in this chapter also comes from Scripture; unabashedly, this work is an attempt to find our predominant images for healing and helping within our own discipline, even as we remain in constant relationship with the behavioral sciences. This attempt is in agreement with the sentiment of numerous pastoral theologians "that in this particular time and place, the stress should be on the second rather than the first word in the title for our field—upon theology and its relationship to the meaning of pastoral, rather than the other way around."[8]

The theological paradigm offered in this chapter as foundational for the pastoral care of women comes from Luke 10, the parable of a Samaritan. This narrative develops the interconnection in the injunction to love God, neighbor, and self (Luke 10:27). Underscoring love of self, this chapter utilizes the parable as appropriate to women in search of the elusive self. A second type of interconnectedness essential to the Samaritan paradigm is reflected by the function of the inn and developed in this chapter as crucial in pastoral practice with those by the side of the road.

Love of God, Self, and Neighbor: A Paradigm of Interconnection

Shepherding has been one of the dominant metaphors in pastoral care and counseling. The art of shepherding as described in John 10 has been extended to pastoral care and developed by pastoral theologians such as Seward Hiltner.[9] Although other theologians such as Carroll Wise have spoken of inherent dangers in the use of this symbol, no other paradigm has been as prominent. Wise expresses his reserve over the symbol of the shepherd in this way: the symbol subtly but powerfully conveys the idea of the shepherd over the sheep.[10] Although Wise points to places in the New Testament that stressed the equality and unity of all believers, he offers no alternative paradigm to that of the good shepherd.

Shepherding was also my favored image in the field of pastoral care until I prepared a sermon on the Good Shepherd passage in John 10. I was beguiled with the phrase "the voice of strangers."

> He who enters by the door [of the sheepfold] is the shepherd of the sheep. To him the gatekeeper opens; the sheep hear his voice, and he calls his own sheep by name and leads them out. . . . A stranger they will not follow, but they will flee from him, for they do not know the voice of strangers.

In this biblical pericope, there is mention of wolves, thieves, robbers, hirelings, and gatekeepers. All of these figures are predictable within the passage. The mysterious grouping is that of the strangers. The "voice of strangers" stands in tension with the voice of the Good Shepherd.

In the biblical setting, Jesus talks to the Pharisees about himself. He speaks about leadership and uses the shepherd as a type. The Pharisees, the religious leaders of that day, could not comprehend the christological import of his metaphor. Yet, I as a pastoral theologian understand it so well. I often imagine myself as shepherd, standing in the door of the classroom or church, greeting the flock by name, feeling responsible for their nurture, becoming so identified with shepherding that it takes all I have. I and others in pastoral ministry give our lives for the sheep. We give exemplary care to others. We become the good shepherd. In doing so, however, we, like the Pharisees, miss the christological import of the metaphor. In becoming the good shepherd of our flock, *we* are the voice of strangers.

With the traditional male developmental emphases on autonomy, individuation, and self-sufficiency as goals of maturity, usurping the place of the Good Shepherd is not difficult for the individual. To warn religious leaders against this propensity, Jesus reiterates twice in John 10 that he is the door of the sheep and that he is the Good Shepherd.

A paradigm other than that of the good shepherd, one with less inherent danger of lone external hierarchical authority, is crucial for the pastoral care of women. As more women in transition move away from reliance on external authority figures, away from passivity, and into a comfort with their own internal authority, we seek a paradigm that avoids the risk of the lone shepherd who can control, cajole, and cavort with the sheep. To see how the isolated shepherd can ravish the flock, we need only glance at the recent documentation of a scandal in the early 1980s in which a winsome and adored pastor sexually abused at least six women parishioners over a four-year period.[11] In the allegations against their pastor, the six women acknowledged they were caught off guard by the attention given them by a male, religious authority. Although the recent book *Is Nothing Sacred?* exposes sexual misconduct, we have yet to document the more prevalent psychological abuse between male authority figures and their parishioners.

With the emerging emphases and goals in female developmental theory on mutuality and interdependence, a paradigm that is appropriate in the pastoral care of women needs to underscore interconnectedness in the helping dimensions of ministry. Two types of interconnectedness are essential. One type is discussed later as relatedness to other disciplines in healing. The other type of interconnectedness is the interplay of love of neighbor, God, and self. North American pastoral theology has been criticized for lack of attention to this interconnection;[12] German theology after World War II has been stamped by the conviction that interpersonal disturbances between people are intimately tied up with disturbances between people and God. Friedrich Wintzer reminds us that the question about the relationship of a person to God, self, and neighbor is a central one to pastoral care and counseling.[13] Surely such an interconnection is present in the injunction in Luke 10:27 to love God with all our heart, and with all our soul, and with all our mind, and our neighbor as ourselves. It is followed by a parable of a Samaritan who stopped to help a wounded person. The parable has been understood by commentators to be an elaboration of what it means to "love your neighbor." The parable also implies that love of neighbor is intimately tied up with love of God. Pastoral care of women must concern itself with the more subtle interconnection implied in the text: love your neighbor as yourself.

Carol Gilligan, in her ground-breaking *In a Different Voice*, has worked with the complex interplay of self and other.[14] She suggests that women's development moves through three phases in this interplay. The first phase pivots on care for oneself. A person cares for the self in order to ensure survival. A transition occurs when this first position is seen as egoistic. A concept of responsibility develops in a growing understanding between self and other. In the second phase of Gilligan's sequence, caring for others is equated with what is good. A disequilibrium occurs as the woman neglects to give care to herself and to receive care. Caring is confused with self-sacrifice that hurts and neglects the self of the caregiver. A transition occurs when this dilemma is recognized. In Gilligan's third caring pattern, a new connection develops between self and other. Self-knowledge is essential for this perspective and leads to healthy relationships. It involves concern with the interrelationship between self and other but a condemnation of self-exploitation.

The movement in Gilligan's sequence is from a narcissism to an altruism to an interdependence between self and other. Imposing Gilligan's schema onto the Good Samaritan text in Luke 10, one could imagine the priest and Levite as illustrative of her first perspective, caring for oneself. The Samaritan could then be seen as representative of her second perspective, that caring for the other equals the good. What then depicts the third perspective, a healthy connection between self and other?

Using the parable of the Samaritan as a paradigm for interconnectedness, one can understand the sequence within the text as follows. The robber represents the infantile position: what is yours is mine. The priest and Levite depict the narcissistic worldview: what is mine is mine. The Samaritan, in caring for the neighbor, exhibits the traditionally "feminine" altruistic posture: what is mine is yours.

In our customary way of reading this biblical text, we women have not acknowledged a crucial aspect to the narrative, an aspect so significant that it shatters the previous sequence. The Samaritan finished his journey. The Samaritan finished his journey while meeting the need of a wounded and marginal person. The Samaritan did not give everything away; in this enigmatic parable, he did not injure, hurt, or neglect the self. He loved himself, and he loved his neighbor. He relied in a sense on the communal, on a type of teamwork as represented by the inn and by the host at the inn. In the pastoral care of women, we can appropriately interpret this last and preferred phase in the complex interplay of self and other as: what is mine is mine, but I have enough to share. Thus, the Samaritan as paradigm represents love of self and neighbor, with love of God understood in the parable. This paradigm can be utilized to describe developmentally mature women from the perspective of the Christian faith. It reinforces recent research in women's development that underscores the fact that all psychological growth for women occurs within emotional connections and not separate from them.[15] This paradigm supports the notion that in genuine caretaking the caretaker is not submerged. The paradigm can be utilized in the new understanding of women's psychological development, which is called "self-in-relation" theory or "being-in-relationship." This theory posits that the core self-structure in women is the relational self.[16]

In using the Samaritan paradigm to describe the developmentally mature woman and to inform our patterns of pastoral caregiving as well, we raise two theological issues. Exegetically, we cannot avoid the christological import of the text. Although we cannot go so far as to say that the Good Samaritan is Jesus Christ in the parable, we can say that Christ was a "unique realization" of the Good Samaritan; however, to say that Christ intended the Good Samaritan to represent himself as he related to wounded and fallen humanity is more than we can know.[17] One commentator has depicted the parable as indication or "object lessons in human scale" of the reign of God's grace, which Jesus deploys.[18] Another sees the life-giving journey of Jesus as "mirrored by this foreigner."[19] Christ himself as realization of the Good Samaritan could be seen to demonstrate a fourth level of interaction in the parable: what is mine is yours. This authentic self-sacrifice stands at the core of the Christian gospel. Moments of authentic self-sacrifice can occur only after a sense of self is formulated. Christine Gudorf, a feminist ethicist, adds that authentic self-sacrifice incurs the intention of mutuality and a goal of interdependence: "The moments of self-sacrifice, such as we find in the crucifixion of Jesus, are just that—moments in a process designed to end in mutual love."[20] Unless we as pastoral caregivers are clear on this last point, we could be guilty of perpetuating a Christian interpretation of self-sacrifice that is self-annihilation. As feminist theologians continue to point out, women have been socialized to be more susceptible to this misinterpretation of *agape* love.[21] Misbegotten or unauthentic self-sacrifice extinguishes the self.

In using the Samaritan paradigm to inform our patterns of pastoral caregiving, another theological issue surfaces with the use of a distinctive verb in the Luke 10 text. The Samaritan is described as "having compassion." Outside the original parables of Jesus, this verb is not used of men and women.[22] It is used as a divine attribute. Yet the verb occupies a central place in three parables of Jesus and there does denote a human quality.[23] The verb, "having compassion" or "moved to pity," is shown to be the basic and decisive attitude in human and hence in Christian acts.[24] It is the foundational attitude in a paradigm for the pastoral care of women. It is a divine attribute that is conveyed in "theological presence." It is a convergence of the divine and the human.

Theological presence is mentioned in Chapter 4 by Mary Dean and Mary Louise Cullen as the one gift most women hope to encounter in relationship to their pastors. Theological presence is an existential posture of receptivity that sometimes results in activity when that activity benefits the health of the other. Theological presence manifests certain characteristics: listening to women's experience of travail and transition; providing responses when they are desired; allowing God to be part of the dialogue even when intense anger is expressed toward God; honoring women's expertise, intuition, cognitive abilities, caring attributes, and interior and often superior strengths; connecting one's experience as a listener to textbook knowledge and classroom exposure; and knowing God is undergirding this process of receptivity as the source of theological presence.

Admittedly, the paradigm offered in this chapter will not speak to or for women who have experienced the robbers, the neglectful Levite, or the uncaring priest. Some women have left the Judeo-Christian religion disappointed and disenfranchised and turned to other traditions such as goddess worship or wicca. With these women, using an image from Bonnie Miller-McLemore's comments in Chapter 3 on Ruth and Orpah, we can only embrace, weep, and part in the wilderness.

Love of self.   In previous chapters we have seen women struggle with shame and guilt in battering and abusive relationships. We have noted women encumbered with low self-esteem in a culture that devalues traditional feminine virtues and places more value on a son than a daughter. In our American culture of fleshly beautification and youthful beatification, women have identified themselves with their bodies and inevitable decay. In power structures that are run by males, in sinister and subtle ways, women as the powerless ones can become the target group, a despised group.[25] They can end up "beaten, stripped, and left for half-dead." That women do not love themselves is small wonder.

To understand what love of self means in the Samaritan paradigm, clarifying what it does *not* mean is helpful. For the purpose of elucidation, I am going to draw from the critiques of individualism in *Habits of the Heart*.[26] This book has deplored the modern therapeutic attitude that reinforces the traditional individualism of American culture[27] and the American dream of the admirable one, "the one who stands out from the crowd of ordinary folk who don't know how," the star.[28] We might add also the lone shepherd, separated from the sheep. By love of self we do not mean this radical and romantic individualism seen as a goal of modern therapy. With feeling good as the objective of radical and romantic individualism, we have only a narcissistic substitute for women's traditional obsession with being good. The type of individualism that posits the person as the only firm reality in the universe, with society as a secondary or artificial construct, is termed *ontological individualism*. This form of isolated individualism is prevented in the Samaritan paradigm by the interconnection—love your neighbor as yourself—that maintains a social realism that is true to biblical tradition[29] and reinforces the view presented in Chapter 3 that women prefer to regard themselves as connected selves, not isolated individuals. By love of self, we do not mean the form of individualism that calculatingly subjugates every relationship and action to self-aggrandizement and self-interest; this attitude is called *utilitarian individualism* and is seen to be fostered by the cost-benefit calculation of the modern therapeutic attitude.[30] Utilitarian individualism analyzes action and effort according to the maximization of self-interest; social relationships revolve around the individual's personal economy and property. This cost-benefit calculation is reversed in the transaction between Samaritan and innkeeper, "Take care of him; and whatever more you spend, when I come again, I will repay you" (Luke 10:35). Unlike the tendency in expressive individualism, in which a person merges through intuitive feelings with others who are like-minded and lives in "life-style enclaves" in cultural insulation, love of self in the Samaritan paradigm has obligations beyond the like-minded and loved ones and a wider social understanding.

Love of self for a woman is the conviction and perception that she is of infinitely great value and immense worth. A woman can come to this awareness of herself as a loved self in a variety of ways. She comes to the understanding that she has absolute value. This understanding may run counter to society's or her family's attempt to grant her relative value. Diogenes Allen, a philosophical theologian, utilizes the Samaritan parable to illustrate the absolute value of a person, in contrast to a person's relative value. The Samaritan acknowledges the intrinsic worth and great value of the one stripped, beaten, and left for half-dead. This compassion is a mirroring of God's perfect love.[31] This kind of compassion in the Samaritan passage is described as "being moved to pity."

> To love a thing is to see a thing as existing in its own right—to go out to its existence. And to go out to a thing in this way when it is a living thing, and particularly when it is a living person, is *fundamentally to have pity for it*. . . . The insight into its existence is at the same time an insight into its suffering, its defenselessness, its profound vulnerability.[32]

The loved self is a self-in-Relation. We have absolute value because we have been created to receive God's presence.[33] Our absolute value is based on God, who alone is wholly good. This philosophical and theological premise offers another dimension to the title *Good* Samaritan.

A woman might come to perceive herself as the loved self in many ways. We must discuss these ways because genuine love of self is the key to pastoral care with women. Let me illustrate one way through the story of one woman whose life was scarred, not marred, by cancer. Following a mastectomy, she experienced her relative value: her close friends avoided her, her teaching contract was not renewed, her husband began to abuse her physically, and her children expressed embarrassment. Most memorable was her account of the afternoon when her children asked her not to wear her bathing suit in the backyard because it revealed the edge of her chest scar.

Fortunately, this woman was given listening and understanding following her radical mastectomy and subsequent familial separation. Listening and understanding came from long-term counseling with a hospital chaplain, from a support group for survivors of cancer, and from a roommate with the same gynecologic diagnosis. In cyclical and imitative fashion, this woman was eventually called to be a compassionate presence to others. She expressed this calling with the following text:

> When I am dying, I want to remember the times when I was real and honest, when I shared myself in open self-disclosure as an act of love. I want to remember the times when I gave to those who were hungry the food of my sharing, to those who were thirsty the drink of my listening and understanding, to those who were locked inside themselves the gentle, extended hands that said, "Come out. You will be safe with me." I want to remember the times when I offered the healing gift of loving and caring to those who were in need.[34]

What prompted her to move from relative value to a loved self was encountering individuals who to her represented the Good Samaritan and who mirrored God's compassion. This woman imaged herself as a self-in-Relation to God; in this relation, she became aware that she was of cosmic concern, of intense value, of immense worth. She understood her absolute value.

Love of God, love of neighbor.   Love of God, love of neighbor, and love of self are the goals of ministry, pastoral care, and theological education. In the 1950s H. Richard Niebuhr, Daniel Day Williams, and James M. Gustafson's classic study of more than ninety theological schools engaged in a process of self-examination concluded that the goal of the church, the ministry, and the theological schools themselves was to increase among people the love of God and neighbor.[35] As developed in *The Purpose of the Church and Its Ministry,* this ultimate objective subsumes all proximate ends of theological education, which includes pastoral theology among its disciplines.[36] Thus, North American pastoral theology has been caught up in this teleology of love of God and neighbor as "law and gospel."[37] In his use of the biblical injunction (Luke 10:37), Niebuhr missed what commentators on the Luke 10 pericope have also overlooked: love of self is integrally interconnected in the text. They have neglected the obvious interplay because they have analyzed the text from the position of male lawyer, Samaritan, Levite, or priest. Women read the text from the side of the road. They raise the question, Who is my neighbor? from the position of the morally inferior group, the group who is "unclean" at regular monthly intervals and contaminated like the wounded traveler who was taken to be dead, and, thus, untouchable for a religious authority. A woman not only reiterates the male lawyer's question ("Who is my neighbor?") but also asks, Who sees her value when she has lost her physical beauty, her worth when she has no economic security, her significance when she is so vulnerable? Who proves to be neighbor to her?

In *The Responsible Self,* H. Richard Niebuhr developed the concept of man as responder or *homo dialogicus.* This man-made-for-society was opposed to the image of man-the-lawmaker or man-the-citizen, living under the law. Man was most himself as *homo dialogicus,* in an I-Thou relationship ("Thou" being God as seen through a fellow human being). The dialogue begins when man answers the greeting or the cry of need of neighbor(s).[38] With the term *women-in-dialogue,* I seek to add the internal conversation that is essential for woman as responsible self. As a woman-in-dialogue, when a woman has an answer to the questions, Who is my neighbor? Who proves neighbor to me? and when she receives the compassion exhibited by the Samaritan in the text, she loves herself and can love the neighbor.

Suffering, sacrifice, and selfless love.   Connecting suffering, sacrifice, and selfless love brings a danger. This danger is a subtle one that lurks in the pages of pastoral care texts. For example, pastoral theologian Wayne Oates has attempted to explain the interconnection of love of God, neighbor, and self by equating love of self with self-sacrifice.

> The love of neighbor *as oneself* does not take narcissistic self-idolatry as its prudential point of reference. Far from it. The Christian has taken up his cross and followed the Lord Jesus Christ. This is *how* he loves himself. This is his calling.[39]

This selfless love becomes the basis for self-respect. Oates's description of the persecution, oppression, and trials that do come to followers of Christ is central to the biblical message. I do not mean to imply that Oates intended to glorify suffering. However, the danger in limiting the understanding of love of self to selflessness and self-sacrifice in this way is the persistent and pernicious tendency of some to glorify suffering, particularly to inflict mundane martyrdom on women.

I would like to underscore Oates's emphasis on the "transformation of tragedy"[40] as represented by the event of the resurrection. However, another more feminine image would have greater import for women: "But God raised [Christ] up, having loosed the *pangs of death,* because it was not possible for him to be held by it" (Acts 2:24). The Greek word for *pangs* is literally "birthpangs" or "pain of birthing." The word might have originally denoted the cries of a woman at the onset of labor. It is used in the Septuagint for two similar Hebrew words meaning "cords" and "what is born."

The imagery becomes clear when we read of the cords of death or the cords of Sheol (Ps. 18:4, 5). It is the imagery of a painful childbirth until, with the severance of the umbilical cord, something is born. In the Acts passage, this imagery is used for Christ. Out of the pain, the pangs, he was raised up, very alive, out of the womb of death or Sheol. The cords of physical decay were broken, the cords of death were severed, and the cords of the womb of Sheol could not hold him.

Pangs can also mean "what is born" (with pain). Women die many deaths in life, but we are not held by these lesser deaths. We are not overcome by the pangs of death. Because of the Easter experience, we know that through the pain something can be born, something can be raised up, and we have hope for the transformation of tragedy.

This book should not be seen as an exaltation of suffering or an elevation of tragedy. The contributors and editors have each known and experienced at least one of the life crises in these pages. Our expose is not a magnificat of travail and transition; rather, it is a manifesto of refusal to capitulate to pain and tragedy. It is a statement that we and other women can take one other to the "inn." It is confidence that we will not be overwhelmed by evil, robbers, negligent Levites, or calculating priests.

Love of God. Luke 10:38-42 extends the meaning of the parable of the Samaritan. The exposition of what it means to love God has traditionally been found in the story of a listening Mary and an industrious Martha in this passage. This account is a continuation of the illustration of what loving God, neighbor, and self entails. One commentator concluded that loving God means receiving from God.[41] Mary has always been the exemplary one, the one receiving.

Yet, we as pastors and counselors have seen ourselves as the ones giving, the pastoral caregivers. The surprise in the text comes from the model offered, a model that moves away from the image of the autonomous individual, for example, the lone shepherd who tends, sacrifices for, and guards the sheep. The model comes not from one individual person but from two individuals, two women, who when taken together offer a picture of what it means to be both caregiver and care receiver. The shocking Christian message is that at the base of our nurturing is the continual need for our own nurture.

One point of clarification is essential at this point: receptivity as exhibited by Mary in the narrative is not to be confused with passivity. Because women have customarily been more silent, because they have not been chief spokespersons for the church, and because they have been invisible in ecclesiastical structures, they have often been seen as quiet partners in communal ministry. On the one hand, a faith issue for women is how to connect our receptivity with activity. On the other hand, in our newfound avenues of activity, we need to guard ourselves from slighting the receptivity at which we have always excelled.

In the narrative of Mary and Martha, we have a model for linking receptivity and activity, being and doing, care receiving and caregiving, tending to self and to others. The portrayal of the two women in the midst of a community of disciples reinforces the new perspective in developmental theory: a woman sees herself as a self-in-relation. In the biblical text, the women are also in the presence of God; thus, each woman in this narrative is also a self-in-Relation. This account of Mary and Martha, which follows that of the Samaritan, offers a balance that undergirds the interconnectedness necessary to pastoral care with women: love of God, love of neighbor, love of self.

Interconnectedness and the Inn

The second type of interconnectedness essential to the Samaritan paradigm is reflected by the function of the inn. As pastoral counselors, pastors, laity, and seminarians, we must sometimes take the wounded to the inn. The inn may be a battered woman's shelter, a Resolve meeting, a Bosom Buddies' support group, a round of chemotherapy. The inn may be represented by other disciplines in healing, such as the behavioral sciences. The inn may be the church. Again, we must acknowledge that some women have been so neglected by the Levite and the priest that the inn as synagogue or church will not be a timely place for restoration. These women recall the damage done when institutional religion fostered the beliefs of male (particularly white) supremacy, women as evil, glorification of suffering, an unquestioning stance toward religious authority, a passive and nondiscerning acceptance of all hardships, and deification of the work ethic.[42] Women who have been devastated by one or more of these distortions understandably view religion as "only for superstitious and sheeplike types."[43] The inn as a place of spirituality and a spiritual shelter (*Herberge*) has more appeal to women scarred by institutional religion. In our exegetical attempt to understand the inn in the Lukan passage containing the Samaritan parable, we do know that the inn was a temporary lodging place, a place where a journeying person found room for the night. At the end of several of the chapters in Part 2, we have suggested places where women might find "room for the night" on their journey.[44]

As a chaplain on an addictive disease unit in a psychiatric hospital, I experienced an "inn" and I witnessed the recovery of Ann, the patient mentioned at the beginning of this chapter. "Restoration at the inn" in this location involved the Alcoholics Anonymous recovery program and a multidisciplinary team of health care providers. Our team was composed of a psychiatrist, a nurse, two patient counselors, one family therapist, one aftercare counselor, and one activities therapist. We had access to the evaluations of a clinical psychologist. The team met three mornings a week to discuss patients before making rounds together. The spiritual component was central to the treatment. As a therapeutic team, although our proximate professional goals sometimes differed, we were united by an ultimate goal: love of Higher Power, love of self, love of neighbor as encouraged by the peer networking of AA. Both types of interconnectedness under discussion in this chapter are displayed here: the interplay of love of God, neighbor, and self; and our relatedness as pastors and pastoral counselors to other disciplines in healing.

Ann made considerable progress under the care of this multidisciplinary team. After leaving the hospital, Ann lived in a halfway house with other professionals in recovery as addicts. While Ann was still an inpatient, I met her on a Sunday after a hospital worship service. She had heard a poem about a great craftsman that went like this: At an auction, no one bid on a battered, weathered old violin. Just as the auctioneer announced, "Going once, going twice," a person entered the room, mounted the podium, took the bow, and played the instrument. A thrilling sound came from the violin; the audience was spellbound. After the person finished playing, the bidding escalated to unheard-of amounts simply because the discarded violin had been touched by the crafter's hand. Ann identified with the battered, weathered violin and had what we called in that facility a "spiritual awakening."

Ann's experience, which I summarized, encapsulates a cyclical movement within the Samaritan paradigm.

And Ann, once half-dead and beaten,
will go back eventually
to a helping profession and family relationships in love
of neighbor,
stronger for having been restored at the inn,
    for having learned to love herself on the journey,
    for experiencing the touch of the Crafter's Hand.

PASTORAL PRACTICE: A VIEW FROM THE SIDE OF THE ROAD

While we were developing this volume, a male colleague asked, "How do women *do* pastoral care differently than I?" His query is similar to that of the male lawyer to whom Jesus told the parable of the Samaritan. The male lawyer's question as he attempted to put Jesus to the test was, What shall I *do* to inherit eternal life?

Neither this chapter nor this book is a how-to manual. Interspersed throughout the book are styles of ministry, recommendations on referral, and issues that affect the functioning of pastoral care with women. Similar to Jesus' response to the male lawyer, we have answered with actual case stories or illustrations from our work with women. We have put our focus on how we *are* as pastoral caregivers rather than what we do differently. We have put our emphasis on what being a woman means. We have reread the familiar story of a Samaritan and interpreted it from the side of the road.

The first part of this chapter presented a model for the paradigmatic interconnectedness that is foundational for the pastoral care of women. This interconnectedness involves the interplay of love of God, self, and neighbor; it also entails interaction and teamwork among various disciplines of healing. The last part of this chapter addresses concerns in pastoral practice: What faith issues effect a pastoral care of women? What does a woman want from her pastor or pastoral caregiver? What kind of caring and understanding are useful in working with women?

Faith Issues Among Women

The proliferation of modern works on women's spirituality, feminine spirituality, and feminist spirituality, as well as the renewed interest in classical works such as those of Catherine of Siena, Teresa of Avila, and Thérèse of Lisieux, attests to women's desire to engage in a deeper interplay of spiritual receptivity and activity, in a specific focus on the interior person, and in an awareness of the significant religious context of the mothering process. When these faith issues are addressed by female and/or feminist theologians, the theme of continuity in both classical and modern texts has been women's need for autonomy and self-direction, as well as mutuality and relationship.[45]

Receptivity and activity.   Women exist in an interplay of receptivity and activity. Women's receptivity is described or illustrated in Luke 1:38, an account of the song of praise or Magnificat by Mary, mother of Jesus. The movement in the song is as follows:

> Here am I.
> I am the Lord's servant;
> as you (angel) have spoken, so be it.

Mary conceived and bore a son; she experienced anxiety when he was missing; she meditated on ideas about her son; she performed many tasks for him as a child; she observed him perform many miracles in the context of an extended family of faith; she stood near the cross where her son hung at a young age. After this life of receptivity and activity as a mother and as a follower of the Messiah, she received some of his last words. These last words to Mary reinforce the developmental view of feminine experience that sees a woman as a being-in-relationship. To Mary he said, "Woman, behold your son" (that is, John, disciple). To John he said, "Behold, your mother" (John 19:26, 27). This more universal feminine experience of being a self-in-relation involves both receptivity and activity.

The Lukan text containing the Magnificat (Luke 1:46-55) is problematic for some women because of its concept of servanthood as self-sacrifice. Admittedly, the church's teachings on servanthood have been misused to restrict and exploit women. Therefore, let me offer another example of the interplay of receptivity and activity.

Betsy Caprio, from a Jungian perspective, employs the concept of androgynous spirituality to include both masculine and feminine modalities of behavior, a harmony of both activity (masculine behavior) and receptivity (feminine behavior).[46] She locates symbols of masculine behavior in certain passages of Scripture as "Ask and it shall be given you; seek and you shall find; knock and it shall be opened unto you" (Matt. 7:7). Aspects of masculine behavior are action, assertion, directness, outgoingness, and analysis. Aspects of feminine behavior are illustrated in other passages such as "Watch therefore, for you know not the day nor the hour" (Matt. 25:13). Thus, aspects of feminine behavior are absorption, contemplation, waiting, listening, practicing stillness, and synthesizing. Caprio depicts the emergence of androgynous spirituality through retelling the legend of St. Barbara.

Through captivity in a tower, Barbara learned receptivity and connection to her earth, air, water, and fire natures. Barbara found one human model of what was "manly" outside herself, established a relationship to it (a priest), and activated the "man within" herself. Subsequently, through action and assertion, Barbara left the prison tower. Caprio's retelling of this ancient legend pointed to not only the balance of complements within each person (earth/air/fire/water) but to a harmony of the masculine and feminine modalities of spiritual behavior in all of us, a harmony that includes activity and receptivity. This concept of androgynous spirituality has already been applied by pastoral caregivers in their ministry.[47]

Note that pastoral caregivers must distinguish between receptivity and passivity or dependency. Both in the biblical account of Mary and in the legend of St. Barbara, we see that receptivity need not be confused with either dependency or passivity. Mary, mother of Jesus, shows us a more basic interplay of receptivity and activity: a woman's capacity to be biologically receptive reinforces her spiritual receptivity.

Homo exterior and homo interior.   For women who have been objectified sexually, pushed onto pedestals, adored and adorned as Madonnas, and worshiped as fertility goddesses, the inner person and inner developmental phenomena are central faith issues. Because women have so often been assessed by externals, we need to see and value the inner self. Hildegard von Bingen, a twelfth-century Benedictine abbess, maintained that faith is a function of the inner self. Her works, now becoming available in English, reveal the distinction between homo interior and homo exterior, two levels of personality.[48] The homo interior has a symbolic set of eyes and ears and resembles the Pauline concept of inner human (Rom. 7:22). Hildegard's six elements of faith present a framework for understanding faith development radically different from "stages of faith," as represented in the works of theologians such as James Fowler.[49] According to Mary Ford-Grabowsky, the Fowlerian cognitive structures correspond to Hildegard's homo exterior, which is egocentric, faithless, and resistant to grace.[50]

Right-brain methods of healing—using dreams, visions, imagination, and visualization—provide one way of ministering to the homo interior. One woman, for example, had been struggling for five years to forgive someone who had betrayed her. She had just read a book about forgiveness, an astute work laden with exegetical comments and theologians' quotes on the power of forgiveness. Yet she continued to struggle with resentment and revenge. She happened to attend a Maundy Thursday service and heard a sermon on betrayal. The female pastor related her experience of being betrayed by her best friend. The sermon led into the feeling Christ must have had on the night of his betrayal. During the Communion liturgy, the pastor asked the parishioners to image Christ, the betrayed Christ, with hands outstretched at the table. The parishioners were asked to each recall a person who had been their betrayer, to take that betrayer's hand, and to lead in the imagination that person to the Communion table. Thus, the unforgiving parishioner stood before Christ at the Maundy Thursday meal and imaged Christ breaking the bread and offering it to her and to the one who had betrayed her. The use of visualization to be in the presence of the One who knew what betrayal felt like, being so understood, and receiving the Passionate Presence into her pain did more for the woman's healing than the tome she had just read or the sermons she had heard preached.

Imaging is one example of the many, varied ways women are initiating right-brain techniques in pastoral care. Some women have called imaging the "primary language of feminist theology."[51] Images are not only inductive, synthetic, and experientially based but also transformational: "Images are a source of spiritual transformation in ways that concepts are not; they replenish our spirits, nurture us, sustain us as we learn to abide in the pursuit of justice, which is our politics."[52]

The mothering process as a context for spirituality. All of us have had mothers, which gives us a common context of experience. This central thesis of Carol Ochs's *Women and Spirituality* leads her to regard traditional spirituality as male-centered: it has been regarded as an extension of the male maturational process, emphasizing individuation or coming into selfhood alone. Her work focuses on the distinctive aspect of spirituality as known by women: "The new spirituality offered here is an extension of the female maturational process that emphasized nurturing—coming into relationship."[53] For example, the empathic identification of a mother with her child is a kind of knowing that is central to spirituality.

According to Ochs, one of the major functions of spirituality is the de-centering of the self, which is described in traditional writing as "killing the self" or "dying to the self." In psychoanalytic terminology, it is "expansion of the ego boundaries." In biblical language, it is "compassion." For Ochs, "de-centering the self" means a focus away from the narcissistic, individualistic egocentric self that cares for others out of its own need. De-centering of the self can be accomplished through motherhood as well as asceticism. Thus, it is accomplished by true devotion and physical caring: "In caring for their infants, mothers don't seek to mortify their sensitivities—they simply know that babies must be diapered and that infants who spit up must be cleaned."[54] Mothering means de-centering the ego: the child comes first for a time. Mothering occasions spiritual insight, according to Ochs and others. Chapter 1 developed this insight in terms of maternal identification.

A word of caution seems appropriate as we consider Ochs's theory. De-centering of the self implies a preexisting sense of self to be given to others. As pastoral caregivers, we can watch for women who lack a clear sense of self; their own development was arrested before an identity consolidated. In these women the pastor may need to reinforce the woman's sense of self as well as a sense of the separate other. The self-in-relation, the compassionate individual, first needs to have an established sense of self available to offer others.

This sense of self has two somewhat overlapping approaches: feminine and feminist spirituality. Some feminine spirituality books present spiritual autobiographies such as that of St. Thérèse of Lisieux, the Little Flower, whose doctrine of "the little way of spiritual childhood" is replete with maternal imagery for God and for her family of faith at Carmel in Normandy, France.[55] Other works present theories of spirituality such as that of androgynous spirituality, discussed earlier in this chapter. Feminist spirituality, unlike feminine spirituality, always has the interconnection that the personal is political. Feminist spirituality raises critical questions about gender expectations and about the relationship between the personal and the political domain, the private and the public sphere, and the interior and the exterior life of an individual.

The women who wrote as The Mud Flower Collective expressed it this way:

> We believe this equation of spirituality with privatized self/God relationships is thoroughly ideological (Euroamerican), a sacralization of the view of the world that makes members of dominant cultures, classes, and races unaccountable to others in their daily lives and religion.[56]

Anne Carr's *Transforming Grace* is an example of feminist spirituality.[57] In this work, she takes issue with traditional views of spirituality that have been religious mythologies of the White Male System. Carr borrows the following lists of characteristics from the work of Anne Wilson Schaef to illustrate the male's stereotypical reflection of the characteristics of God.[58] The female stereotypical characteristics closely resemble childlike, weak, and sinful humankind.

God	Humankind	Male	Female
male	childlike	intelligent	emotional
omnipotent	sinful	powerful	weak
omniscient	weak	brave	fearful
omnipresent	stupid, dumb	good	sinful
immortal, eternal	mortal	strong	like children

Feminist spirituality can only enhance our pastoral caregiving as we critique a culture in which so many women have suffered. The perspectives offered by feminist spirituality refine our sensitivity to stereotypes of race, class, and sex.

What a Woman Wants from Her Pastoral Caregiver

Throughout this book, we have concerned ourselves with what a woman wants from her pastor or pastoral caregiver. This section supplements the previous chapters with three additional expectations: A woman desires that her identity be reshaped by a theology of grace, that her experience be affected by a theology of hope, and that intimacy needs be addressed by connectedness within the family of faith. Above all, she seeks pastoral pointing toward God as Primary Relationship.

A theology of grace; a theology of hope.   A woman hopes to experience, hear, and see a theology of grace. She wants to bathe herself in grace as extended within the family of faith.

The following example of that need and hope is not atypical. A woman attended a support group of Christian women and asked for prayer. She came into the circle of women and told her burdensome story. A few days before, she had gone to a free health clinic, had some tests run, and discovered she had glaucoma and high blood pressure. When she returned from the health clinic, her daughter's school called to say the daughter was running a fever. She brought her daughter home from school. When she was getting ready for the trip to the pediatrician's office, with her little son already in the car, her daughter had to make one more trip to the bathroom. The mother accompanied her. When they emerged from their house, they saw that the family car had rolled down the driveway, the open door of the car was caught on a chain-link fence, and the bumper was dented by a tree. The little son was safe in the car. The sobbing woman recounted this near-tragedy. Then the anxious woman confided in her support group the cause of her weeping. She was afraid of her husband's anger when he got home from his trip and saw the car. She was afraid of the rage of this conscientious churchman, her husband.

Women like this have had enough judgment, law, and fear of punishment. In excessive and outrageous ways, women have been made to feel guilt and shame. Some women fall prey to a tendency to perfectionism, as evidenced by their attempts to be the perfect lover, wife, or mother.[59] Yet, women know they are not perfect. They know they fall short of certain biblical and societal standards. This awareness can contribute to an underlying depression. What a woman wants from her pastor is the preaching, teaching, and counseling of grace. Women encouraged to see themselves enveloped in God's grace can be all they ever wanted to be.

A "horizon of hope"[60] is crucial for the pilgrimage of women who have known travail, travesty, and tragedy. Neither supportive therapeutic relationship nor acceptance is enough. Hope is essential to transition. Women are not misguided in their sense that things are not improving for women. We know, for example, that violence to women is increasing. False hope that our society is now healthier for women should not be engendered. At the same time, with our different language worlds, we women seek an authentic horizon of hope beckoning us forward in our journeys.

Recently, in Basel, Switzerland, I attended a worship service conducted by an ecumenical group of women. Men and children were also present. The songs, liturgy, and Scripture, however, were geared to offer much to women. What impressed me was the focus on the theme of hope. In Basel, February is often a grey, rainy, cold month. Many Swiss experience a mild depression. Christmas is over; Easter is not yet. On the altar of this church service were traditional Christian symbols, including the cross and chalice. In addition, a pot of fire was ready to burn paper containing our painful reminiscences from which we sought forgiveness or release. Also, water and bread were ready to refresh us for our journey home. But there, in the midst of all these things on the altar, was a little vase with lilies of the valley. This symbolized hope: that in the midst of the dismalness, the mist, the depression-conducive weather, spring would come. Among the aching memories and feelings expressed that day, symbols of hope were present lest we be left in the February of our feelings.

Authentic biblical hope has as its threefold dimension the ground of its hope in Christ, the horizon of its hope in the promise of the *basileia* and the object of its hope in "strategies and possibilities that the church devises as inroads of the dawning kingdom of God in the midst of an idolatrous and suffering world."[61] This book is one of those strategies. Our concern as pastors and theologians is both the individual woman in travail and the whole of creation. As we connect the gospel of God's suffering love in Christ with a gospel of hope, there will be varying reactions. Not all women will allow Jesus as a male to be a model for brokenness and recovery. For others, the maleness of Jesus is irrelevant. For still others, the fact that Jesus as male voluntarily gave up power and access to power is a message to a patriarchal church.[62] For these, Jesus is hope.[63]

Connectedness within the family of faith. We have already discussed in Chapter 4 that women desire in their pastor a theological presence, a listening, supportive, nonthreatened and compassionate presence. A pastor can be a woman's introduction into support groups within the church. Women may prefer prayer groups, Bible study groups, and support groups with only other women. Jesus relating most vulnerably to twelve other men is a model for such a group.

Women desire a sense of connectedness within the family of faith. Women's support groups may have certain characteristics conducive to this. For example, one effective prayer group placed the woman desiring prayer in the center of all the women gathered. Hands were placed on the shoulders of the one in the center; when large, the group had inner and outer circles, always with hands on shoulders. Touching was significant for these women. Women who have traditionally carried their best recipes to the Wednesday night suppers, caressed babies, and washed the antique lace on the baptismal gown are very sensitive to the sense of touch.[64] The configuration of the prayer group resembled the spokes of a wheel with the woman in need standing in the position of the hub, at the center of connectedness within her family of faith. The constellation also resembled a womb, from which some women experienced either the birth or rebirth of self-esteem.

Again, some men have abused a sense of pastoral closeness through sexual misconduct with woman parishioners.[65] When such abuse and mistreatment are absent, connectedness and closeness within the family of faith can be a means of restoration through relatedness.

Reinforcement of a primary relationship.   Throughout this chapter, I have asserted that a woman sees herself as a being-in-relation. Her development occurs in or within relationships. Many women hope their pastors will reinforce the sense of Primary Relationship because women want to know who they are in the presence of God.

Although we have developed a paradigm in this chapter around a male Samaritan (Luke 10), there is another Samaritan—a female, often called the woman at the well (John 4). The conversation between the woman and Christ gives us a model for the gracious disclosure of who we are in the presence of God. It involves not only a revelation or understanding of who we are but also a disclosure of who God is. This passage is the first instance that Jesus divulged his messiahship; this disclosure was to a woman, a woman who, as a female and a Samaritan, was relatively insignificant in terms of other relationships in the Gospel of John. Yet to her Jesus revealed who he was. This reciprocity and mutual self-disclosure as we stand in the presence of God is the foundation of a woman's sense of Primary Relationship. She is a self-in-Relation.

Caring and Understanding Helpful to a Woman in Crisis

A family of faith can supplement the caring and understanding women need. This network of relationships is not defined by denominations, religious orders, or nondenominational groupings. It is not limited to a particular culture. Women can experience the family of faith deeply because they are relationally oriented. Many women never receive adequate support from their family of origin, the biologic family. Because both biologic and faith types of families are subject to abusive relationships, we as pastoral caregivers seek to establish or maintain the health of both. This support means that a woman can find sisters and brothers, perhaps even a temporary spiritual mother, father, or children, within this family of faith because it is based on a New Testament understanding of caring and nonabusive relatedness. In a relationship with God through Christ, the Firstborn of the family, we are adopted as daughters and sons (Eph. 1:5). This adoption profoundly alters who we are as women. It gives many women an empowered sense of lineage and inheritance, a realm of resources, and entitlement through their spiritual genealogy.

The community of faith can extend and augment its caring through understanding issues of vital import to women. Three areas calling for enhanced pastoral sensitivity are mentioned here: greater awareness of forms of psychological abuse; recognition of the significance of the maternal matrix; and a redefinition of "weakness."

Awareness of forms of psychological abuse.   Pastors are paying more attention to physical abuse. As pastoral caregivers, we need to be in the forefront of recognizing the tyrannical behavior and verbal abuse that debilitate many women. In particular, I would include psychological neglect, for example, neglect experienced by women whose husbands have mistresses in their professions. If a woman's husband has an affair with a secretary or nurse at work, then traditionally the woman has received an outpouring of sympathy. If the husband has an affair with his corporation, his ministry, or his job, however, then this liaison is more likely to be sanctioned by society—and the church.

Recognition of the maternal matrix.   Bearing life, with its pleasures and pain, is an aspect of pastoral care that deserves more consideration. When the traditional Mother's Day sermon is preached, are we aware that one of five couples experience infertility? Do we remember the couples waiting three to seven years for adoption? Do we remember the singles who do not desire marriage? Do we recall the couples who have lost children?

Drawing upon the role of maternal identification for women (chap. 1) and the gynecologic issues involved (chap. 4), we can offer women more understanding when we continue to explore both the pain of phenomena like premenstrual syndrome, menstruation, menopause, and hysterectomy, on the one hand, and the privilege of pregnancy and parenthood on the other. In the tradition of the Christian church, that Jesus was born of a human mother points to the pivotal place of the maternal matrix. This matrix will continue to disclose more insights for an effective pastoral care of women.

Redefinition of weakness.   Understanding women necessitates a re-definition of the word *weakness.* In dispensing with the label "the weaker sex," we have cause to question the word *strong*. Does strength have to do with body and bulk?

Recently, in the waiting room of a pediatrician's office, I saw a man emerge in a wheelchair. He rolled himself through the waiting area and left the complex followed by his two healthy children. His wife stopped to pay the bill. In the pediatrician's waiting room, two women were talking about their struggles with infertility. The wife, after paying the bill, joined in the conversation. This is a part of her story: Shortly after she and her husband were married, he was drafted to the war. He was terribly injured and returned home without legs and one arm. For thirteen years, they endured infertility. Without his limbs, the heat of his body concentrated and killed his sperm. This lithe and attractive woman remained faithful to an infertile, maimed, and mutilated man. Eventually they were able to conceive two children. The woman told this story to us with deep and genuine affection for her husband. Then she left the waiting room, this woman whose gender has traditionally caused her to be classified as the "weaker sex." For me, she mirrored the tenacity and fidelity of God. These characteristics and others in which women have excelled need to be seen and redefined as strength.

By the phrase "women in travail and transition," we have attempted to depict realities, crises, and movements in women's lives. At one time the entire Christian tradition in macrocosm and one marginal woman in microcosm were in travail and transition; this woman was Mary Magdalene, and, according to John 20, she was alone at the empty tomb of Christ. This woman had known shame, guilt, and ostracism. She was well acquainted with psychological abuse and sexual objectification. She had been by the side of the road. She had cause to weep at the empty tomb; she had lost a relationship which had given her life meaning. It was her time of travail. It was also a time of travail for the whole Christian tradition. There is a time to weep. There is also a time to learn a new way. There is a time to discover self-esteem and worth, to hear one's name. There comes a time of transition, a time to refrain from weeping. When Mary Magdalene's time of transition came, she was encouraged to go back to the gathered disciples, to a supportive and caring community. In writing this volume, in our focus on women in travail and transition, we as editors and contributors have sought to be a part of that understanding and caring community.

NOTES

1. Lillian B. Rubin, *Women of a Certain Age: The Midlife Search for Self* (New York: Harper and Row, 1979). The issue of identity was a troubling

question for the 160 women in Rubin's study of mid-life women. This cultural cross-section was of women between the ages 35 and 54 who had taken out at least ten years from their profession after their first child was born. Their difficulty answering the question, Who am I? was attributed to the mystery about women's nature, the elusive self. Twenty-five percent of Rubin's sample could not answer the question at all. The remaining 75 percent generally started with physical attributes, which agrees with a previous chapter's premise—my body is my self. Eventually the respondents moved beyond physical description to stereotypical "feminine" personality traits such as sensitive, caring, and kind. "Mother" and "wife" were often used as answers to the query, Who am I? Most fascinating to Rubin was the fact that not one of the women described herself in relation to her work, although 50 percent held paid jobs outside the home. Women had disconnected being from doing. "All her life, she's been expected to *be*—*be* good, *be* pretty, *be* kind, *be* loving. *To be*—the quintessence of woman" (p. 59). Not so for man, who from infancy is trained to *do*—master, conquer, achieve.

Both genders traditionally live with repressed aspects of themselves. For women, Rubin argues, the repressed aspects are more painful because they are the most valued by society (pp. 50–51).

2. Orlo Strunk, *The Secret Self* (Nashville: Abingdon, 1976), 96.

3. Linda Tschirhart Sanford and Mary Ellen Donovan, *Women and Self-Esteem: Understanding and Improving the Way We Think and Feel About Ourselves* (New York: Penguin Books, 1984), 13. Sanford and Donovan found six self-esteem problems among their interviewees. Two findings are of special interest: Some women feel they have no true self to like and value (p. 12); Some women experience *self-concept dislocation*, which is precipitated by a major event such as a mastectomy (physical trauma) or such as a divorce (relational disruption) (p. 17).

4. Rubin, *Women of a Certain Age*, 68.

5. Valerie Saiving, "The Human Situation: A Feminine View," in *Womanspirit Rising* (San Francisco: Harper & Row, 1979), 37. These feminine "sins" and similar characteristics result in an "underdevelopment" or negation of the self.

6. Rubin, *Women of a Certain Age*, 68.

7. Christine Downing, "Gender Anxiety," *Journal of Pastoral Care* 43 (Summer 1989):156.

8. Charles V. Gerkin, in response to Don Browning and James Lapsley, "On Beginning a New Chapter: Pastoral Theology as a Practical Theology of Care," paper for the Society of Pastoral Theology, Denver, 27 June 1986, 7.

9. Seward Hiltner, *Preface to Pastoral Theology* (Nashville: Abingdon, 1958).

10. Carroll A. Wise, *The Meaning of Pastoral Care* (Bloomington, Ind.: Meyer Stone Books, 1989), 2.

11. Marie Fortune, *Is Nothing Sacred? When Sex Invades the Pastoral Relationship* (San Francisco: Harper & Row, 1989).

12. Dietrich Stollberg, *Therapeutische Seelsorge. Die amerikanische Seelsorgebewegung. Darstellung und Kritik. Mit einer Dokumentation*, Studien zur praktischen Theologie Nr. 6 (Munchen: Kaiser Verlag, 1969).

13. Friedrich Wintzer, ed., *Seelsorge: Texte zum gewandelten Verständnis und zur Praxis der Seelsorge in der Neuzeit* (Munchen: Kaiser Verlag, 1978).

14. Carol Gilligan, *In a Different Voice* (Cambridge: Harvard University Press, 1982), 74.

15. A number of papers from The Stone Center for Developmental Sciences and Studies at Wellesley College, Massachusetts, reinforce this developmental perspective. See Jean Baker Miller's "The Development of Women's Sense of Self," *Work in Progress* 12 (1984):4.

16. The reader is referred to another work in progress: Janet L. Surrey's "Self-in-Relation: A Theory of Women's Development," *Work in Progress* 13 (1985).

17. Alfred Plummer, *A Critical and Exegetical Commentary on the Gospel According to Luke*, International Critical Commentaries (New York: Chas. Scribner's Sons, 1898), 289.

18. David Tiede, *Luke*, Augsburg Commentary on the New Testament (Minneapolis: Augsburg Publishing House, 1988), 210.

19. David P. Moessner, *Lord of the Banquet* (Minneapolis: Fortress Press, 1989), 144.

20. Christine E. Gudorf, "Parenting, Mutual Love, and Sacrifice," in *Women's Consciousness, Women's Conscience*, ed. Barbara Hilkert Andolsen, Christine Gudorf, and Mary Pellauer (Minneapolis: Winston Press, 1985), 186.

21. Ibid., nn.17, 190, 191.

22. Helmut Koster, *Theological Dictionary of the New Testament*, ed. Gerhard Kittel, vol. 7 (Grand Rapids: Eerdmans, 1971), 554, esp. σπλγχνίζομαι. The Samaritan passage, one of the three parables mentioned, comes from the oldest stratum of the Synoptic tradition.

23. Ibid., 554.

24. Ibid.

25. Rubin, *Women of a Certain Age*, 69.

26. Robert Bellah, Richard Madsen, William Sullivan, Ann Swindler, and Steven Tipton, *Habits of the Heart: Individualism and Commitment in American Life* (New York: Harper & Row, 1985).

27. Ibid., 98, 104.

28. Ibid., 285.

29. Ibid., 334.

30. Ibid., 336.

31. Diogenes Allen, *Love: Christian Romance, Marriage, Friendship* (Cambridge, Mass.: Cowley Publications, 1987), 12.

32. J. R. Jones, "Love as Perception of Meaning," *Religion and Understanding* (New York: MacMillan, 1967), 149–50, quoted in Allen, *Love*, 12.

33. Allen, *Love*, 21.

34. John S. Powell and Loretta Brady, *Will the Real Me Please Stand Up? So We Can All Get to Know You!* (Allen, Tex.: Tabor Publishers, 1985).

35. H. Richard Niebuhr, *The Purpose of the Church and Its Ministry* (New York: Harper & Row, 1956), 31. "When all is said and done the increase of

this love of God and neighbor remains the purpose and hope of our preaching of the gospel, of all our church organization and activity, of all our ministry, of all our efforts to train men and women for the ministry, of Christianity itself" (p. 39).

36. Ibid., 32.

37. Ibid. I am grateful for Alice E. Hickcox's insight into the exegesis of Luke 10.

38. H. Richard Niebuhr, *The Responsible Self* (San Francisco: Harper & Row, 1963), 56. Although Niebuhr would most likely have used inclusive language if he had written *The Responsible Self* in the current decade, I am purposely retaining the masculine terminology here to underscore the differentiation between men and women in dialogue.

39. Wayne E. Oates, *Christ and Selfhood* (New York: Association Press, 1961), 181.

40. Ibid., 182.

41. Chas H. Talbert, *Reading Luke: A Literary and Theological Commentary on the Third Gospel* (New York: Crossroad, 1982), 126.

42. Sanford and Donovan, *Women and Self-Esteem*, 160–74.

43. Ibid., 162.

44. Chaps. 4–8.

45. Joann Wolski Conn, ed., *Women's Spirituality: Resources for Christian Development* (New York: Paulist Press, 1986).

46. Betsy Caprio, *The Woman Sealed in the Tower: A Psychological Approach to Feminine Spirituality* (New York: Paulist Press, 1982).

47. Edward Morgan III, "Implications of the Masculine and Feminine in Pastoral Ministry," *Journal of Pastoral Care* 34 (December 1980):268–77.

48. Mary Ford-Grabowsky, "The Fullness of the Christian Faith Experience: Dimensions Missing in Faith Development Theory," *Journal of Pastoral Care* 12 (March 1987):39–47.

49. Ibid., 43.

50. Ibid., 42. Women's reactions to faith stages are not uniform. For example, some women find the notion of linear progression and stage theory problematic and suitable only for a male metaphor of the spiritual "journey"; see Carol Ochs, *Women and Spirituality* (Totowa, N.J.: Rowman and Allanheld, 1983), 3. Other women utilize stage theory as developed by James Fowler and see stage 5 conjunctive faith as opening to voices of the deeper self; see Conn, *Women's Spirituality*, 230.

51. The Mud Flower Collective, *God's Fierce Whimsy: Christian Feminism and Theological Education* (New York: Pilgrim Press, 1985), 157.

52. Ibid., 161, 162.

53. Carol Ochs, *Women and Spirituality*, 2.

54. Ibid., 19.

55. *The Autobiography of St. Thérèse of Lisieux: The Story of a Soul*, trans. John Beevers (Garden City, N.Y.: Image Books, 1957).

56. The Mud Glower Collective, *God's Fierce Whimsy*, 162.

57. Anne E. Carr, *Transforming Grace: Christian Tradition and Women's Experience* (San Francisco: Harper & Row, 1988).

58. Ibid.

59. Sanford & Donovan, *Women and Self-Esteem*, 309.

60. J. Christiaan Beker, *Suffering and Hope* (Philadelphia: Fortress Press, 1987), Preface.

61. Ibid., 67.

62. Diane Tennis, *Is God the Only Reliable Father?* (Philadelphia: Westminster Press, 1985), 104.

63. Ibid., 112.

64. Barbara Barksdale Clowse, *Women, Decision Making and the Future* (Atlanta: John Knox Press, 1985), 133.

65. Fortune, *Is Nothing Sacred?*